Managing School System Change
Charting a Course for Renewal

Managing School System Change
Charting a Course for Renewal

by

Serbrenia J. Sims
and
Ronald R. Sims

INFORMATION AGE
PUBLISHING

80 Mason Street • Greenwich, Connecticut 06830 • www.infoagepub.com

Library of Congress Cataloging-in-Publication Data

Sims, Serbrenia J.
  Managing school system change : charting a course for renewal / by
Serbrenia J. Sims and Ronald R. Sim [i.e. Sims].
      p. cm.
Includes bibliographical references and index.
  ISBN 1-59311-078-2 (pbk.) – ISBN 1-59311-079-0 (hardcover)
  1. School improvement programs–United States. 2. School management
and organization–United States. 3. Educational change–United States.
I. Sims, Ronald R. II. Title.
LB2822.82.S47 2003
371.2'00973–dc22

                                              2003018591

Printed in the United States of America

CONTENTS

PREFACE

No matter which way you turn schools and school systems are increasingly expected to respond to the change challenges presented by the expansion social renewal, political pressure, economic trends, the expansion of knowledge, and a variety of internal and external stakeholders. Are schools and school systems prepared to successfully respond to these challenges? Can they avoid being crippled by their own inability to bring about the necessary changes? How can schools and school systems become more effective in managing change? Are there ways administrators can improve on their existing efforts to manage change? If so, then what should they be doing differently? These were some of the questions that inspired us to write *Managing School System Change: Charting a Course for Renewal*.

The book you are reading reveals our collective wisdom based on years of teaching and consulting in K–12 and higher education institutions. *Managing School System Change: Charting a Course for Renewal* is our attempt to identify viable strategies for improving on the existing efforts to manage school system change. Although no book can address every potential manifestation of school system change management, this book is an attempt to: look closer at the challenges of school system change; the roles and competencies necessary for administrators and others to successfully manage school system change; the importance of identifying and mapping stakeholder issues, interests, and commitment to heighten their involvement in school system change; articulate the importance of culture to school system change; and discuss the use of the balanced scorecard and other approaches to enhancing school system change.

While we clearly recognize the important role that teachers, parents, community members, students, and other school staff play in successful

Managing School System Change: Charting a Course for Renewal, pages vii–ix
Copyright © 2004 by Information Age Publishing, Inc.
All rights of reproduction in any form reserved.

school system change we focus primarily on administrators (principals, central office personnel, and so on) as key actors or change agents in the school system change process. We believe the good and not so good school system change management habits administrators can learn from this book will prove useful—even critical—for change success, not only in increasingly complex education environment but also in an increasingly demanding and unforgiving world of education. In the end, we hope that this book will stimulate dialogue, feedback, and suggestions in current and future efforts to continuously improve and change schools and school systems that make-up the K–12 landscape.

OUTLINE OF THE BOOK

Chapter 1 discusses the forces driving school system change, changes in education over the years, and the importance of a systems view of school and school system change. Chapter 2 looks at change failures, the various roles that school system members play in the change process, a simplified model of the change process, and the relationship between teachers, principals, and change. Chapter 3 presents a contemporary view of administrators as agents of change, with an overview of the key roles that they must be willing to fulfill in order to engage key stakeholders, and the personal competencies that they must develop in order to be capable of doing so. Chapter 4 delves deeply into stakeholders, their roles in school system change effort, and the application of stakeholder theory and analysis to school system change.

Chapter 5 turns to a look at the need for administrators to create the case for school system change by providing to such basic questions as: "Why change?" "What needs to change?" "What outcomes do we want from this change?" and "Why should we include others in the change process?" The chapter also discusses how administrators can use the "force-field" analysis model to diagnose the need for school system change, a framework and process for selling and communicating the case for school system change.

Chapter 6 turns to the important role of stakeholder participation, involvement and cooperation in school system change efforts. The extent to which administrators strive for stakeholder participation, involvement, and cooperation, will increase the likelihood of successful school system change. Chapter 7 discusses the importance of culture in organizations, exploring the nature and levels of organizational culture, and investigating how to create, maintain, and change a culture in organizations in general, and school systems in particular. Chapter 8 explains how the balanced scorecard, which has been successfully used in the for-profit sector to promote and sustain change may be used by administrators to revitalize and change a school system. Finally, Chapter 9 revisits the challenge of change facing today's school administrators before taking a look at employee and administrator reactions to change and how schools or school systems can overcome resistance to change. The chapter also offers some strategies available to administrators for building support for school or school system change.

ACKNOWLEDGEMENTS

A very, very special thanks goes to Herrington Bryce who continues to serve as our colleague, mentor, and valued friend. The administrative support of Larry Pulley, Dean of the School of Business Administration at the College of William and Mary, is also acknowledged. We are also indebted to Eric Valentine, former Managing Editor at Quorum Books who provided an outlet for our ideas over the last decade or so.

Our thanks and appreciation goes to our gang, Nandi, Dangaia, Sieya, and Kani who have supported us during the times when it seemed as if we would never complete this book. A special "we've set the bar for you" goes out to Ronald, Jr., Marchet, Vellice, Shelley, Sharisse, Taylor, and Amaya.

CHAPTER 1

AN INTRODUCTION TO MANAGING SCHOOL CHANGE

INTRODUCTION

There should be no doubt that education in the United States is a big issue. Many scholars, laypeople, and others have discussed the need for educational change or reform over the years while also observing the phenomena of its deterioration, discussing causes of its serious problems and offering suggestions to its possible solutions. It seems to have been accepted by most people that a major change or radical transformation must take place in our schools, the education system or in the education industry. It also seems to have been accepted by many that such things as information technology, restructuring, increased accountability or outcomes assessment, and many other levers should be exploited as a part of the solution to the various calls for change, reform, transformation or whatever one chooses to call the need for moving away from what some might refer to as a "business as usual" approach to education. As educators it is our intent to take the opportunity to make a conscious effort to ponder on and contribute to the dialogue on the need for school, school system or educational system

Managing School System Change: Charting a Course for Renewal, pages 1–13
Copyright © 2004 by Information Age Publishing, Inc.

change. The authors, being both K–12 and higher education teachers, share and agree with the above views as expressed by many but further concludes that there is still much work that needs to be done to make continuous improvement and change a significant outcome for schools, school systems, and educational systems. The purpose of this book is to stimulate dialogue, feedback, and suggestions for making continuous improvement and change a part of the K–12 landscape. Hopefully, collective wisdom will guide us all to accomplish the positive impact of change in schools and school systems in a shorter, more proactive, and satisfactory way.

FORCES DRIVING SCHOOL CHANGE

As we advance toward the future, our entire society is changing in a global context. Major institutions, including government, industry, and finance, are seeking ways to restructure that will increase their flexibility and effectiveness in this climate of change. Education is often pointed to as the key sector of our society that can prepare us for this new world and ensure our success.

K–12 schools like other educational institutions must recognize that the world has changed. Employers and students have needs that our current delivery system is not meeting. We face financial constraints that will not quickly disappear, as well as both global and private competition. Doing more of what we are currently doing will not solve these problems. To survive these challenges, we must find new ways to deliver education to our students. For example, the use of technology combined with other measures will dramatically change the nature of the teaching/learning process.

Mark Twain once said, "In the first place God made idiots. This was for practice. Then He made school boards" (Cummings & Worley, 2001). Fortunately, more of today's critics of schools are more kind in their analysis. Driven by greater social complexity and increasingly competitive demands of a global economy, societal pressure to improve educational effectiveness has increased during the past couple of decades. Shifting demographics, for example, have produced a culturally diverse and multilingual student population. Other societal trends, such as increased rates of divorce and dual-career families, manifest themselves in children who arrive at school poorly prepared and lacking the supportive and active involvement of their parents. Schools are being asked to do more under difficult circumstances.

Clearly, schools do not exist in a vacuum. They are influenced by the societal or local community events constantly occurring around them. For example, as briefly noted in the preceding paragraph changes in student demographics present new challenges for an educational system that is already under extreme stress. Further, recent developments in the workplace, changes to student demographics, and the economic trends are forcing schools to change. Consider for example the political and economic background and the changes in the world of work.

Political and Economic Background

With the end of the Cold War, the political agenda which had provided the basis for American foreign policy and many domestic issues as well was suddenly gone. As we have tried to redefine our role in the international arena, Americans have begun to see ourselves in a new world, one demanding a greater understanding of many cultures and histories. We have also begun to focus more on our domestic policies, looking at how we can reform our education, health care, welfare, campaign finance, and other systems. Much of this is in response to dramatic shifts in our economy and social fabric that are demanding new policies.

Within the U.S., our nation's economic base has shifted from industry to information. This change brings with it a demand for new skills and emphasis in the work place. To make an automobile takes 40% ideas, skills, and knowledge and 60% energy and raw material. To make a computer chip takes 98% ideas, skill, and knowledge and 2% energy and raw material (Sims, 2002). Human capital has become crucial to the success of American business.

Meanwhile, national economies are becoming increasingly internationalized with greater movement of capital, products, technology, and information. This brings American industry into direct competition with industries from around the world. Standards for skills, products, and worker knowledge are derived not only from our domestic agenda, but from our needs for competing in this international arena.

The World of Work

Indeed, the very concept and expectations of work and career have changed dramatically in the past decade or so. For example, while computers have created more jobs than they have destroyed, companies have used computer-based technology to eliminate unskilled jobs without giving the displaced workers the training needed to move into the new high-skilled jobs. In low-tech companies, 15% of all workers are managers and professionals while 36% are unskilled. In high-tech companies, the numbers are 31% managers and professionals and 10% unskilled workers. With corporate downsizing and organizational restructuring, workers are increasingly making multiple career changes. These new trends accentuate the importance of lifelong learning and adaptability.

The nation's economic shifts have social parallels. There are shifts in family structure, increased child poverty, inadequacy of social welfare and social service programs, and what some have called a decreased sense of civic responsibility. All of these combine to exacerbate existing inequities in our society, reflected vividly in the education system. One has only to read Jonathan Kozol's decade old *Savage Inequalities* (1992) and his descriptions of the schools in such areas as East St. Louis, Chicago and New York to see the extent of this problem that still exists today.

Impact on Individuals and Organizations

We are increasingly inundated with information in our daily lives. From the news media to advertising to the World Wide Web, the amount of information available to individuals in today's society is staggering. This has prompted some to say that we have indeed moved out of the information age into the knowledge age. They point out that we now only need ways to sift and sort this information, a way to gauge what is useful and what is not.

The defining characteristic of the knowledge age is perpetual change. Unlike previous transformations, the transformation to the knowledge age is not a period of change, followed by stability. It has ushered in an epoch of continuous change on an accelerating time cycle. This means that the kinds of knowledge that will serve each individual and our society as a whole are constantly evolving. Consider these present and future change facts:

- Every two or three years, the knowledge base doubles.
- Every day, more than 7,000 scientific and technical articles are published.
- Satellites orbiting the globe send enough data to fill 19 million volumes in the Library of Congress—every two weeks.
- High school graduates have been exposed to more information than grandparents were in a lifetime.
- Only 15 percent of jobs will require college education, but nearly all jobs will require the equivalent knowledge of a college education.
- There will be as much change in the next three decades as there was in the last three centuries (Mourier & Smith, 2001; Anderson and Anderson, 2001b).

Ongoing Issues Observed in Education

There are numerous ongoing issues and problems observed and reported on education by various stakeholders (teachers, administrators, social scientists, parents, child psychologists, economists, politicians, various professional and community groups, and students). Only a number of important observations are listed below to set the stage to illustrate the magnitude and seriousness of challenges confronting education. These are:

- cost of education (budget crises, burden shifting, high overhead, operational costs...)
- effectiveness of school systems (drop out rates, test scores, meeting government and professional association standards...)
- school facility (outdated equipment, maintenance costs, increasingly demanding physical space requirements, lack of sharing and cooperation...)
- education system (nonuniformity, poor entrance, testing and graduation standards, nonselective enrollment in public schools, local politics...)
- attitude of parents or homemakers (not participating enough, impact and use of technology, single parent, no parent at home...)
- students' discipline and attention span (learning attitude, no discipline, too much TV watching, too many distractions...)
- teacher quality (low pay, low incentive, frustration, continued education, need to adjust to new technology...)
- teaching methodology (traditional, inflexibility, rigid, sequential...)

Although the above is a non-exhaustive list, it amply demonstrates the magnitude and seriousness of the challenges confronting schools and broader school systems. Many (and the authors) agree that continuous improvement or ongoing transformation must take place in school systems to facilitate an effective change. In fact, one need not look very far to realize how many stakeholders contend that entire educational systems are in a crisis state. The issue at hand is to recognize the inevitable changes, to sort out the positive and correct changes emerging and to accelerate them with a thoughtful change plan that is executed in a way that increases the likelihood of success wherever and whenever possible. Let's examine below some of these fundamental changes.

A BRIEF LOOK AT CHANGES IN EDUCATION

Several fundamental changes are expected to become commonplace in most school divisions across the county within the next decade. First, school systems will see an influx in the need for technology in order for its students to remain competitive with more affluent school divisions. Students should have access to more than one or two computers in the classroom. Second, as suggested in our earlier discussion on changing student demographics (e.g., immigration) teachers and other administrators must be sensitive to race and cultural differences as the country becomes more and more diverse. Third, increased calls for accountability as demonstrated by mandated federal and statewide testing and accountability, increased graduation requirements, and learning standards for every subject. In addition, it is expected that each individual school will be expected to complete an annual report card documenting their success over the year. To successfully implement these changes requires a corresponding change in teaching styles, learning approaches, and access to required information. The authors make the following observations based on their own experiences. These changes may be viewed as a variety of forces or viewed as challenges or problems, which are calling upon administrators and other stakeholders to provide solutions.

Never Ending Calls for School Change

Never-ending calls for school reform or change over the last few decades have led only to the consensus that American education needs improvement. The problem, according to Thomas Wagner, is that people are confused about what's really wrong with public schools (2001). Worse, many of the accountability systems established in the last five years to improve schools are having the opposite effect. The standards movement, once touted as the cure-all for failing schools, "has degenerated into the 'standardized testing movement,' in which teachers teach to the test, students become scores, and everyone feels less motivation to learn and achieve. Inadequate attention gets paid to the development of the complex reasoning and problem-solving abilities necessary in a rapidly changing world or to the citizenship skills needed in a pluralistic society. And perhaps most troubling, high stakes testing attached to grade retention has led to increased dropout rates, especially among minorities.

Like Wagner we favor accountability systems that focus on what students can do with their knowledge, rather than what they can remember for a test; localized authority that holds teachers and administrators accountable for student learning, but allows them choice in curriculum and methodology; and smaller schools, where teachers and students know each other and children feel valued. None of these ideas is revolutionary; each has merit in the struggle to continuously improve and change schools to make them places of genuine, relevant learning.

Effect of Implosion of Physical Space

Due to advances of technologies in electronics, transportation, computers, and communications, the meaning of physical space continues to change. A parent can converse with a child over an intercom. A principal can address the entire school via broadcasting.

Using video conferencing, lectures may be shared among multiple sites (distant classrooms) so that lecturers' travel is minimized. This need not be limited to lectures in classrooms it can be extended to laboratories with experiments. With computers and computer networks, collaborative experiments are not only possible between labs in Williamsburg and Charlottesville with supercomputers but also between facilities in an elementary school and a university. Cable TV networks have been used to link some K–12 schools with the Cable in The Classroom programming.

The above phenomena are the consequence of implosion of physical space. It is clear we need to redefine the meaning of school systems, schools, classrooms, and laboratories. Over the years school districts have increased their use of distance learning technologies. We must continue to examine further what information technologies are required to cope with these and other changes. For example, how much can video technology serve as a solution for distance learning? How is distance or space an issue in learning, teaching or education?

The Uniqueness of Schools

Schools are different! How so? Schools differ from for-profit sector organizations in their tasks and technologies, environments, members, and structures. The primary task carried out by schools is the education of young people so that they can contribute to society. Educating children is a complex and uncertain task. There is, for example, considerable ambiguity and disagreement concerning educational content of the required curriculum and little public (and at times professional) consensus as to valid measures authenticating mastery of that curriculum. Further, the methods or technologies used to carry out this task are ambiguous, particularly in their effectiveness. The impact of a particular teaching strategy may be difficult to discern, and its applicability may vary for students with different characteristics (e.g., learning styles). These uncertainties create problems for each teacher as well as for the school or school system as a whole.

Not unlike for-profit organizations, schools are highly dependent on and vulnerable to their environments. Their enrollments rise and fall with birth and immigration rates, and their funding base erodes, as citizens demand lower taxes. In addition, as will be highlighted in Chapter 4 their customers or stakeholders are characterized by different and often mutually exclusive sets of interests. They are subject to close public scrutiny and to occasional "crises" that may arise within their communities. Unfortunately, still too many school administrators react to these forces by retrenching and defending, and their schools or school systems evolve into reactive, rather than proactive, organizations.

However, public schools in particular still enjoy near-monopoly status and generally lack an environmental force (despite the growth in charter, private or other types of schools) for matching that of competitive pressure. Although various types of competitive schools have increased in number, their total share of the market is still slight, accessible only to a relatively small percentage of the population.

Although some structural differences exist between schools and other organizations, these differences are not always very great. The administrative structures of schools originally were modeled after those of business organizations (Flynn, 1976), and schools have been characterized by their centrality of decision-making and their standardization of activities (Cummings & Worley, 2001). However, schools also have been called "loosely structured" and "loosely coupled" organizations (Weick, 1976). Those labels have been applied partly because teachers mostly carry out their work in self-contained classrooms; are highly autonomous; and are weakly interconnected in influence, interpersonal support, and the flow of information. Thus, the administrative (or horizontal) structures tend to be weak. Although these structural characteristics are similar to those of many for-profit organizations, they are not entirely appropriate for schools, given the uncertainties of their task and technologies. As suggested by Cooke (1993) better developed collegial structures would be particularly useful in schools for solving the problems experienced by those directly responsible for carrying out the primary tasks of the organization.

Implications for School Change

The organizational characteristics of schools have important implications for the design of school change initiatives. First, schools traditionally have highly developed administrative structures that enable them to interact with their environments, although not necessarily in a proactive manner. For example, all schools are subjected to public oversight concerning the academic achievement of their students. As a result, these sophisticated structures are quite good at collecting and reporting on the students' academic progress. Yet, despite the repetitive nature of annual standardized testing, still too few states have sought to achieve public consensus regarding the test instrument in advance of public criticism.

Second, the tasks performed by schools are somewhat uncertain. This uncertainty can create difficulties in task performance and can complicate other problems, including those of coordinating activities and allocating resources that routinely must be solved by all organizations. In states such as California, Texas, and Florida, for example, the number of non-English-speaking students continues to change dramatically from one year to the next. Although teachers and other members of the school community may be able to solve some of these problems by relying on traditional authority structures, other problems may be resolved only through the use of collaborative decision-making structures that often do not exist.

Third, teachers committed to their work are likely to receive greater intrinsic rewards if task-related issues are resolved properly. However, teachers typically do not have access to structures for collaborative problem solving or do not possess the skills needed to use such structures effectively should they exist.

Finally, despite their obvious bureaucratic characteristics, schools paradoxically may be regarded as underorganized systems. Communication among teachers is typically fragmented, curricular responsibilities between and within grade levels are frequently unclear, and the output requirements of the system are somewhat ambiguous. Correspondingly, many school districts exhibit characteristics of transorganizational systems. Schools within a given district can be said to be "loosely coupled" because leadership and power are typically dispersed among principals at largely autonomous school sites.

These four points explain why many school change initiatives focus heavily on creating collaborative decision-making structures that include teachers and parents and other stakeholders who must develop skills necessary to use such structures. These interventions can provide the school community with a base for identifying and solving problems that involve task and technological issues and that require the collective expertise of the entire school staff as well as the active support and involvement of parents and other stakeholders. Furthermore, they can provide a base for change initiation within schools and can make them more proactive vis-à-vis their environments. And although the appropriateness of collaborative structures depends on the precise nature of the school's or any organization's environment and tasks it is our contention that collaborative participation and decision-making structures should be a thread within all schools.

School change advocates will continue to call for large-scale reform in educational systems that require a systems approach to any change initiative. The next section offers a more in-depth discussion of school change and the need for a systems approach to such efforts.

SCHOOL CHANGE:
A SYSTEMS APPROACH IS ONE ANSWER

In response to the challenges and demands being placed on schools today, those calling for radical change continue to advocate changes in all aspects of the bureaucratic network that constitutes and surrounds K–12 education. Educational change has focused on the individual school site as well as on the complex policy-making machinery that directs and simultaneously constrains schools. School change advocates seek higher standards for all children, smaller class sizes, bona fide measurement systems and greater accountability, and more effective school organizations. In short, school personnel are being asked to attain higher standards, carry out their tasks differently, and organize differently to do so.

As organizations, schools are regarded by educators and many non-educators as completely unique and distinct from other organizational types. However, some advocates of school change view schools as no different, than the typical bureaucratic systems one might find in the for-profit and government sectors. For example, Cooke (1993) has indicated that there is some validity in both these views. Schools share certain characteristics with all open systems and can be diagnosed and changed along variables common to all organizations. At the same time, schools differ from other organizations with respect to such things as the tasks they perform and the technologies they use to accomplish those tasks. Considering both the similarities and differences between schools and for-profit organizations, a case can be made that change programs designed for business and industry are neither entirely suited to nor entirely inappropriate for school systems. Change techniques and theories developed for other organizations can be used constructively in schools but only if they are refocused and modified to be responsive to the special needs of these systems. However, one technique or theory that can be applied to all organizational change efforts is that of a systems view of the organization and an approach to bringing about change. The remainder of this section discusses the systems view in more detail.

Like others we suggest the need for a comprehensive, systemic approach to school change. As noted earlier, administrators and other school system stakeholders have been trying to address change for a long time. We agree with Saul Rockman (Banathy, 1991) that the problem is that, "Our reform efforts have dealt with practically every instructional issue one-at-à-time— and still we persist in our belief that schools are not performing as well as we would like and are in need of additional reforms." Like their for-profit counterparts, many disgruntled school stakeholders have come to call new efforts in this parade of reform programs the "flavor of the month." As a result, many are reticent to engage in new change initiatives.

Despite this reticence we agree with others before us that there is a need to take a systemic approach to any school or school system change effort. Systemic change offers an opportunity to enact change while moving beyond thinking about individuals and individual organizations, single problems and single solutions. It entails thinking about *systems*—policy systems, education systems, social service systems, information systems, technology systems.

Systemic change is a cyclical process in which the impact of change on all parts of the whole and their relationships to one another are taken into consideration. In the contexts of schools, it is not so much a detailed prescription for improving education as a philosophy advocating reflecting, rethinking, and restructuring.

Essentially, systemic change entails working with stakeholders throughout the system to:

- Create a change vision of what the stakeholders want the school or system to look like and accomplish (to include the prevailing culture—or "the way we do things around here").
- Take stock of the current situation.
- Identify strengths and areas of opportunities of the current system or school in light of the change vision.
- Identify or target several priority items for improvement or change.
- Establish a change plan (direction, execution, and evaluation) for addressing these priority items and for defining and measuring success.
- Monitor and assess progress regularly and revise change interventions or actions as needed.
- Take stock again and use execution and evaluation feedback to revisit the change vision and keep the change momentum going at critical points in the change effort.

As suggested earlier, our current information—or really knowledge-based society—necessitates a comprehensive redesign of our educational system. For example, educational technology is a key player in this change process. It is important to learn not only to manage it—to implement educationally sound applications of technology—but also to guide and facilitate the evolution of instructional *systems* in which such innovation will survive and flourish.

Today's administrators must face the change challenge head-on. And to do this, they must be facilitators of change, working alongside parents, community leaders, and other stakeholders, to design and implement learning systems that ensure that students can achieve *their* full potential. They must view every school change effort through a comprehensive or systemic change lens. Today's school change efforts must pay particular attention to the nature of the learning experiences, the instructional system that implements those learning experiences, the administrative system that supports the instructional system, and the governance system that governs the whole educational system.

HOW DO YOU CHANGE SCHOOLS THROUGH SYSTEMIC CHANGE?

At this point, you should understand a few of the basic ideas of systems theory, including the characteristics shared by most dynamic systems. The next step is to apply some of these ideas to education—one system with a deep need for systemic change.

School change is defined in many ways by different people. Traditional school change leaves the basic educational system intact, while fixing up or adding on discrete parts. Often, such change fails to consider how these parts *interrelate* to form the complete system in which they are intended to function. This frequently leads to superficial and short-lived change, as feedback loops—triggered by introduction of a change not clearly compatible with the rest of the system—reject it like a transplant patient rejects an incompatible organ.

Early advocates of systemic change often assumed this to mean that the only way to achieve lasting change was to discard the old system in its entirety and design a new one, meeting the new requirements, to take its place. Unfortunately, this ignored the practical reality that some existing subsystems remained a "good fit" with the new system's design, and would just have to be rebuilt if the new system started from scratch. It also neglected the *political* reality that those who control the existing system have a personal stake in the *status quo.*

Gradually, the fusion of the traditional school change perspective with the radical paradigm of early systemic change led to a more recent systemic change movement. For example, the Council on Systemic Change recognized that effective, lasting change *must* be systemic; that is, it must reflect the interrelationships among education's stakeholders and subsystems. With this view the Council also stressed the importance of understanding that it was or is often neither practical nor necessary to change the entire system at once—only to ensure that its old and new components reinforce rather than undermine one another.

Systems theory provides the *strategy* for school change, ensuring that a "critical mass" of coordinated change interventions takes place, and that stakeholders' needs are addressed (see Chapters 4–6 for a more detailed discussion of stakeholders). Aided by the previous work of others interested in successful school change, change agents in schools today will have a more versatile toolbox for undertaking change initiatives.

CONCLUSION

Advocates for school change continue to call for radical change in educational systems that may require schools to become organizations capable of tapping the vast underutilized potential of teachers, parents, and the community to find better ways to educate children. Principals, teachers, and parents are not being asked simply to do their jobs better; they are being asked to do different jobs as part of the demands for school change.

Principals and other administrators are being asked to lead radical change at a time when the task of educating children is more difficult than ever. Teachers are being asked to participate in improving the quality and performance of the school; to collectively solve problems and generate new and more effective approaches to teaching and learning; and to demonstrate new ways of relating to each other, to students, and to the community. Parents are being asked to participate more fully in the decisions affecting the direction, content, and delivery of their children's education.

This change process requires establishing new and effective structures and processes to promote broader participation in school governance, organizational or school improvement, and enhanced delivery of service; creating systems to measure results and share information; developing broader and deeper skills and knowledge through extensive training and development; and establishing appropriate systems to reward improvement.

A number of factors in schools will continue to make a positive response to demands for change and present special challenges. The loose coupling of various aspects of schools and the isolated functioning of teachers conspire against a systemic approach to change. Schools are still struggling with the institutionalization of well-developed or accepted strategy formulation, goal setting, accountability, and performance management systems. School administrators and other staff personnel will have to continue to get used to examining results, talking about goals and how to achieve them, watching trends collectively, solving problems, and being held accountable. We hope that by the time you finish reading this book that you have a better comfort level and understanding of what they can do to proactively identify the need for, execute, evaluate, and institutionalize school change. The reality is that we as educators, schools, school systems, educational systems, and the education industry has little choice but to proactively respond to the calls for more and more school change.

CHAPTER 2

CHALLENGES TO LEADING AND MANAGING SCHOOL SYSTEM CHANGE

INTRODUCTION

Leading or managing school system change—the phrase sounds reasonable enough, and yet, "leading" or "managing" change is probably one of the most troubling and challenging tasks facing schools or school systems today. Executing a major and lasting change requires principals, other school administrators and employees to develop skills akin to a juggler's. Instead of balls, however, administrators must juggle tasks, striking a delicate balance between individual and collective actions, paying attention to the content as well as the process of change, and pursuing both short-term and long-term goals.

Considering the complexity of the task, it is no wonder that many administrators feel overwhelmed—unable to keep all the balls of change in the air at the same time. The principal is too busy to add "change" related tasks to their already crowded schedule of "normal" activities, the science

Managing School System Change: Charting a Course for Renewal, pages 15–38
Copyright © 2004 by Information Age Publishing, Inc.

team leader nods his head during the meeting on managing curriculum change, but forgets the message as soon as he's back in his classroom; or the school system launches a change effort with great fanfare and enthusiasm, but then loses momentum into the second grading period and calls it quits. Consider the situation where an administrator recognizes that personal commitment helps create more teacher commitment to change, yet other demands prevent them from devoting more time to communicating.

To help address such problems, change experts have devised tactics over the years to help administrators do a better job on everything from crafting a vision to rewarding employees for productive behavior. Many of today's school administrators have been exposed to these tenets. However, it would not be surprising to find that many of the tactics are not used in school system change efforts. Despite volumes of literature on planned change, legions of consultants, and the best efforts of for-profit and not-for-profit organizations, school system change too often appears to be a chaotic process. It is frequently mismanaged, beset by unexpected developments, and often largely unfilled.

In the first part of this chapter, we briefly look at change failures and some factors contributing to these failures. Next, we take a more specific look at obstacles that must be overcome to decrease change failures. We present two broad themes: (1) School system change is extraordinarily difficult, and the fact that it occurs successfully at all is something of a miracle. (2) School system change is furthered, however, if and when a school system can strike a balance among key stakeholders in the process. No one person or group can make school system change "happen" alone—not the top of the school system mandating change, nor the middle executing what the top had ordained, and not the bottom "receiving" the efforts. A simplified model of the change process is incorporated in our discussion of the two broad themes. The chapter concludes with a discussion of the relationship of principals, teachers and school system change.

CHANGE FAILURES

Today's and tomorrow's school systems will evolve, not through random mutation, but through purposeful strategies to effectively lead and manage change initiatives that are predictable and respond effectively to unpredictable and shifting demands. Administrators and others responsible for school system change will need to change the way they lead or manage change. This means that more and more administrators and others will need to rethink old assumptions about what it takes to achieve the overall vision, mission, and goals of educational institutions (e.g., educating students) while doing so in an environment that is demanding change,

change, and more change. And they will have to do it "on the fly." They will need to improve the quality of discussions amongst key stakeholders and the speed with which they make decisions. Decisions will have to be made in an environment that is in large part unique. Perhaps the best place to start in understanding the administrative challenges to leading school system change initiatives is to take a brief look at change failures.

In efforts to respond to demands for change, schools and school systems like their for-profit counterparts are structuring and managing themselves differently to the traditional approaches in the past. Schools and for-profit organizations are all being challenged to be quality organizations, to be learning organizations, to be customer focused, to be at the forefront of the technology revolution and yet to be flatter and leaner organizations. The environmental rules have changed and so too have the design of organizations, management or administrative philosophies and techniques used to manage in this new environment. In short, there have been and continue to be a number of organizational change efforts across all sectors.

Over recent years many change failures have been reported. For example, the failure of many programs has been linked to a variety of factors, such as "lack of vision and commitment from senior management, limited integration with other systems and processes in the organization, and ill-conceived implementation plans." Perhaps Anderson and Anderson (2001a) sum up best what we know about change failures as they note:

> Organizations' track records at change are not very good. The vast majority of today's change efforts are failing to produce their intended business results. These struggling efforts are producing huge costs to budgets, time, people, customers, and faith in leadership. Organizations are spending tens of millions of dollars on change efforts such as reengineering and informational technology installations, yet not obtaining their intended return on investment. Furthermore, the very methods used in these failed efforts are causing tremendous resistance and burnout in people, loss of employee morale, and turmoil in the cultures of organizations. Put simply, organizational leaders are falling short in their efforts to lead change successfully (pp. 1–2).

While the reports focus mainly on change in the for-profit sector it is our contention that the lessons learned are easily generalizable to school system changes. Some of these change failure lessons are as follows:

1. they tend, for example, to focus on broad and longer-term issues which are not always perceived to be in the short-term "critical path" of the organization;
2. they rely heavily on education and training methods which encourage representational learning (through acquiring a new administra-

tive language, complete with jargon, catch-phrases, etc.) rather than behavioral learning (through doing);

3. they are too often driven by an exclusive core group who are seen to be the sole or main owners of the problem (and therefore of its solution);

4. such groups are often insensitive to the history, culture, and priorities within sub-parts of the organization (amongst the masses that really must be brought on board any change);

5. all this serves to set up a tension between "rhetoric" and the "reality."

Another way of viewing the problem with many change efforts to date is the failure of the responsible change agents to integrate content, people, and process. "Content" refers to what about the organization needs to change, which are usually the components found in the external domain, such as strategy, structure, systems, processes, technology, and work processes. "People" refers to the behaviors, emotions, minds, and spirits of the human beings who are designing, implementing, supporting, or being impacted by the change (mostly internal domains). "Process" refers to how the content and people changes will be planned for, designed, and implemented. In other words, process denotes the actions that will produce both the external (content) and internal (people) changes (Anderson & Anderson, 2001b). The failure of change efforts to achieve their objectives to date suggests a number of obstacles that administrators responsible for school system change must overcome if they are going to decrease the likelihood of school system change failures.

OBSTACLES TO OVERCOME

There is considerable evidence that most change programs don't achieve their objectives. Post-audits of failed efforts have identified a variety of potential problems that can be applied to school or school systems, including:

Absence of Clear Change Leadership

Nothing will derail a school system change program faster than absence of leadership. If the presumptive school or school system leaders lack credibility or credentials, demand politically acceptable solutions, or can't bring the rest of the administrative team to consensus, the whole effort is likely to be futile.

Change Initiative Burnout

A daunting obstacle is the weariness that settles on schools or school systems that have been forced to change more or less continuously as strategic' or environmental priorities change. Some employees will have seen five or six widely heralded change initiatives in their time with the school system, each promising salvation and each soon supplanted by yet another initiative. This leads to a bewildering mix of approaches with distinct methods, vocabularies, deliverables and teams of outside consultants, and these compete for a shrinking share of the organizational mind. When this syndrome prevails the cynics refer dismissively to the "fad of the month" and conclude that if they just wait patiently the latest one will soon pass. The beleaguered cartoon character Dilbert is a master at this passive resistance.

Stifling School System Cultures

School system cultures in which administrators, teachers and other staff are suspicious of ideas outside the status quo can quickly derail a change process. Often the rules of conduct and practice thought to be behind a school's earlier success are codified into rigid operating standards and styles. A more subtle form of resistance arises when the employees or administrators think they are doing well and regard the new program as an implicit criticism of their efforts.

Top Leadership (Administration) Turmoil

Too many initiatives have stalled or failed during turmoil in the leadership ranks. Not only is the champion of the change program gone, but the new team may not have accepted the initiative or may want to make their mark by doing something different. If there is a lot of turnover at the top no one can remember why various initiatives were started, and the school or school system becomes progressively more confused and disenchanted. These signals strengthen the status quo. Those clinging to the past are encouraged by inconsistencies in the picture of the future. They are further encouraged when the picture changes rapidly and for no apparent reason.

Lack of Urgency

If administrators, teachers, and other staff, for example, don't feel the change is urgently needed, other more pressing concerns (such as immediate state-mandated test results) will push it aside. This lack of urgency leads to the argument that "we're too busy now, and can't possibly spare the time." Others may protest that "We're already doing it," or "This is a waste of money." Furthermore, "we already know what the government or parents want and expect, which should be obvious since we're doing well right now."

Poor Change Execution

Execution problems range from not allocating enough resources or time, to the benefits and goals not being clearly understood by key stakeholders in the school system. It is also very hard to sustain enthusiasm if there is a lack of early success or if the successes aren't celebrated properly. If early encouraging results do not occur, it is important not to allow impatience to short-circuit key steps in building support or putting systems in place.

These obstacles or conditions provide some clarity about why the success rate of change efforts is so bad. Regardless of the reasons change efforts fail and whether or not things have or are still as bad when it comes to managing change, the reality is that even if only 50% or 25% of future school system change efforts were to fail, administrators would still need to be attentive to these obstacles to change success.

Administrators must recognize that school system change failure statistics may be just as alarming as those reported in the for-profit sector and that the only way they can decrease their own numbers is through continuous improvement, change execution, learning, and constantly transforming themselves. Administrators must do everything possible to try to understand and reduce the reasons for school system failures. Internal and external stakeholders will continue to expect better student performance and other results for the money they invest in schools, school systems, and these change efforts. The bar is being raised dramatically, and the already faltering latest change fad techniques being used today or thought up for tomorrow will certainly fail unless administrators can figure out what they need to do differently than in the past.

The key in our view is to move away from what appears to be a common practice of separating content change and people change to better integrating the two. It is our premise that this integration is best achieved by an increased emphasis on such things as maximizing stakeholder involvement and cooperation in school or school system change initiatives. Chapter 6 will discuss stakeholder involvement and cooperation in more detail. Before moving on to further discussion of the challenge of leading change initiatives, we suggest why, based on our own experiences, change initiatives oftentimes fail to meet objectives.

In our experience the failure of change initiatives can be attributed to factors found in the change process itself and its misuse. Thus, we believe the following factors, all of which can be directly tied to our later discussion on insufficient stakeholder involvement, contribute to the ineffectiveness of change efforts:

- Relying on the few versus the many.
- Not eliminating the "us" versus "them" mentality between organizational leaders and other members.
- Failing to link the various steps of the change process (i.e., design, execution, evaluation).
- Organizational culture shifts are secondary to process improvements.
- Incongruency in the change process itself.

THE CHALLENGES OF CHANGE

We dispel the difficulty of change efforts to discount well-intentioned attempts to portray "change" as a discrete process, which when followed "correctly" leads more or less inevitably to the new desired state. Implicit in this notion is the idea that the benefits of change, while perhaps not immediately perceived, will eventually be realized, and the whole school system will go forward thriving on the chaos that the process drags in its wake. Anyone who has been even marginally connected with a school system change effort knows this isn't so.

Our second theme—that no one makes change happen alone—sounds a more positive note. Successful change builds on constructive interactions and cooperation among multiple stakeholders within a school system. Three basic groups must be coordinated if the change is to be effectively executed: visionaries (future shapers), executioners, and beneficiaries. Each group carries its own assumptions, agendas, and reactions. Unless these are considered both at the outset and during the unfolding of the change process, the most well-meaning efforts will be thwarted.

A brief illustration makes this point. A consultant describes an experience she had teaching principals in a large school system about engineering change:

When I went to this school system, it seemed that at all their efforts to change were stricken with paralysis. I started off by talking to the principals. The group seemed very receptive, but afterwards, someone came up to me and said, "That was a very well-done workshop with interesting ideas, but you had the wrong group here. It's not principals who make change happen. It's our bosses at central office."

So I offered the same workshop to school administrators, minus the superintendent, from central office. Again, the crowd responded eagerly, but an administrator broke in near the end and declared, "That was a fascinating workshop, and we know there are many changes we have to manage. But you really ought to be talking to the superintendent and school board members.

Finally, assuming that the school system's most senior leaders would readily accept responsibility for executing change, I presented my ideas one more time to the top of the school system (superintendent and school board members). "That's all very well," simultaneously responded the superintendent and one school board member. "But there's a limit to how much we can do. Most of the time, it's the principals who actually determine whether the change gets executed or not" said the superintendent.

While each level acknowledged its dependence on the others, there was clearly no process for working through change issues together. As a result, change in this school system seemed destined to fail. In more successful school or school system change efforts, the key players have developed a process that enables them to work together. Chapter 6 discusses processes that enable key stakeholders to work together during school system change efforts.

THE MUDDLED LANDSCAPE OF CHANGE

How are you supposed to change the
tires on a car when it's going 65 miles per hour?

—Epitaph of a change agent

Real-life stories of school or school system change rarely measures up to the tidy experiences related in books and popular education magazines. The echo of the enthusiasm of those responsible for executing change fades as the hard work of change begins. No matter how much effort schools or school systems invest in preparation and workshops they are invariably insufficiently prepared for the difficulties of executing change. The responsibility for this situation lies in several areas.

In too many instances the change literature and popular press tend to consider school system change as a step-by-step process leading to success. However, recent writings have grown more sophisticated taking into account the often divergent methods called for in different scenarios (Sims, 2002); acknowledging that school system change should be a continuous, ongoing process rather than a short-term fix; and recognizing change as a reciprocal learning process between all levels of the school system. But still too often we find that many writings on school system change fail to concede that difficulties lie along the way.

The unrealistic portrayal of the school system change process can be dangerous. In too many instances school systems are inclined to push change faster and stop earlier than the process requires. Such inclinations are further strengthened by an illusion of control that in fact does not exist. School administrators are sometimes misled by authors or consultants who make change seem like a bounded, defined, discrete process with guidelines for success. They feel deceived; instead of a controllable process, they discover confusion.

In the real world, school systems cannot plot one change to be rationally and tenaciously pursued. Like other organizations, school and school systems must stakeout multiple changes at once and the change goals themselves must be continually reexamined, altered, added to, or even abandoned. Successful school system change efforts require a clear vision and teams of collaborating and cooperating individuals or stakeholders (e.g., parents, teachers, students, etc.) who hammer out the emerging details of the change process through bargaining, compromise, and negotiation.

The larger and more complex the school system change, the more likely it is that this kind of overlap and complexity occur. Any large-scale school system change entails at least some of the following characteristics:

- *Multiple changes.* Rather than being confined to one change, complex changes often involve many different changes. Some may be explicitly related; others not.
- *Incomplete changes.* Many of the changes that are initiated do not get completed. Events overtake them, or subsequent changes subsume them.
- *Uncertain future states.* It is difficult to predict or define exactly what a future state will be; there are many unknowns that limit the ability to describe it. Even when a future state can be described, there is a high probability that events will change the nature of that state before it is achieved.
- *Changes over long periods of time.* Large-scale school system changes take a long time to execute—in some cases, as much as two to four years. The dynamics of managing change over this period are different from those of managing a quick change with a discrete beginning and end.

Today's school system change efforts require that administrators wrestle with complex, real-time issues day after day in a changing environment composed of and affected by so many different individuals and stakeholders—each with their own hopes, dreams, and fears. For these school systems, operating in an increasingly demanding environment—with all the calls for accountability and complexity that implies—managing school system change does indeed require a juggler's skills.

Unfortunately, the unsettling nature of this process is often neglected in change "success stories," leading those who "make" change to judge their own performance too harshly. Instead of the crisp, logical and forward-moving process they have seen described, their own best efforts may feel like just "muddling along"—poking their fingers in the dikes as a flood of demands and forced modifications threatens to pour down over them. One school administrator executing multiple changes at a large school system described the sensations this way: "I feel like I need to be smarter. There's just no way I can do it. Then I realize it's not related to my inexperience at all, it's just the situation and the constant demands of change, change, change that come from the state, teachers, parents, students, and others!"

This kind of frustration is part of the landscape of school system change. In fact, while the change process has often been portrayed as an organization's quest for change like a brisk march along a well-marked path, those administrators in the middle of school system change are more likely to describe their journey as a laborious crawl toward an elusive, flickering goal, with many wrong turns and missed opportunities along the way. Only rarely does a school system know exactly where it's going, or how it should get there. In fact, in many instances in nearly every change project, especially in the middle, doubt exists on the original change vision because disruptions or problems mount and the end often seems like it is nowhere in sight.

School system change is often chaotic, messy, and painful, no matter what administrators do to smooth the process. Take the case of the administrator of a school system confronted with severe budget cuts. After a careful analysis of the options to respond to the budget cuts, the administrator decides to cut several programs. To further respond to the budget cut, she must lay off 5% of the school system's teachers. Although she does her best to make the reduction in force humane, both the teachers who leave and those who remain respond with anger, bitterness, and distrust. Did the administrator botch this change effort? Probably not. In fact there is no way to make laying-off teachers pleasant, and yet it can be an important and necessary step in responding to a force for change like a dramatic budget cut. Administrators responsible for change generally make unpopular decisions. A school system is made up of many different stakeholders, and each stakeholder is likely to be affected by—and to react to—any given change differently.

Administrators who undertake a change effort must grapple with unexpected forces both inside and outside the school system. No matter how carefully the administrators prepare for change, and no matter how realistic and committed they are, there will always be factors outside their control that may have a profound impact on the success of the change process. Those external, uncontrollable, and powerful forces are not to be underestimated, and they are one reason why there is a question on the manageability of school system change at all.

Given the number of forces that buffet a change process any number of events outside a school system's control can render the best change plan obsolete. Shifts in government regulations, funding, and stakeholder' expectations are all realities of school system life today, and administrators cannot expect to implement their plans free of such interruptions. All forms of action are in play simultaneously. The world does not stand still while administrators manage a change.

This, then, is at least part of the landscape of change and the resultant challenge of execution. School change is unusually more complex than expected. School administrators responsible for change may feel overwhelmed with frustration, or "lost" in the middle of the process. In order to realize the change goals, administrators may have to make decisions that are unpopular with at least part—if not all—of the school system. And throughout the process, the rest of the world continues to change and make demands. School change management is not a neat, sequential process. Unfortunately, it is a process that defeats many who strive for substantive school change.

A SIMPLIFIED MODEL OF STEPS IN THE CHANGE PROCESS

A number of models outlining steps for change have been developed over the years. Kurt Lewin's change model (1947) was one of the first, giving an overview of the change process. Lewin's model is based on the idea of force field analysis. Although force-field analysis may sound like something out of a *Star Trek* movie, it is a technique that can be used to analyze a change and help overcome resistance.

Lewin's model contends that a person's behavior is the product of two opposing forces; one force pushes toward preserving the status quo, and another force pushes for change. When the two opposing forces are approximately equal, current behavior is maintained. For behavioral change to occur, the forces maintaining status quo must be overcome. This can be accomplished by increasing the forces for change, by weakening the forces for status quo, or by a combination of these actions.

For school administrators, the first step in conducting a force-field analysis is to develop a list of all the forces promoting change and all those resisting change. Then determine which of the positive and which of the negative forces are the most powerful. The forces can be ranked in order of importance or by rate of strength. To facilitate the change, administrators try to remove or at least minimize some of the forces acting against the change in order to tip the balance so that the forces furthering the change outweigh those hindering the change. The complete steps in force field analysis are:

1. Identify the forces for change;
2. Identify the forces against change;
3. Brainstorm actions to reduce forces against change;
4. Brainstorm actions to enhance forces for change;
5. Assess feasibility of each action specified;
6. Prioritize actions;
7. Build an action plan from ranking actions, and
8. Develop timetable and budget for action plan.

Lewin's change model suggests that every change require employees to go through three steps. The three steps are: unfreezing, changing or moving, and refreezing. In order for change to be fully executed, the administrator must help provide a way for the new behavior to become an established practice.

Before reviewing each stage in more detail, it is important to highlight the assumptions that underlie this model:

- The change process involves learning something new, as well as discontinuing current attitudes, behaviors, or organizational practices.
- Change will not occur unless there is motivation to change. This is often the most difficult part of the change process.
- People are the hub of all organizational changes. Any change, whether in terms of structure, group process, reward systems, or job design, requires individuals to change.
- Resistance to change is found even when the goals of change are highly desirable.
- Effective change requires reinforcing new behaviors, attitudes, and organizational practices.

Let us now consider the three stages of change in more detail.

Unfreezing

In the unfreezing stage, employees must see the status quo as less than ideal. The administrator responsible for executing the change must spell out clearly to affected beneficiaries why the change is necessary. Allied Signal's former CEO, Lawrence Bossidy, described this step colorfully, as the "burning platform theory of change":

> When the roustabouts are standing on the offshore oilrig and the foreman yells, "Jump into the water," not only won't they jump but they also won't feel too kindly toward the foreman. There may be sharks in the water. They'll jump only when they themselves see the flames shooting up from the platform.... The leader's job is to help everyone see that the platform is burning, whether the flames are apparent or not. (Tichy & Charan, 1995)

In essence, unfreezing means overcoming fears about the change and other resistance to change. Organizations often accomplish unfreezing by eliminating the rewards for current behavior and showing that current behavior is not valued. Unfreezing on the part of individuals is an acceptance that change needs to occur. In essence, individuals surrender by allowing the boundaries of their status quo to be opened in preparation for change.

According to Ken Blanchard, a behavioral scientist, a major reason many efforts to change fail is that management does not consider the employees' point of view (Blanchard, 1992). Many changes require not only performing new tasks but also adopting new attitudes, such as teachers' willingness to assume additional decision-making responsibility or increasing the use of technology in the classroom. Beneficiaries may have difficulty changing their attitudes, especially if they are unsure about administration's sincerity.

Changing or Moving

When employees appreciate the need for a change and have received any necessary training, they are ready to begin altering their behavior. It is practical to begin by attempting to make basic changes in employees' behavior, rather than trying to change their values. Values, by their very nature, are more resistant to change. To induce changes in behavior, administrators should offer tangible and intangible rewards. As employees' attitudes become more positive, their values may shift as well.

The key to successfully executing school system change is to build on success. Administrators should determine those aspects of the change over which they have control and then try to carry them out successfully. An administrator should point out each change success along the way. This positive reinforcement will help employees to change their behavior and their attitudes.

Refreezing

The change process is complete only when employees make the new behaviors, attitudes, and values part of their routine. In school systems that do not manage change effectively, administrators may assume a change effort has succeeded simply because employees merely fulfill the basic requirements of a change without adjusting their routines or their attitudes. For example, technology is available in the classroom but teachers rarely use it to enhance student learning. In such cases, backsliding is likely. Employees may revert to their old practices when the initial pressure for change eases, because new procedures are less comfortable than the old familiar ones. Changes in the reward structure may be needed to ensure that the school system is not rewarding the old behaviors and merely hoping for new behaviors.

Backsliding is a natural response to change, but it can become a problem unless the administrator acts to get everyone back on track. An administrator should remind employees about what they have achieved so far and what is expected of them in the future. It is important for the school system to continue to reinforce and reward employees for behavior that shows they have made the desired change.

A brief example of an application of Lewin's model helps to understand change in action. One school system's approach to increasing the diversity of employees in the system is an illustration of how to use the Lewin model effectively. First, the school system emphasized unfreezing by helping employees debunk negative stereotypes about others. This also helped overcome resistance to change. Second, the school system moved employees' attitudes and behaviors by diversity training in which differences were emphasized as positive, and principals and others learned ways of training and developing minority employees. Third, the school system changed its reward system so administrators were evaluated and paid according to how they rewarded and institutionalized diversity, which helped refreeze the new attitudes and behaviors.

Lewin's model proposes that for change efforts to be successful, the three-stage process must be completed. Failures in efforts to change can be traced back to one of the three stages. Successful change thus requires that old behaviors be discarded, new behaviors be introduced, and these new behaviors be institutionalized and rewarded.

Given that change is far more complex than consultants and the literature often suggests, is there anything useful to be drawn from such advice? Should administrators simply fold up their tents and forgo any attempt to executive change systematically? Of course not! Moreover, there are many examples of successful change that have been built on reasonable advice. Our point is that rational suggestions for executing change are most useful when they are addressed to the entire range of people involved in the change process.

LEADING OR MANAGING CHANGE: CHANGE ROLES

Over the years, organizational change is typically modeled as a three-part process (similar to that suggested in Lewin's model) that takes the flawed organization, moves it through an arduous transition stage, and deposits it at the end in the enriched, desired state (see Lewin, 1947; Kanter, 1983; Nadler & Tushman, 1989). For example, whether the three phases follow Lewin's change model (unfreezing, changing, and refreezing), or a transition from current state to future state, the same major themes emerge:

- The school system must be awakened to a new reality and must disengage from the past, recognizing that the old way of doing things is no longer acceptable.
- Next, the school system creates and embraces a new vision of the future, uniting behind the steps necessary to achieve that vision.
- Finally, as new attitudes, practices, and policies are put in place to change the school system, these must be "refrozen" (as Lewin put it) or solidified.

As noted earlier, many forces "conspire" to frustrate change and to destabilize the process. Moreover, change is effected by a combination of actors, a much more varied group than is often suggested. Because there are multiple parties (and stakeholders) involved in making change happen, and because their assumptions, perspectives, and even agendas may not always converge, there is in fact a natural instability built into the change process. Thus, both external and internal dynamics are at work to rock the school system change boat. But whereas many of the external forces are truly uncontrollable, or at a minimum unpredictable, school systems can control the way the various actors in the change drama interact. And if these players share an understanding of what change is needed, of how that can be effected, and of the "price" to be paid, then the change process has a far better chance of succeeding. Chapters 4–6 build on the importance of a shared understanding of and cooperation between the various actors or stakeholders involved in school system change.

Who, then, is really involved in executing change? We would argue that change is successful only when the entire school system participates in the effort. But the school system isn't a monolith; it can be divided into three broad change categories; future shapers, executioners, and beneficiaries. Chapter 3 offers further discussion on the key roles and competencies administrators have to play in their role as change agents.

Future shapers lay the foundation for change and craft the "vision." They oversee the links between the school system and its environment (i.e., local community, other external stakeholders) that give the school system its identity; they speculate in managing the first of our three kinds of action. Future shapers are responsible for identifying the need for change, creating a vision of the desired outcome, deciding what is feasible, and choosing who should sponsor and defend it. They tune in to the external and internal environment, assessing the forces for change. School board members, superintendents, and principals typically, but not exclusively, are future shapers. They involve themselves in broad change design issues related to the resources the school system change would absorb; they do the big-picture work, reading the external signs and the perceived pressures for change. With their overview of the school system, they attempt to master the possibilities.

Executioners develop and enact the steps necessary to bring the vision to fruition; they manage the coordination among parts and the relationships among various stakeholders that give the school system its internal shape and culture, specializing in our second kind of action, the internal development of the school system. Executioners "make it happen," managing the day-to-day process of change. They are concerned with the action inside the school system, with coordination and habits. They are often assigned their role and given a mandate to institute the change on behalf of the future shapers. Depending on the extent of the "vision" that is handed down to them. Simultaneously, they must respond to demands from above while attempting to do so with the cooperation of those below. Principals primarily serve as executioners of change in school settings. However, the smart school systems show an increasing number of teachers fulfilling this role.

Beneficiaries, finally, adopt—or fail to adopt—the change plan. Their response to the promised distribution of tasks and rewards determines whether interest groups mobilize to support or oppose the change effort, either "refreezing" the organization in new habits or resulting in political turmoil—corresponding to our third kind of action. Beneficiaries, in fact, give the desired change its ultimate shape and sustainability. Beneficiaries are the institutionalizers: their behaviors determine whether a change will stick. Future shapers and executioners who fail to take that fact into account do so at their peril.

Breaking all the dramatis personae in a school system into three distinct groups is, of course, an oversimplification. The roles often overlap, and any given person in a school system is likely to assume each of these roles at some point during the different phases of the change process. Nevertheless, these players roughly correlate to the phases of the ideal change process; each group also more or less embodies the tasks that accompany the effort. And there are concrete numbers involved; for a given school system change, the future shapers are few; the executioners constitute a larger group; and the beneficiaries are the most broadly represented.

Beneficiaries are often portrayed as sources of resistance to change. However, understanding how beneficiaries perceive the change and how they experience it is key to successful school system change. This point of view is all too often underplayed by administrators. Indeed, if the majority of the school system that "uses" a change is considered only in terms of potential resistance, a self-fulfilling prophecy can result-treated as likely resistors, they fight the change.

PRINCIPALS, TEACHERS, AND CHANGE

Because principals are seen as the primary leaders in the individual school, this section examines how the principal is both a part of the environment or context while feeling the impact of the environment. Because specific strategies used by principals or other school administrators leading school system change efforts are central to any change initiative this section is intended to heighten awareness regarding the existence of factors that appear to facilitate or impede change. Without awareness of their existence, school administrators like principals cannot possibly address the problems they present to change, or the help they may provide for change might be overlooked.

There is no doubt that the impact of the school system environment on administrators responsible for change is profound. Factors such as the size or complexity of the school system or school district, the number and types of programs, teacher experience and stability, school level, district support and expectations, and other factors shape the principal's approach to leadership in general, and during change initiatives in particular. In addition, features of the community such as homogeneity, socioeconomic status of families, parental expectations and involvement, and geographic location simultaneously constrain the principal and provide different change opportunities. Principals who are aware of the inorganic factors of the school system environment and their influence on school change efforts may take steps to reduce or enhance the impact of those factors depending on the change needed in a particular school or school system.

Principals committed to continuous improvement or change will nurture the norms of school culture that support improvement and ongoing change. Developing collaborative and cooperative work cultures to help teachers and others deal with school system change efforts is a major responsibility of the principal. The important message for principals and other administrators about the leadership role they must play in school systems is best captured in Schein's (1985) observation: "The only thing of real importance that leaders do is to create and manage culture" (p. 20). An additional challenge for principals is that they are also part of the culture of the school system through their attitudes and relationships with others.

Like other leaders, past experiences can influence a principal's beliefs. Experiences as a teacher can cause principals to view going into the classroom for purposes of evaluation and change as a hostile intrusion. A belief that the power to legislate change is no guarantee that the change will occur also may be based in part on the principal's experience as a teacher. These experiences create "the tendency to deny that problems exist in the school" (Sarason, 1990, p. 147). A denial that can contribute to the development of a culture that is resistant to or aversive to change.

The active support of principals powerfully affects a school change effort's execution and institutionalization. The principal's contribution to positive cooperation and change execution lies in giving moral support to the staff and other stakeholders while also helping to create a culture that gives the change initiative "legitimacy" rather than simply in "how to do it" advice. To the extent that the principal is the gatekeeper of change he or she will give teachers the support and sanction necessary to their involvement in and perhaps acceptance of the need for school or school system change.

Principals' actions serve to legitimate whether a change is to be taken seriously and to support teachers and other staff both psychologically and with resources. The principal is the person most likely to be in a position to shape the organizational conditions necessary for change success, such as the development of a shared vision and goals, a climate of stakeholder collaboration, cooperation, change execution, and procedures for monitoring results. If principals do not understand and support them, if teachers do not view them as relevant to their own goals and needs and if the community and central office do not provide ongoing encouragement, support, and resources for school or school system change, it is doomed to fail.

While it may appear that principals have a great deal of power and freedom to act in a school in reality there are many restrictions, formal and informal, that limit the principal's freedom of action. One principal faced with impending restructuring described the conflicting feelings the prospect evoked: "I feel like a bird that has been caged for a long time. The door is now open. Will I dare to fly out? I am beginning to realize that the bars of the cage that have imprisoned me have also protected me from the hawks and falcons out there" (Barth, 1991, p. 128).

Like many other school administrators, principals have little formal preparation for managing school change. The principal must face problems of change that are as great as those that confront teachers. And, as is the case with their for-profit sector leader counterparts those who aren't in the role of the principal responsible for a school change effort don't understand the complexity of the problems they face. One thing we have learned about change over the years is that administrators, just like teachers, need partners, someone to nurture them, and persons with whom they can collaborate and cooperate with during change efforts.

The Relationship between Principals and Teachers

As it goes between teachers and the principal so will it go between other stakeholders involved in school or school system change' initiatives. If the teacher-principal relationship during a change effort can be characterized as helpful, supportive, trusting, so too will relationships between other administrators, teachers, students, and parents. A principal must recognize, and work toward building a collegial and collaborative relationship with teachers who are key stakeholders before, during, and after any planned change effort. Failure to avoid putting themselves in direct conflict with teachers during a change effort will doom the change initiative. However, such conflict may be unavoidable if the relationship between teachers and principals are already strained as a result of factors such as a growing emphasis on teacher empowerment and increased calls for "accountability." Principals must deal with the need for change along with issues of accountability, control, and change. And these are all values that increase the likely friction between principals and teachers. Without mutual respect, trust, and support between a principal and teachers no significant school change will occur.

Change will be undermined if misconceptions held by teachers regarding principals/administrators and by principals/administrators regarding teachers are not dealt with. In addition, as noted earlier in this chapter, broad participation in developing school system change effort program is essential to successful execution.

The degree to which the superintendent supports school system change affects the ability of principals or a particular school to change. The superintendent and central office administrators are key figures in stimulating and facilitating change efforts. Like their for-profit counterparts principals and teachers know they should avoid taking any change seriously unless the school systems (central administrators) demonstrate through actions that they should.

Principals are accountable to parents, the central office, school boards, and the state department of education. The school principal is the agent through which others seek to prevail on teachers to do their bidding. Barth (1990, p. 27) asserts "Principals are judged on the basis of how effectively they can muster teachers to the drumbeats of these others, by how well they monitor minimum competency measures, enforce compliance with district-wide curricula, account for the expenditure of funds, and implement the various policies of the school board." With these many forces exerting pressure on the principal, focus on the change effort may be difficult. However, stakeholders like teachers can play a key role in helping a principal to execute change.

Principals and Stakeholders

The support of the local community for a school and school or system change are vital for lasting change execution and institutionalization. Because, as noted in Chapter 7 the school's culture is impacted heavily by the external environment, the introspection and critical examination of the school by those who are responsible for a school or school system change effort cannot occur without a supportive community. If schools are to be successful in changing when necessary, parents and other members of the community must be actively involved in the school and school change effort.

Stakeholder group support and buy-in are key ingredients in reducing opposition to change. As will be discussed in Chapter 4, it is important, first, to identify stakeholder groups that are essential for effecting change. And as noted previously, some of the critical groups include teachers and teachers' organizations; school administrators (superintendent and other central office administrators) and the groups that represent them; school boards; parents; civic, business, and political leaders, including governors and legislators; and taxpayers generally. There is little chance to undertake successful school or school system change without the appropriate stakeholders.

Caught between the external demands of various stakeholder groups and the needs of teachers and students, as well as the community and institutional contexts, school administrators at both the district and school building level have a difficult role to fulfill. A principal's attitudes, beliefs, and values, like those of teachers and students, profoundly impact school or system change efforts.

Administrators must often take risks regarding what the system will allow. It is they who provide support, both psychologically and through the allocation of resources, to give credence to change execution efforts. Without this support, these efforts will not succeed. Administrators demonstrate this support through power sharing and relationships with teachers. Establishing and nurturing a culture of shared power and decision making, with norms of introspection for continuous improvement and change, is an important task for school administrators/principals. It is a task that is shaped by the community and institutional context in which administrators find themselves.

Implications for Principals and Change

Administrators responsible for school change efforts must understand that schools are complex organisms, with all parts interrelated and interdependent. The fact that the principal as a change agent is also part of this organism creates difficulty. The principal both acts on and is acted upon by the environment of the school. The school environment plays a vital role in school change efforts. Principals must understand and learn how to work with elements of the school environment if they want a school change initiative to succeed.

Many elements of the school environment impact the efforts of those seeking to undertake school change. For example, the size of a school and the policies it establishes may encourage the development of an environment or culture necessary to support change.

As discussed in Chapter 7 the culture of the school exerts a powerful and pervasive influence over everything in the school. It is important to understand the beliefs, values, and norms that make up a school's culture. The interaction of administrator, teacher, and other stakeholder' beliefs in a school powerfully impact what teachers and administrators do, what they see (in terms of what the problems are and what solutions can be considered), and what they are willing to change. Before a principal can work to change, if necessary, beliefs of key stakeholders, the beliefs held by teachers, as well as the principal's own beliefs, need examination. If the internally held beliefs and perceptions that truly guide behavior do not change, neither will the school, at least not for long.

Because actions reflect deeply held and often unquestioned beliefs and myths, the culture of the school may need alteration. This task requires understanding the culture, being open to criticism, and confronting those beliefs that act as barriers to change success. Changes in "the way we do things around here" will be made. A knowledge of factors identified by Schein (1985) which affect internalization can be used by administrators to help staff internalize the new school culture. (See Chapter 7 for a more detailed discussion of these factors).

Cultural norms of continuous improvement or change, a shared sense of purpose that includes a vision of "new way of doing things" as a major goal, and collaborative relationships provide support for school change efforts. Norms of continuous improvement, experimentation, innovation, and change imply that teachers constantly seek and assess potentially better practices inside and outside their own schools. This culture of continuous introspection helps build a school community where collaboration, collegiality, and involvement by many stakeholder groups in decision-making and the need to change may exist. This is vital to the development of a shared vision that is, in turn, vital to successful change execution. Not only should this shared vision include the outcomes desired by those involved, it also should include a shared vision about "how to get there," which includes the change process itself. A shared sense of purpose creates ownership of the change effort among all players. Administrators and others in a school or school system must be open to the idea that criticism is necessary because it exposes areas of weakness. If these weaknesses are denied or ignored change cannot happen.

All participants in school (or any other) change are asked to rethink their beliefs, recognize unproductive patterns, and change them. People confronting change seem primarily interested in three things when confronted with changing the informal rules they have worked out about how things are to be done. They are:

- How will this change affect me, and what I personally do?
- Why do you have reason to believe this can be implemented?
- Once implemented, why do you think it will work?

Principals can help resolve fears and provide support both emotionally and with necessary resources, including time. The resource of time is especially important considering that changing the culture of the school is extremely time consuming and costly. Teachers and others need to know what the new "thing" looks like when fully executed, and what modifications they can make, if needed, without sacrificing the integrity of the new way of doing things.

Teachers and Change

Teachers need to believe that they are the essential ingredients in the success of the change effort and to act in ways that confirm this belief. Principals can focus attention on the need for autonomy, independence, and a sense of efficacy on the part of teachers. Principals need to investigate past attempts to change the school and explain why this innovation is different. They also must understand that teachers are resistant to change based in part on past experiences with change and their belief system or mental model of schools. Change support and commitment cannot be mandated.

Teacher input into school matters is not new, of course, but charging teachers with responsibility for assessing needs, determining the school's direction or focus, proposing changes, and seeing that they work is still far less common. Furthermore, giving teachers authority to enact their recommendations is a significant change in the governance of many schools. However, it is our premise that successful school change cannot occur unless teachers play an active leadership role in the change process.

In some instances, teachers are playing a more active leadership role in school change. For example, school reforms such as site-based management and restructuring efforts over the past decade or so have included broader roles for teacher participation and leadership. Teacher leadership roles have also increasingly involved teachers as mentors, team leaders, curriculum developers, and staff development providers as part of efforts to improve the quality of public education while allowing teachers greater leadership in the development of those improvements and other change efforts. These roles continue to involve teachers in decision-making processes and facilitate teachers becoming leaders of change. As advocated by Nickse (1977) more than twenty-five years ago teachers should be involved in leadership roles in change efforts for four reasons:

- teachers have a vested interest, "they care about what they do and how they do it and feel a sense of responsibility for their efforts;"
- teachers have a sense of history, they are "aware of the norms of their colleagues;"
- teachers know the community, "have information concerning the values and attitudes of the community;" and
- teachers can implement change, they "are where the action is . . . in the position to initiate planned change on the basis of need" (p. 5).

Teachers must accept the responsibility of being active participants and leaders in school change efforts and with this comes the need for administrators to pay particular attention to the importance of teacher' cooperation in change processes.

Like other leaders in the for-profit sector, teachers must help to shape and foster a change vision, and build a collaborative partnership between various stakeholders. They must be proactive and take risks. In addition, they must strongly believe that the purpose of schools is to meet the academic needs of students and be an effective communicator and listener.

CONCLUSION

Leading or managing school change is probably one of the most troubling and challenging tasks facing administrators and schools today. As emphasized in this chapter school system change is and will continue to be extraordinarily difficult. Change will be furthered, however, if and when administrators strike a balance among the key stakeholders involved in the school system change process. Successful school system change will only happen when all levels of the system are involved in the change process: senior administrators at the top of the organization mandating change, the principals in the middle executing what the top has mandated, and the bottom "beneficiaries" receiving the efforts.

Successful school change requires understanding of the challenges of change, relationships between the various levels of the school or school system, and particularly the relationship between principals and teachers. For it is the strength of these and other relationships that will have the most impact on the likely success of school change efforts. Chapter 3 discusses the key roles and competencies, like building relationships between teachers and principals, which administrators must fulfill if they are to be successful agents of change.

CHAPTER 3

SCHOOL SYSTEM CHANGE

Key Roles and Competencies
for Administrators

INTRODUCTION

Those responsible for school system change cannot expect to rely on methodologies and theories to guide the change process itself, instead they must put an increased emphasis on the key competencies required of administrators as change agents that ultimately drive successful change engagements. In short, while there is a need to focus on the process (change management) it is equally important to pay particular attention to the human resource (administrators as change agents) component of the school system change equation.

This chapter provides a framework to address both of these issues. The framework presents a contemporary view of administrators as agents of change, with an overview of the key roles that they must be willing to fulfill in order to engage key stakeholders, and the personal competencies that they must develop in order to be capable of doing so.

Managing School System Change: Charting a Course for Renewal, pages 39–64
Copyright © 2004 by Information Age Publishing, Inc.
All rights of reproduction in any form reserved.

THE KEY ROLES OF SCHOOL
ADMINISTRATORS AS CHANGE AGENTS

Today's administrators must develop the personal competencies necessary to holistically approach their school system change efforts with the *brains* to understand and intellectually influence their school system, the *heart* to meaningfully connect with the people in various stakeholder groups, the *courage* to proactively change their school system, and the *vision* to define what their school system should look like in the future. Each of these— *brain, heart, courage,* and *vision*—are personal sources that must be collectively drawn upon by administrators (as change agents) as they operate within the following four *key roles:*

- School Partner—master the school system operations and the tools of a change agent
- Servant Leader—selflessly serve their school system's needs, both personally and professionally
- Change Champion—exhort the school system to strive for excellence throughout the change process
- Future Shaper—assist the school system and all stakeholders in defining the long-term future of the system

Each of these key roles is independent of one another, yet *interdependent* at the same time. That is, each provides administrators as change agents with a *decidedly different* platform from which to drive school change and yet intentionally progressing through each of the key roles results in administrators operating in an increasingly broad sphere of influence.

THE KEY ROLES AS SPHERES OF INFLUENCE

The School Partner Sphere of Influence

The *brain* must serve as the initial source of credibility for administrators as they strive to build internal and external networks as part of any school change initiative. Without first establishing this "brain-powered" credibility, the efforts of administrators undertaking school change are doomed to failure. Without it, administrators are regarded as "empty suits" with "soft" hearts, unnecessary school change missions, and misguided visions of the future.

The Servant Leader Sphere of Influence

Once a credible school partnership is established, the *heart* becomes the source of selflessness necessary for administrators to gain the full commitment and trust of key stakeholders. The administrator's main goal as Servant Leader is to demonstrate wholeness in approaching school life and work—a wholeness that compels a school system's stakeholders to fully engage (hands, mind, heart, and spirit) in the effort at hand and to trust that the administrator is committed, first and foremost, to the school system's (and their) success.

The Change Champion Sphere of Influence

Garnering the commitment and trust of the school system's stakeholder groups through selflessness earns the administrators the right to employ *courage* and champion change throughout the school system. Based on credible school system analysis conducted within the School Partner sphere, administrators can now proactively address school system dysfunction and manage change efforts to improve school system performance.

The Future Shaper Sphere of Influence

This final and broadest sphere of influence allows administrators to leverage *vision* and become a major driver of long-term strategic direction for their school systems. In order to operate in this sphere of influence, administrators' need to demonstrate a proven track record of results over a significant period of time within their school systems.

It is important to note that while administrators must *initially* progress through each of the four key roles successively to achieve increased breadth of influence, operating in one sphere does not mutually exclude the others. For example, once administrators have operated effectively in the School Partner sphere they will continually "regress" as needed to operate within that sphere; or, at times, they will concurrently operate in any combination of the four spheres. This dynamic is clearly demonstrated in Figure 3.1, which portrays the key roles as increasingly broad, but not mutually exclusive, spheres of influence.

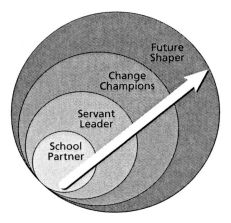

Figure 3.1.   Administrator as change agent: Key roles as spheres of influence.

PERFORMING THE KEY ROLES:
REQUIRED PERSONAL COMPETENCIES

Associated with each of the key roles are five personal competencies or keys to success that administrator's as change agents must master in their quest for excellence. Each competency is a *sine qua non* of personal success as a change agent. *None* can be excluded from an administrator's change toolkit if their goal is holistic school system change and stakeholder engagement. These "building blocks" are laid out in the unified model (Table 3.1), and a discussion of each follows.

Table 3.1.   Model for Administrator as Change Agent Success

Source	Brain	Heart	Courage	Vision
Key Role	School Partner	Servant Leader	Change Champion	Future Shaper
Competencies or Keys to Success	• Stakeholder Relationship Skills • Systems Thinking Skills • Organizational Analysis Skills • Change Agent Experience and Skills	• Servantship • Stewardship • Emotional Empathy • Teachability	• Change Alignment • Conflict Resolution • Forthrightness • Learning Facilitation	• Reflective Learning • Comfort with Ambiguity • Gained Wisdom • Visualization • Results Engineering

OPERATING IN THE FIRST KEY ROLE: SCHOOL PARTNER

As noted earlier, without first establishing a School System Partnership, administrators are regarded as "empty suits" with "soft" hearts, unnecessary school change missions, and misguided visions of the future. Many administrators have the desire to make their school system a better place, but may lack the frontline change agent skills to gain credibility. Thus, they lack the competencies for establishing a true *school partnership*. To gain credibility as a change agent in any school or school system, requires the ability of an administrator to reach into a tool kit for the knowledge, skills, and abilities the school system stakeholders will take seriously.

Such a tool kit is, then, an absolute prerequisite for administrators responsible for bringing about school system change who want to work with their stakeholders as School Partners to solve problems, create opportunities, capitalize on strategic windows, and leverage school system strengths. Without something to offer the partnership, promising administrators never get to first base, are never considered a player, and are forced to stay on the bench while the real work of the school system change happens around them. What specific skills are essential for promising administrators to become a driving force for change within school systems?

Stakeholder Relationship Skills

Participating in school change initiatives requires the ability to work with people and to be recognized as someone who will add value to the school system's efforts to meet its objectives and change as needed. While it would be nice for stakeholders to view the relationship between themselves and administrators as a partnership, it does not happen enough in our experience. Consequently, administrators face difficult challenges in developing stakeholder relationships as will be discussed in Chapter 6 on building stakeholder collaboration and cooperation during school system change efforts.

Listening, observing, and empathizing are skills that are extremely important for administrators as agents of change in school systems. Experience has taught us that too often administrators in unsuccessful school system change efforts seek to be the one listened too, instead of the one doing the listening. Administrators must strive to really hear what others are saying and to pick up on what is "between the lines" of a message. The first rule in relationship building with a stakeholder must be listening, truly hearing what stakeholders are saying, both verbally and non-verbally.

Similarly, too often administrators want to be the one being watched instead of the one watching. Administrators must be vigilantly observant in order to develop an accurate idea of the school system situation confronting them. Only then are they able to identify where the leverage points are in the school system, what the norms of behavior are, how the school system gets things done, and most importantly, how they can position themselves to add value to the school system's change efforts. Chapter 7 will discuss the importance of administrators taking the time to understand a school's culture before undertaking a change initiative.

People in school systems, like any organization, long to be understood. Although this process begins when administrators pay attention to others so they feel as if they are being "heard," it is most powerfully unleashed when an effort is made to walk in someone else's shoes. Stakeholders in the school system have a desire for administrators to make a connection to their reality in a very real and tangible way in general and even more so during a change effort. The real question that must be answered is "Does the school system's stakeholders truly believe you can relate to them in addressing the need for change given their interests or issues?" Chapters 4 and 6 will discuss stakeholders' issues, interests and issue selling. Developing the reflective skills of watching and listening are important to developing empathy, which translates into greater participation, collaboration, cooperation, and greater influence in most organizations or school system, as discussed in detail in the section on the key role of Servant Leader.

Systems Thinking Skills

Administrators must have the ability to identify gaps between what is (current state) and what should be (desired future state) in their school system's interactions with the external environment. To do so requires that administrators develop an understanding of the characteristics and dynamics of open systems and systems thinking in particular as discussed in Chapter 1. These characteristics form a framework for appraising a school system's internal environment, isolating problems, and identifying relationships critical to school effectiveness.

At its core, viewing and understanding a school as an open system requires that an administrator have detailed knowledge of the inputs, throughputs, and outputs of a school system, as well as the critical connections and *disconnections* existent therein. This is true both for the current state, as well as the evolving state, of the school system. The input-throughput-output cycle flows "smoothly" (albeit dysfunctionally at times) as long as the school system maintains its current processes and procedures. However, the change process itself will cause further breakdowns or disconnections that must be addressed as the school system evolves towards the desired future state. Successful administrators determine how existing school system policies and procedures help to preserve order, and are able to identify which policy and procedure changes are necessary to adapt to or anticipate changing external and internal environmental conditions. In short, administrators must keep the "macro-level" issues facing their school systems squarely in focus, while concurrently remaining connected to the "micro-level" workings of the same school systems. Put another way, administrators as change agents must learn the art of seeing both the forest and the trees (Senge, 1990). This challenge is only becoming taller as the demands for change and accountability increase and school systems become increasingly more complex.

School System Analysis Skills

Administrators must think of school system (organizational) analysis as a process, not an event. It involves all key school system decision-makers, stakeholders, and employees, and should be influenced by a clear understanding of the school system's performance needs, as well as its strategic goals and objectives. As a process, school system analysis is used to examine every aspect of school life.

School system analysis must be perceived as a daily philosophy and practice. As such, school system analysis is an everyday process for administrators. Most importantly, when uncertain of usefulness, effectiveness, or credibility administrators must conduct the appropriate analyses. Then and only then are they able to determine the viability and utility of various planned change activities, initiatives, interventions, and processes.

Change Agent Experience and Skills

Effective administrator change agents ensure that they have significant change-specific or technical training in their toolkit. Specialized change agent skills are needed in any school system change effort, including diagnostic or process analysis and redesign, outcomes or performance assessment and management, teacher, staff and administrative development, and change execution, and more. However, administrators cannot expect to be taken seriously in their school system change efforts without first having cut their teeth in undertaking change with increasingly significant responsibility. Thus, administrators must build their experience base around appropriate areas of change management. For example, an administrator like Joe Kitchen, the district superintendent for Western Heights Public Schools in Oklahoma City, first cut his teeth in undertaking change in his efforts to improve the use of technology to improve education through the Virtual School in Oklahoma Network (or VISION) project (Applegate & Saltrick, 2002). Through his collaborative work on the first phase of the VISION program he further developed change agent skills like: communicating a vision, getting stakeholders' buy-in, and developing a sound plan for assessing the performance of the project.

Despite the relative depth of change management technical expertise administrators who successfully undertake school system change avoid using jargon when explaining school system problems, instead relying on straightforward language to describe processes and approaches to solving problems or identifying the need for changes. Successful administrators understand the school and school system-specific language that other stakeholders (parents, students, teachers, staff, etc.) utilize every day. "Talking their language" allows administrators to establish joint partnerships that are more likely to involve stakeholder collaboration and cooperation. Employing the language of stakeholders is critical to issue selling, garnering stakeholder buy-in and the execution and institutionalization of any change or new school culture.

To aid in this effort administrators must take the initiative to remain current. This includes reading relevant educational journals, popular change management articles, and research on school system change, and reviewing school system documents which are critical to providing information about a school system's history, vision, mission, strategic goals, and performance measures. The discussion on balanced scorecard in Chapter 8 can assist administrators in their efforts to garner such information.

OPERATING IN THE SECOND KEY ROLE: SERVANT LEADER

The administrator's main goal as Servant Leader is to demonstrate wholeness in their approach to organizational life and work—a wholeness that compels the key stakeholders to fully engage (hands, mind, heart, and spirit) in the effort at hand and to trust that the administrator in their role as change agent is committed, first and foremost, to their (stakeholder's) and school system's success. Accessing the hearts of others is what enables administrators to bring about true individual and school system transformation. But accessing the hearts of others requires that administrators selflessly humble themselves. Therefore, administrators must become Servant Leaders, focused first and foremost on the success of those around them, recognizing that the school systems' stakeholders (particularly students) success is, ultimately, their own success.

Make no mistake about it—this is not a "soft" issue with no real connection to the "bottom line" of a change initiative. This is an imperative for administrators serious about truly gaining the trust and commitment of school system stakeholders, which of course is one of the most important goals of school system change agency. Operating in the key role of Servant Leader requires that administrators internalize and model the following four personal competencies: servantship, stewardship, emotional empathy, and teachability.

Servantship

In his seminal work on leadership and power, Robert Greenleaf (1970) introduced the American corporate world to the ideal of leadership as servantship. To be sure, Greenleaf's message initially fell mostly on deaf ears. However, in recent years, Peter Senge, Max DePree, Peter Block, Stephen Covey, and other pioneers of modern managerial and organizational thought have lent significant focus and legitimacy to the idea. And servant leadership has found its way in educational institutions at all levels and as evidenced in the development of organizations like the Servant Leadership National School Network. This leadership paradigm has been eloquently modeled through the lives of service and enduring accomplishments of some of history's most influential change agents, among them Mohandas Ghandi and Jesus Christ. Both men can be viewed as change agents who brought about transformational change through *radical selflessness* and *radical expressions of love.*

Radical Selflessness

As Greenleaf (1996) emphasizes in one of his posthumously published essays, Ghandi was perhaps the greatest leader of the common people the world has ever known. He achieved independence for India and catalyzed an end to the abuses of colonialism. Similarly, Jesus has been referred to as one of the most successful managers and change agents of all time (Briner, 1996). He established 2000 years ago what has since become one of the largest and most successful "organizations" in the world by forcefully challenging the hypocritical religious and oppressive civic forces of his day. Both men ultimately achieved their goals principally through radical selflessness, a willingness to put the needs of their followers above their own, and both eventually made the ultimate sacrifice to that end.

Does this mean that an administrator's success as a change agent depends on their willingness to submit to execution on behalf of the various stakeholders? Yes and no. While servantship in the world of school system change agency may not entail physical death, it does often entail administrators putting their professional necks on the line for their school systems—taking unpopular stands, occasionally in direct opposition to the powers that be. More directly, the success of administrator's school system change efforts depends on their ability to demonstrate a servant heart towards others, intentionally serving the needs and goals of various stakeholders before their own—making *them* their overriding focus, their purpose for being an administrator and advocate of school system change in the first place. This is how real trust and commitment are born, and equally important, it's the way an administrator's track record of servantship eventually becomes a source of significant leverage as they operate in the key roles of Change Champion and Future Shaper.

Radical Expressions of Love

As a change agent, Jesus was continually looking for ways to communicate to his immediate change project team (the twelve disciples) how valuable they were to him both personally and professionally, how much he appreciated their being a part of the same "engagement"—in short, how much he loved them. Perhaps one of the more compelling examples of this is the familiar story of Jesus humbly kneeling before the disciples and washing their feet, a job normally reserved for the lowliest slaves of Jesus' time.

Once again this does not mean that an administrator's school system change success depends on their willingness to *literally* wash the feet of their change team members, as a United States Senator recently did upon his successful election and the experience was apparently overwhelmingly moving for both the Senator and his election team. Rather, the message is how important it is for administrators to tangibly communicate appreciation to others who work with them during a change effort in meaningful ways, and to walk on common ground with them. Such communication can take many forms, and can be as simple as administrators rolling up their sleeves up and staying late to help photocopy change effort status reports due out first thing next morning; publicly praising the work of key change executioners, or sending one of the change team members an encouraging personal e-mail, just because. Acts such as these demonstrate in concrete ways that administrators and their change team members are all "in the same boat," and can go a long way towards creating a change team that is "radically committed" to the school system change initiative at hand.

Stewardship

While servantship entails intentionally putting the needs and the success of stakeholders above those of your own, stewardship takes it a step further and requires that you also be held *accountable* for meeting those needs and ensuring those successes (Block, 1992). And administrators must do so without employing a traditional command and control style, lest they slip back from being their school systems' steward to being their patriarch. It's one thing to operate as a brilliant yet humble administrator, consistently sharing the glory and giving other change team members' credit for change successes. It's another thing altogether to ensure that *they* have actually helped achieve the change success through clearly identifiable actions on their part, and thus have truly earned the praise. Administrators must approach their efforts as a steward—a change agent that *equips* and *empowers* others during school system change efforts.

Equip Others

Stewardship requires that administrators equip other members of the change team with the knowledge, work skills, and resources necessary for successful school system change. Administrators must make significant up-front and on-going investments in change-skill training for their change team members. Successful administrator change agents spend a good portion of every day imparting their personal wisdom, expertise, skills, and experience with teachers, staff, and others, always remembering that their goal in doing so is not to impress, but to equip for current or future change efforts.

Empower Others

Being a steward means that, once other members of the school system or change team have been equipped for a change battle, administrators let them fight it without unnecessary intervention. Successful change agent administrators give school system members the authority and autonomy to make significant change-related decisions. However, this does not mean sending them out to the wolves without any protection. Administrators must legitimize the empowerment of their change team members, formally articulating to the school system the extent and reason for a certain degree of autonomy by the team. Administrators must blaze a trail for the empowered change team members. If administrators are unwilling to do this, then they're not ready to empower the change team. For successful school system change to take place administrators must always remember that when a school system change effort fails, they fail as well.

Emotional Empathy

Today's administrators must view school life as being all about change (remember our discussion of the forces for and history of change drivers in school systems like the No Child Left Behind mandate)—both for them as the change visionaries or initiators of change, and for their school systems and employees as the recipients of change. They view change as a personal mandate, a challenge, a calling to proactively guide school systems in the right direction. However, successful change agents also understand that change is messy, and at times, decidedly emotional (Jick, 1993), especially for their school system, who often don't have the same adaptability to change as they do.

Thus the turmoil of school system change results in a great deal of emotional, transparency between administrators and other stakeholders in the school system. This transparency needs to be handled with great care and sensitivity—or put simply, with emotional empathy. The following steps are necessary for administrators to employ emotional empathy in working with various stakeholders during school system change initiatives.

1. Administrators must articulate to various stakeholders that it is normal, and even healthy, for them to feel what they are feeling.
2. Administrators must openly share their own feelings and emotions surrounding the change with the stakeholders on a regular basis.
3. Administrators must provide individual or group forums and outlets for stakeholders to express their emotions and feelings about the change.
4. When stakeholders do share their feelings and emotions administrators must actively listen to them, in an open and non-judgmental, yet discerning, manner.
5. Based on what they learn, administrators must then design and implement additional individual or group interventions as necessary.

Fulfilling the role of Servant Leader requires that administrators are empathically attuned to the emotions and feelings of teachers, students, parents, and others. Successful change agent administrators remember that these emotions are not only normal and inevitable, and therefore can't be ignored, and more importantly that practicing emotional empathy allows them to more holistically understand and engage stakeholders, thereby gaining more change leverage.

Teachability

Administrators must recognize that they don't always have the right answers and thereby embody a teachable nature, openly embracing situations in which they can learn. In a traditional, hierarchical school system change model the administrator has all the knowledge and viable ideas, and the followers simply soak up what the administrator espouses and spit it back as "good" followers are supposed to do. Under such a model the risk of the school system making poor change decisions is greatly increased because the successful execution of a change effort is dependent on the ideas, knowledge, and wisdom of just one person as opposed to many. The consequences often include severely handicapped school system change performance at minimum, and outright disaster at a maximum like the experiment of building the culture at the new school system discussed in Chapter 7.

An important connection to make here is that teachability not only results in administrators personally practicing continuous learning, but more importantly, almost always results in other members of the school system following suit. This in turn leads to greater levels of organizational learning, and as Senge and others have so passionately exhorted us to embrace over the last 10 years, it is precisely an organization's ability to learn that dictates its long-term success. Administrators must develop school cultures built on organizational learning if they intend to be successful in school system change efforts.

Administrators must demonstrate teachability. Administrators must be able to harness the collective energy and genius of the people in his or her school system if they are to be successful in school system change. This means that they must demonstrate teachability and harness the energy of teachers, students, and staff. They must tap into the ideas and expertise— the "genius" of other stakeholders—learn from it, and achieve greater school system change success as a result.

OPERATING IN THE THIRD KEY ROLE: CHANGE CHAMPION

Garnering the commitment and trust of various stakeholders through self-lessness earns administrators the right to demonstrate *courage* and champion change throughout the school system, proactively addressing organizational dysfunction and managing change efforts to improve school system performance. School system change is not for the weak. It requires that administrators possess the ability to tolerate rejection, even failure. Administrators who try to bring about change are in many instances considered "outsiders" by various stakeholders even though they are personally invested in and held accountable for the success of a school system. Further, they are often thrust into the latest school system change "political hot topic," for which they may be conveniently blamed, at some future date, for its failure or less than satisfactory impact on the school system. Kotter (1996) has clearly suggested that change agents need a healthy dose of courage as they confront the powerful organizational complacency and inertia around them. The world of school system change is not one for cowards. To fulfill the key role of Change Champion or what we referred to as Change Visionaries in Chapter 2, administrators must develop change alignment, conflict resolution, forthrightness, and learning facilitation competencies.

Change Alignment

Successful change agent administrators have a thorough understanding of the organizational behavior (OB) dynamics associated with the change process. Far too many change efforts have involved an attempt to design a fail-safe, lock-step change process without adequate focus on the overarching OB elements of the equation. These efforts are futile, and such detailed "recipes for success" must be replaced with a broader set of change imperatives that greatly enhance the probability of success for any school system change initiative.

SEVEN KEYS TO SUCCESSFUL SCHOOL SYSTEM CHANGE

To operate as a Change Champion with the courage to see the process through to the end, administrators must be equipped with, and be willing to hold themselves and others involved in the change effort accountable to the seven keys to successful school system change.

1. *Provide Strong, Highly Visible, and Personal Leadership.* Administrators must display an unswerving commitment to the goals of the school system change effort at hand. Further, they must claim a personal stake in the success of the change initiative and demonstrate a willingness to be held accountable for achieving that success through teamwork rather than through individual effort alone. Additionally, they must ensure that a clearly dedicated and visible administrative sponsor is 100% behind the change effort and is driving it at all levels of the school system.

2. *Institute Stakeholder Involvement Early And Often, at All Levels.* Administrators must ensure that as many stakeholders as possible, as early as possible, are actively involved in planning and conducting the change effort in some capacity.

3. *Build a Clearly-Articulated, Shared Vision.* Administrators must take the time to develop a shared and formally articulated vision for the change effort at hand, personally endorse it, and build support for it throughout the school system.

4. *Provide Frequent, Consistent, and Open Communication.* Administrators must ensure that as much information as possible is passed along to all the members of the school system at the appropriate times, and in

the appropriate manner. It's better to err on the side of providing too much rather than too little information, even if the details are still being developed.

5. *Leverage Talented and Trusted Stakeholders as Co-Change Champions and Agents.* Administrators must identify those teachers, staff, and other stakeholders that are most enthusiastic about the transition effort and have the highest level of credibility among their peers; and then give them opportunities to lead the charge by exhibiting modeling behavior.

6. *Set Measurable Operational and Behavioral Goals.* Administrators must work with the stakeholders to develop meaningful individual and system change goals that are designed to measure operational results and reinforce the development of teacher and staff work skills, competencies, and behaviors consistent with the desired future state of the school system.

7. *Celebrate Successes and Re-Address Shortcomings.* Finally, administrators must hold themselves and the rest of the school system accountable to the stated individual and school system change goals. They must take every opportunity to publicly and positively reinforce successes, while re-addressing shortcomings in the spirit of development and opportunity.

Conceptually it may help to connect the seven keys to Lewin's classic change model introduced in Chapter 2—the first three with "unfreezing," the next two with "changing," and the last two with "re-freezing"—as illustrated in Figure 3.2.

Thus, the overarching strategy for effective school system change alignment is clear—administrators must employ the seven keys to build momentum for the change effort, deploy the change plan, and provide performance accountability for the various stakeholders and the school system as a whole. Administrators must clearly articulate these seven principles as non-negotiable elements of the change strategy, and then remain unswerving as they employ the list and insist on the on-going commitment of others involved in the change effort to the seven keys.

Conflict Resolution

Conflict is a common by-product of *all* organizational change initiatives. Administrators must have the courage to work proactively to both prevent unnecessary conflict and aggressively resolve the inevitable conflicts that do arise. Doing so elevates change agents to the vital role of peacemaker

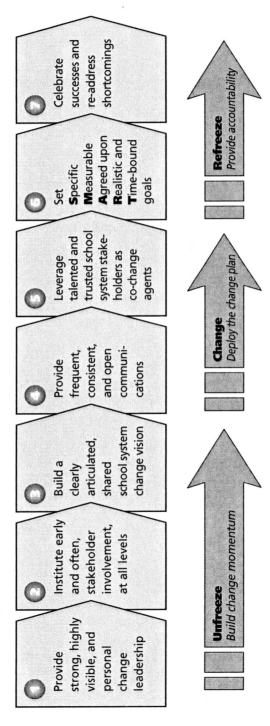

Figure 3.2. Lewin's Model and the Seven Keys to Successful School System Change.

(Goleman, 1998). Moreover, healthy conflict and aggressive conflict resolution can be leveraged to catalyze school system change.

Leveraging Conflict

Change Champions have the courage to embrace conflict as a natural and often beneficial outcome of the change process, and work with school or school system stakeholders to bring those conflicts to a healthy resolution. Leveraging conflict in this way depends on the ability of administrators to implement the following steps.

1. Proactively monitor individual stakeholders and the school system for sources of conflict. Administrators must always keep their conflict radar in full deployment, recognizing that the sources of conflict may be both human (personality clashes, team dysfunction) and inhuman (operational process inefficiency, information system crashes).

2. Once conflict is detected, work aggressively to constructively resolve it. When change administrators allow conflict to fester, it simply becomes a cancer to the school system change effort at hand. As the old saying goes, "deal with the elephant in the room."

3. Bring the parties involved in the conflict together to work through the issue. Attempting to resolve the conflict without directly involving all the parties concerned at the same time may enable administrators to avoid some heated discussions, but the end result is simply a prolonged conflict life-cycle and a greater potential for lingering resentment and misunderstanding. Through the 1990s, Jack Welch, former Chairman of General Electric championed a conflict resolution and organizational improvement process at GE called *Workout* that, simply put, involved sitting the people involved in a conflict in a room together until the conflict was brought to a constructive resolution. In short, administrators must have the courage to bring people together to "slay the elephant."

4. Ensure that the proposed resolution is implemented immediately. Nothing will damage an administrators' reputation for leveraging conflict more quickly than lack of follow through on the resolution. Successful administrators have the courage to decisively implement the solution, even when it will cause individual and organizational or school system pain.

Confronting conflict is messy and even personally and professionally painful at times. However, administrators must remain steadfast in their commitment to proactively and aggressively searching out conflict, embracing it as a change catalyst, and constructively bringing it to resolution. Those that fail to do so find that the "elephant" eventually sits right on top of them, effectively crushing their efforts as change agents.

Forthrightness

During complex and challenging school system change initiatives change administrators are often required to critically examine the behavior or performance of change team members or various stakeholders. How can this be done and still maintain positive collaborative and cooperative working relationships among the change team members? It certainly can not be accomplished through overly aggressive, rude, abusive, or sarcastic tactics all too often employed by some administrators to force changes in behavior. These methods only create resentment and seldom help resolve the problem. Moreover, avoiding problems and pretending they do not exist will only lead to prolonged and exacerbated conflict situations, as previously discussed. Unfortunately, many problems are not addressed until behavior or performance has deteriorated to such a point that drastic action must be taken. Often such action makes the situation even worse.

Successful administrators recognize the critical balance that must be struck between getting change work done and maintaining positive working relationships among those responsible for bringing the school system change to fruition. The only way this is achieved is through forthrightness.

An appropriately assertive and forthright message is nonjudgmental in tone, includes a transparent disclosure of the feelings incited by the behavior, and a clarification of the effects of stakeholder's behavior on the change initiative at hand (Bolton, 1986). Put simply, successful administrators ensure that they forthrightly address performance and behavior problems among those responsible for the change effort with clarity and with respect. Doing so greatly enhances stakeholders understanding of the dysfunctional effects of undesirable behavior, and leads to smoother and quicker resolution of the problem.

Learning Facilitation

Successful school system change requires that administrators also employ the courage to facilitate active and meaningful individual learning in conjunction with the school system change effort at hand. Since the publication of his seminal work on organizational learning Senge (1990) has called change agents to the critical task of learning facilitation. In our view, this means taking on this responsibility requires administrators to master the art of balancing "advocacy"—*teaching members of the school system,* and "inquiry"—*engaging stakeholders in the learning process* as part of any school system change effort.

Teach Stakeholders. Learning facilitation requires that administrators have the courage to teach others throughout the school system. To that end, administrators must employ the following list:

1. Clearly articulate knowledge transfer as a top priority. Successful administrator change agents unequivocally commit to knowledge transfer from themselves to others in the school system, and build into the change plans the infrastructures and interventions that enable this to happen.

2. Take advantage of "teachable moments." In the regular course of organizational life, let alone in the middle of a tumultuous school system change effort, numerous situations arise in which administrators are presented with ideal opportunities to teach. Administrators must have the courage to seize these moments as opportunities to reinforce knowledge transfer, whether the moments are positive or negative.

3. Hold members of the school system accountable for learning. Successful administrators integrate learning expectations and measurements for individual stakeholders into the change efforts' performance management process.

Engage Stakeholders in the Learning Process. In order for administrators to be effective facilitators of learning for others in the school system, they must draw them out and engage them in critical dialogue. To do so requires that administrators have the courage to employ the following strategies.

1. Ask questions. It is as simple as that. Successful administrators continually ask questions, never falling into the cowardly routine of pretending to know something or understand a situation simply because they don't want to appear ignorant. Equally important, if administrators sense the same dynamic in one or several stakeholders they ask the question for them, thereby seizing the situation as an ideal teachable moment for the stakeholder, and as an ideal opportunity to reinforce their commitment to knowledge transfer among the change team members and the school system as a whole.

2. Make connections. As administrators draw out the ideas, knowledge, and expertise of various stakeholders they must take every opportunity to make connections among that collective body of critical information.

3. Forgive failure. Some of the greatest learning that administrators and other stakeholders experience as part of change happens as a direct result of individual or school system failure. Successful administrators forgive failures, and embrace them as opportunities to engage stakeholders in the learning process.

OPERATING IN THE FOURTH KEY ROLE: FUTURE SHAPER

Operating in the fourth and most broadly influential key role of Future Shaper enables administrators to leverage *vision* and become a major driver of long-term strategic direction for the school systems. As a Future Shaper, administrators are responsible for identifying the path ahead and making midcourse corrections to avoid dangerous water. To do so, administrators must rely on past experiences as a source of information and wisdom. Moreover, visionary administrators continue to solicit the wisdom of various stakeholders and others with experience in school system change, and examine conditions before making commitments. Accordingly, they demonstrate faith in others while dynamically balancing optimism and realism, intuition, and planning. Such was the case in Joe Kitchen's efforts to bring his vision to fruition as he sought the wisdom and support of Oklahoma state legislators, business executives, teachers, parents and others to recognize and commit to a long-term strategic vision for Western Heights Public Schools and other K–12 schools in the State. Joe Kitchen's vision for VISION was a bold plan to bring the power of a digital infrastructure not just to one school district but, to an entire state system.

While in some rare cases visionary ability seems to be a birthright, for most school administrators such talent comes only over a period of time. Just as fine wine needs to age and single malt whiskey needs to mellow, the true development of administrator, as Future Shaper is most typically a developmental process. There is rarely a moment of enlightenment change administrators can point to as the moment when they "finally got it". Instead, administrators evolving towards Future Shapers find themselves on a journey that can only be described as a process of "becoming" that involves the development of the competencies of reflective learning, comfort with ambiguity, gained wisdom, visualization, and results engineering. Again, Joe Kitchens serves as an excellent example of such a school administrator's journey as he moved forward to achieve his dream. For example, despite the state of technology during the early 1990s, lack of financial, teacher, and political support, Kitchens continued to gain knowledge and visibility in the K–12 technology arena by evolving from attending technology conferences to presenting at them, building private/public partnerships, and garnering teacher, student, and parent support for VISION.

Reflective Learning

What seems to separate true visionary administrators from the crowd is their inquisitiveness, their impatience with the status quo—in themselves, in others, and in the school systems they impact. Thus, long-term effectiveness as a agent of change is directly correlated with a personal commitment to intentional and reflective lifelong learning.

Many organizations such as the Center for Creative Leadership offer leadership development process models with reflective learning built into them that are highly applicable to administrators desiring to become Future Shapers (McCauley, Moxley, & Van Velsor, 1998). Such models must require assessment (identifying a gap in present and desired states), challenge (experiencing disequilibrium), and support (reflective guidance before, during, and after the experience), thus requiring administrators to begin with an honest critical assessment of where they stand today in relationship to their future goals, expose them to new experiences while concurrently requiring them to experiment with different solutions, and through the process metamorphasize them into better equipped change agents. Successful administrators understand that true reflective learning only happens when *all three* of the components are present. Assessment itself will not change anything. Experience without assessment and reflection is simply a ride. Reflection without prior assessment and experiences on which to reflect is empty.

Further, truly visionary administrators also recognize that the reflective learning process is not strictly a personal one and that it must also be a system-wide process. Such change administrators implore their school systems to employ system employee development programs that encourage assessment, risk taking, and reflection in an effort to improve long-term school system learning and performance.

Comfort with Ambiguity

Seasoned administrators must develop within themselves a comfort level with ambiguity. Too often administrators struggle with this issue from two different directions. On the one hand, sensate—oriented administrators struggle with *analysis paralysis,* not allowing decisions to be made until *all* the data has been gathered and analyzed and *all* the unknowns have become known. The notion that decisions cannot be made until all the facts are in and all the variables are known simply will not work today with the increased demand and pace of change required in most school systems. A second type of struggle is the *back seat driver* approach to administrator change agency. Here, the administrator appears to be comfortable with delegation and decision making but then hovers so closely to "inspect" change team member progress that performance is stifled. Visionary administrators recognize the futility of both of these approaches to school system change.

Future shapers recognize that decisions must be made with wisdom and intuition based on the known available facts at hand, and that they must also be made in "real time" given the numerous opportunities and threats facing their school systems. They further recognize that moving their school systems forward to meet their strategic goals and objectives can only happen if the power of individual performance is unleashed through real delegation in a "freedom to fail" environment. Max DePree, widely regarded as a contemporary sage of leadership and management theory, has commented that "the more comfortable you can make yourself with ambiguity, the better leader you will be." (De Pree, 1992, p. 57). Successful and seasoned change administrators heed DePree's words, and develop comfort operating in the "gray" areas of school system change.

Gained Wisdom

Listen, my sons, to a father's instruction; pay attention and gain understanding . . .
Do not forsake wisdom, and she will protect you; love her, and she will watch over you.
Wisdom is supreme; therefore get wisdom. Though it cost you all you have,
get understanding.
—Proverbs 4:1, 6–7

Written three thousand years ago by King Solomon, one of the "wisest men who ever lived," these words have a timeless applicability to school system change. As administrators evolve into Future Shapers they experience many things and work with many seasoned administrators, teachers and other staff that afford them opportunities to develop wisdom. Successful administrators embrace those opportunities, enabling them to draw on that wisdom as they map out the future state of their school systems.

An important reality for administrators to accept right away is that wisdom is most often gained through practical experience and instruction from more experienced colleagues. Many hard-charging administrators of the 21st century find this difficult reality hard to swallow, but successful school change administrators recognize that it is consistent with their makeup as teachable Servant Leaders, as discussed in the previous section. To this end, administrators must commit to the following list of absolutes in their quest to develop gained wisdom.

1. Tap into the wisdom of the "elders" in the school system -Despite the "generation gap" that exists between younger administrators and

older stakeholders in the school system savvy administrators tap into their wisdom and understanding. Often their insights into the culture, history, and people of the school system prove to be invaluable to the change effort at hand, and are available from virtually no other source. Listen to their stories. Observe the artifacts in their offices. In short, honor their wisdom and absorb as much of it as possible.

2. Build a "Wisdom War-chest"—As an administrator's change experience base grows so too do their battle scars. Future Shapers have the hindsight and vision to see those experiences within the broader contexts of both the past as well as the future, continually asking themselves the following questions: "What can/did I learn from this change/incident/experience?" and "How can I apply the lessons from this change/incident/experience in the future?"

3. Patiently and progressively wield wisdom-based influence on an organizational level. Seasoned change administrators must never be in a rush to display their rich wisdom to the rest of the school system. Remember that wisdom is gained, and that administrators must patiently earn the right to influence the direction of the school system when drawing from their wisdom-base as the source of that influence. Once they have done so, administrators can then gradually broaden the scope of their wisdom-based influence.

4. Share wisdom with others on an individual level—Once administrators have become established as a true source of gained wisdom at the organizational level they must then commit to sharing their insights with others throughout the school system. This must be done in an intentional yet casual way, as a mentor of future change agents who will in-turn become future sources of wisdom for the school system.

Understanding and employing this list enables administrators to differentiate themselves as "wise" change agents as opposed to "foolish" ones—change agents that have earned the right to influence and shape the future of their schools or school systems. Thus, the implications of demonstrating gained wisdom are clear. Seasoned administrators wield a source and breadth of influence during school system change efforts that is much more significant than mere intellectual knowledge, extensive practical experience or even seniority.

Visualization

Future shapers serve a unique role in their school systems. In a sea of change, choppy water, and uncertainty, Future Shapers are called on to find the horizon for those on board. The definition of what the school system is fundamentally about, what it will and will not do, where it will and will not go, and where the boundaries are, is the work of Future Shapers. Accomplished athletes use the technique of visualization often in preparation for competition. Michael Jordan, Jack Nicklaus, Jackie Joyner Kersee, Wayne Gretzky, and others could visualize the performance before the moment of truth and then turn that vision into reality during the heat of competition. So it needs to be for Future Shapers in charting the course for change in their school systems.

Such visualization of the future is not always clear, which is a critical reason that comfort with ambiguity is so important. Often, the first glimpse administrators have of the future will be fuzzy, unclear, and seem ludicrous. Think of John F. Kennedy's bold prediction of sending a man to the moon. An inspirational moment to be sure, but at the time he uttered those words, that reality seemed incredible to most and even for Kennedy must have been a bit of a stretch. However, his ability to go to the edge of present reality to define a future state demonstrated the brilliance of his change agency. To become Future Shapers, administrators must be like Kennedy and break away from certainty. They must rise above the known to see another, altogether different and higher plane. They must allow their feet to leave the solid ground of the present.

Results Engineering

Future shaping administrators don't simply have their heads in the clouds visualizing unrealistic dreams of the future. As bold as his prediction was, Kennedy knew in his gut that he would be able to deliver on his promised deliverable, and he engineered the results of the space program to that end. Thus, the final competency of a seasoned administrator change agent involves an unyielding commitment to results. Once the future reality is defined, effective change agents focus with laser like precision on the journey to that reality.

The purpose of any administrator during a change initiative is to secure results for their school, from increasing student learning to improving the healthfulness of the school system culture. Successful administrators accept the fact that the ultimate accountability surrounding change results is theirs, and theirs alone. However, they are also acutely aware that they will only achieve the desired results in concert with other stakeholders—in short, that results are ultimately achieved *through other people*. Thus, administrators must employ the following components of results engineering.

1. Clearly articulate the driving needs for the change. Without legitimate and widely understood business-driven needs school system change initiatives are doomed to failure. Seasoned administrators ensure that "felt-need" exists within their school or school systems.

2. Clearly define the desired deliverables and results. Administrators must outline, as early as possible, the specific deliverables and results for which those responsible for the school system change will be held accountable. They must also ensure that these deliverables and results are concretely related to the needs for the change initiative at hand.

3. Integrate a performance management process into the change effort infrastructure. Results engineering requires that administrators abandon the traditional "one-time-annual-event" model of performance evaluation and instead commit to an on-going *process* of evaluating and managing the performance of those responsible for a school or school system change and the overall change effort.

Future Shapers are obsessed with achieving results. By engineering their change effort infrastructures in such a way as to create a culture of results-orientation (via the use of tools like the balanced scorecard) among those stakeholders' ultimately accountable for change success, they better ensure that the desired school system change results will be achieved.

CONCLUSION

The state of contemporary school system life dictates that administrators and other stakeholders must accept responsibility for continuous improvement and change. Administrators cannot approach the demands for change being placed on school systems to change as solely school system analysts, student advocates, change drivers, or strategic planners. Rather, they must concurrently embody each of these approaches to be successful change agents. Further, they must turn their attention within the school system to focus more time and energy on equipping themselves as change agents.

The ideas offered in this chapter presents contemporary administrators with four distinct, yet critically connected platforms from which to drive successful school system change initiatives. The competencies required for effectively operating in each of the four roles—School Partner, Servant Leader, Change Champion, and Future Shaper—have been clearly articulated above. While it may appear overwhelming and perhaps even impossible for any single administrator to effectively fill all four roles the contemporary school system change landscape demands nothing less. Successful administrators will begin by critically reflecting on their toolkit in relationship to the ideas offered above, assessing where the gaps exist, and taking concrete measures to eliminate those gaps. Aspiring administrators recognize that school system change begins with them.

CHAPTER 4

MANAGING SCHOOL SYSTEM CHANGE

Stakeholder Theory Analysis

INTRODUCTION

There are a variety of stakeholders who have significant and legitimate interests in a school system change effort. Clear understanding of the potential role and contributions of the many different stakeholders is a fundamental prerequisite for a successful school system change initiative. These multiple stakeholders with vested interest in the success of the school system change effort must interact and come to a workable consensus on the various activities or components of the planned change. It has been our experience that oftentimes institutions tend to limit the number of stakeholders who participate in various change efforts. This can prove fatal to a school system change initiative.

After first defining what is meant by stakeholders this chapter discusses stakeholder theory and analysis along with identifying some of the key stakeholders and their roles involved in a school system change effort. The chapter also discusses the application of stakeholder theory and analysis to school system change.

Managing School System Change: Charting a Course for Renewal, pages 65–86

STAKEHOLDERS DEFINED

The past century of education has seen an expanding number of services that schools are expected to provide to students as a part of their education. Historically schools have served two purposes: education and socialization. Education is viewed as a development of the mind. As the mind develops, students are expected to begin to think critically and understand various subjects. In addition to education, schools have also served a socialization component where they are expected to prepare students for adult life and active roles as members of society. More recently a third component of schools have been added. This third component is nurturing. Schools are now expected to nurture students' physical, moral, and emotional development (Gunn, 1995). As more components are being added to the education system more stakeholders are also being added. These stakeholders must now compete for limited resources.

The 1980s and early 1990s was a peak period for valiant educational reforms. Each proposed/adopted educational reform meant that more and more stakeholders became involved in the educational system. Thus resulting in a tumultuous time period for education. Decentralized or school-based management and shared decision-making became the norm for many school systems after the 1980's and 1990's. School-based management meant that decision-making authority was shifted from the state level to the individual schools. This resulted in more shared decisions where principals called on others in the school and community to aid in the decision making process. It is believed that decisions that are made with multiple groups input are likely to be more responsive to the specific, individual school problems (Stevenson, 2001). After a few years of relatively calm waters, education is once again at a turning point. Numerous groups and individuals have voices and opinions that they would like to see reflected in the educational system. Some view these groups/individuals as "partner" whereas others view them as "stakeholder" in the educational system. Gunn (1995) offers the following definitions to distinguish the two groups although the terms are oftentimes used interchangeably. Partners work together in a common enterprise. Thus a partnership is viewed as a give and take relationship where the best interest of the student is always given top priority. On the other hand a stakeholder is generally defined as any group who have an interest in, or impact on, an educational system.

The primary goal of a stakeholder is the achievement of their objective (stake). Stakeholders are viewed as having something to gain or lose as they participate in the educational system. Oftentimes stakeholder groups are in conflict with one another in achieving what they want from the educational system. For the remainder of this book, we will use the term stakeholder to refer to any group or individual who participates in a school system change process.

STAKEHOLDER THEORY AND ANALYSIS

At least 100 articles and a dozen books have been written on stakeholder theory (Garrison & Borgia, 1999). The purpose of stakeholder theory is to explain and guide the structure and operation of an existing organizational system and the level of achievement or financial success within that system. When applying stakeholder theory and analysis to education, one must focus on how to define quality in an educational system and how to serve the needs of its various constituents. With this in mind the educational system is viewed as an organizational entity through which numerous and diverse participants can accomplish multiple purposes (Donaldson & Preston, 1995). These diverse participants may include a myriad group of participants such as university personnel, government officials, political candidates, religious leaders, business leaders, and possibly social service agents. One must also keep in mind the typical stakeholders that come to mind when educational change is considered. Figure 4.1, for example, identifies a typical group of stakeholders that principals must interact with as decisions are made. These stakeholders include students, teacher,

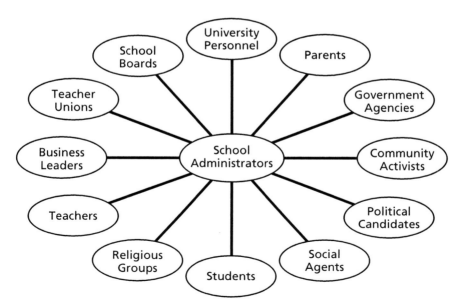

Figure 4.1.   School System Stakeholder Map

administrators, parents, and the community. By including these stakeholders in defining educational achievement and quality, more useful benchmarks may be established. These benchmarks may include graduation rates, higher standardized test scores, reduction in achievement gaps, student independence, and dropout rates, just to name a few (Garrison & Borgia, 1999).

Stakeholder analysis is a basic tool available to administrators for achieving understanding of the multiple stakeholders like those identified in Figure 4.1 that will play particular roles and make contributions to school system change efforts. To ensure a balanced representation, the analysis should examine and identify stakeholders across a number of different dimensions. For example, the analysis should separately identify relevant individuals and group's interests within and outside the school system. In addition, the analysis can seek out potential stakeholders to ensure proper representation in relation to students, parents, teachers, government and private organizations, local community, etc. Cutting across these categories the analysis can also look at stakeholders in terms of their information, expertise and resources applicable to the school system change effort. However, stakeholder analysis by itself only identifies potentially relevant stakeholders—it does not ensure that they will become active and meaningful participants; other measures to generate interest and sustain commitment, participation, and cooperation will be necessary as discussed in Chapter 6. One place administrators can begin to increase their understanding of the multiple stakeholders is by considering the political environment in which change and other decisions are made in a school system.

A STAKEHOLDERS' MODEL FOR SCHOOL SYSTEM CHANGE: POLITICAL LENS

The term "stakeholders," which today has entered the basic vocabulary of educators, lies at the core of a political perspective on the school system environment. Stakeholders are the social actors who play a role in the survival and success of the school system and who are affected by a school system's activities—that is, they have a stake in its operations. The stakeholder model of the school system environment extends the political lens's focus on power, interests, influence, coalition-building, and negotiation beyond the formal boundaries of the school system to provide a way to assess the environment's influence—and potential influence—on the school system, and the school or school system's bargaining power vis-à-vis that environment when undertaking a change initiative.

As noted earlier, key stakeholders for school systems include, students, teachers, administrators, parents, local communities, accrediting agencies, and government just to name a few. Often a distinction is made between internal stakeholders—those who are formally members of the school system—and external stakeholders. But this distinction, while useful in many ways, is difficult to maintain rigorously because many internal stakeholders have multiple stakeholder identities. School employees, for example, are also members of the local community, some may be members of a teachers union, and others (especially top administrators) may be part of school boards. Some external organizations also play multiple stakeholder roles. In public schools, state and federal governments may be simultaneously a regulator and customer.

In the stakeholder model, two of the variables on which principals or other administrators responsible for system change must focus are:

- Interests (What does each set of stakeholders want? How clearly defined are those interests? What are the priorities assigned to those interests, and can priorities be altered?)
- Power and influence (What is the basis of power or influence of each set of stakeholders?)

The key processes in school system-environment change efforts on which this model focuses are negotiation between the change champion (e.g., principal or other administrators) and key stakeholders to build support for their change agendas, and vice-versa.

In today's environment of school system change, stakeholders are becoming more diverse and often draw the members of the school system more aggressively into recognizing and identifying with their interests: in other words, stakeholders are becoming more densely networked across the boundaries of a school system.

The stakeholders' model calls attention to groups that are often not formally organized but are potentially important and can be mobilized, such as parents and alumni(ae). It also includes unions, which organize subsets of the employees (in some schools, for example, teachers who are affiliated with a union at other school systems, or employees charged with maintenance of the school system's physical facilities are often members of craft or industrial unions). And it includes the local community, for which the school may be important in a number of ways: as an employer, a source of attraction for businesses, and occupier of land and user of services that pays lower (or no) local taxes than businesses.

A stakeholders' approach to a school system change should begin by asking questions such as the following: Who are the key stakeholders who will be affected by this decision? What is their reaction likely to be? Can or should we make efforts to increase the involvement of the stakeholders favorably disposed to this move? How will it affect the relative power of current stakeholders?

The model draws attention to the fact that although interests of various stakeholders may be compatible, they are not identical. The local community may share with the school system an interest in the school system maintaining its reputation as a leading K–12 institution or system, for example. But if the school system decides that in order to do this it needs additional land to build a new school, the local community's interests in maintaining a lower citizens' property tax rate and protecting citizens from increased taxes may override the shared interests, and require the school system to engage in intensive negotiations with the local community before it can carry out its plans.

STAKEHOLDER ANALYSIS IN THE SCHOOL SYSTEM

As suggested previously in this book school administrators/principals are faced with unprecedented demands for change. Leading change and integration, both within a school system and across schools, has become and will continue to be a leadership requirement.

School administrators must also be able to assume the roles required for strategic and transformational change. They must be able to lead, direct, and guide large-scale change as well as continuous change. School administrators are increasingly asked to assume the role of change champions and change agents.

Balancing paradox, ambiguity, and change requires flexibility. Today school administrators must be able to be mentors as well as controllers, innovators as well as producers, power brokers as well as information processors. Additionally, they must balance and manage different stakeholders, inside and outside the school system. In the contemporary *stakeholder approach* a school system and its culture are effective to the extent that its leadership meets the obligations and requirements of its different constituencies—stakeholders group. Here effectiveness depends on the extent to which a school administrator can satisfy and balance the competing demands of all groups internal and external to a school system and have a "stake" or claim on its activities, policies, and performance.

In this approach, the values, strategic assumptions, and norms can be evaluated not only from the viewpoint of focal or central organization, but also reciprocally from the viewpoints of different key stakeholders. Many different views can be obtained when school administrators are faced with change decisions, thus giving an accurate picture. The accompanying list of stakeholder questions address a diagnostic process that school administrators can follow in their efforts to identify all stakeholders who have a stake in the outcomes of a particular change idea or initiative and manage competing stakeholder interests:

- What is the presenting problem, issue, opportunity, or change needed?
- What are our goals and objectives in this change effort?
- Who is the primary (i.e. central) stakeholder?
- What is at stake for this stakeholder, why?
- Who are the other primary stakeholders?
- What are their stakes in this situation? Why? Prioritize the primary stakeholders.
- What outcomes would effectively resolve/solve the problem, issue, opportunity, or lead to the desired outcome?
- Who benefits and who looses from this solution or change? Why? How?
- What strategies can the "focal" stakeholder plan and implement toward each primary stakeholder to achieve this "end result"— change?
- What support and from who does the "primary" stakeholder need to achieve the outcome—change?

As school leaders interact with multiple stakeholders, they must keep in mind that this process is indeed a competition for limited resources and attention in the form of prioritization. Stakeholders in their truest form exist to ensure that their expectations take precedence over other stakeholders. Most stakeholders will push to have their issues established oftentimes at the expense of the educational program, teaching strategies, or overall student concern. Stakeholders tend to be deliberate and masters at political strategies. Thus it is important for school administrators to take the time to better understand each stakeholder. One way of doing this is for the administrator to take a political view of the school system. In addition, administrators should develop a guide or map that identifies each stakeholder and important information about the roles that they play in a particular decision. The remainder of this chapter focuses on these points.

MAPPING AND UNDERSTANDING SCHOOL SYSTEM STAKEHOLDERS

Power is shared in organizations and it is shared out of necessity more than out of concern for principles or organizational development or participatory democracy. Power is shared because no one person controls all the desired activities in the organization (Salanick & Pfeffer, 1977, p. 7).

In our view a principal or any other administrator makes a mistake when they view a school or school system as a monolithic, strategic, machine-like entity, where administrators are capable of making and implementing rational decisions in pursuit of achieving either the goals of the school or school system or of a change initiative. This "strategic" depiction of a school system does not jibe with our vicarious or real-life experiences of politics and power in educational institutions. As the quote above expresses, sharing power is a necessity in organizations, but that necessity is itself a contested struggle for power and control among individuals and groups with quite different goals or interests. To manage or lead change in a real world school system, a principal needs to augment the "strategic" view of the school system with a political perspective.

A political perspective views a school system as composed of multiple "stakeholders," i.e., individuals and groups who contribute important resources to the school system and depend on its success but who also have different amounts and sources of power to bear in school system or school interactions. To use a political perspective a principal must

(a) identify and map the relationships among the different stakeholders involved in school system change;
(b) uncover the most salient interests and goals the different stakeholders bring to the change initiative and the extent to which they conflict or are congruent; and
(c) assess the amount and sources of power of the different stakeholders.

With this analysis in mind, any principal can then design and implement processes to produce joint gains or acceptable compromises among the stakeholders and their interests during a school system change initiative. Putting a political analysis to work requires acknowledging and legitimating differences in interests and goals, exploring ways to better align them so the proposed change can produce joint gains, building coalitions and stakeholder cooperation to achieve the school system change and stakeholder' goals, negotiating solutions or outcomes, and resolving conflicts where the change situation does not lend itself to results that are joint gains for all stakeholders. Over the longer run, a political perspective is useful to the principal in designing and implementing school system change since any change will reconfigure and alter existing interests and power distributions and thereby encounter resistance from some and support from other stakeholders. Thus, the political perspective depends heavily on a principals' ability to negotiate and manage conflict

The School System Stakeholder Perspective

Again, a school or school system consists of multiple stakeholders with varying interests. These interests arise from a variety of sources. Some reflect horizontal division of labor and organizational structures such as differences in functional responsibilities within the school system (i.e., teachers, support staff, administrators, etc.). Others reflect one's position in the vertical division of labor or hierarchy (e.g., differences between employee's interests in jobs and careers and the accompanying pay, employment security, and professional autonomy and their supervisors/ administrators' interests in controlling costs and stretching a school's budget as far as they can, maintaining flexibility, and coordinating or controlling her or his unit [e.g., science or math department] or school). And still others reflect the different concerns of numerous external and internal constituencies the school system depends on (i.e., students as customers— parents, taxpayers—individual and corporate, government and accrediting bodies). All of these stakeholders, both internal and external to the school system, have different goals and interest that they are trying to maintain and expand. It is this part of organizational life—the natural struggle or conflict amongst interests or stakeholders—that a viewpoint on schools or school systems as political systems helps to clarify and demystify for the principal responsible for bringing about educational change.

Interests and Goals

Mapping the stakeholders involved in a given school system change initiative and their general interests provides only an initial portrait of the interests that may be represented in given interactions during the change effort. As such, it provides a first approximation of the specific goals the different stakeholders will carry into a given change situation. Organizational theorists Herbert Simon and James March (1958) defined goals as the specific preferences individuals use to evaluate and rank the potential outcomes of a decision or interaction. Thus, the next step is for the principal to uncover how the parties translate their broad interests into specific goals or preferences that will guide their behavior and the outcomes they will seek as part of any school change effort.

Accepting Goal Conflict

Accepting goal conflict is a reality of being in organizations. To do this effectively, a principal must first overcome what is often a psychological barrier. Identifying and working with the range of goals individuals and stakeholder groups bring to a school system change initiative requires a principal to accept the legitimacy and ongoing nature of goal conflict among individuals, groups, various departments, and stakeholders. Although trying to create congruity among the numerous goals the various stakeholders may bring to a change initiative is a large part of the administrative task and is what lies at the heart of many organizational change efforts—goal conflict will not go away. Indeed, goal conflict is consciously built into the design of most organizational interactions (for example, cross-discipline teams are created to ensure that different requirements and knowledge bases are considered in a curriculum decision or change). Acknowledging, legitimating, and surfacing the goals stakeholders bring to school system change efforts are essential to effective change management by a principal.

Discovering and Surfacing Differences

Success during any change initiative requires that principals also discover and surface differences between them and other stakeholders. The challenge is as noted earlier that individuals have multiple interests and stakeholder or group affiliations. So assuming goals or preferences based on group (e.g., teacher) identity or stakeholder roles can be risky. And because stakeholders have multiple affiliations and interests, often the goals they will favor may be unclear at the outset of any given school system change and emerge and are shaped by the process itself. Thus, uncovering and surfacing stakeholders' interests and goals is an emergent and ongoing process of discovery for a principal undertaking change in their school. A critical part of a political analysis of any change situation therefore is for a principal to map the interests and goals most salient to the different stakeholders in the school system change effort and to assess the degree to which the goals that emerge are congruent or conflicting.

Power and Politics in School System Change

A political perspective defines power as the ability to get things done when goals conflict (Dahl, 1957, p. 203), or in simpler terms, the ability to get people to do something they would not do if acting alone in their own self interest. But power is not a fixed commodity or a "zero sum" game such that any power a principal gains is power that another stakeholder loses. There are two basic reasons why such a narrow conception is wrong. First, if a principal can find ways to realign stakeholder interests or achieve solutions that produce joint gains for the different stakeholders, all parties are not only better off but have increased their "ability to get things done" as part of a school change effort without giving up their power or sacrificing their self-interests. There are a number of models of negotiations available to a principal that are specifically designed to search for these types of mutual gains' outcomes. Second, individuals, groups or stakeholders bring different sources of bases of power to bear in school change initiatives that can be combined or utilized in complementary ways. This second point is worth exploring here since it offers a considerable potential for a principal to utilize power creatively and positively in school system change, rather than simply viewing power as a "struggle" over who will come out on top.

Different bases of power. Table 4.1 lists some of the different bases or sources of power commonly found in any school system interaction involving multiple stakeholders. A sampling of these include formal authority or position power, contacts to or alliances with individuals or groups with higher power, the control of sanctions and rewards, specialized or technical knowledge, type of associations or referent groups, and access to critical information.

Table 4.1.   Typical Sources of Power

- Formal authority—position power
- Control over scarce resources
- Rules, structure, regulations, standard operating procedures
- Control over decision process—access to decision making
- Information, knowledge, or specialized (scarce) skills
- Gatekeeping or control over the flow of information or access
- Ability to cope with uncertainty and ambiguity
- Alliances—ability to call on powerful resources
- Symbolic use of power-creating the perception of influence
- Countervailing power—ability to create new institutions
- Empowerment of weaker parties—use of third parties or legal rights
- Negotiating skills—shaping the process

One theorist summarizes the numerous sources of power in three groups (Mintzberg, 1983). The first group consists of resources, technical skills or specialized bodies of knowledge. These will be a basis of power if they have one or more of the following characteristics:

1. They are essential to the functioning of the organization.
2. They are concentrated, in short supply, or in the hands of a few individuals.
3. They are non-substitutable or irreplaceable.

The second group is formal power. This type of power lies in the ability to sanction behavior or impose choices—whether that is a through formal position, legal rights or responsibilities, or ownership. The last group derives its power through access to individuals or groups who have power. This access may be through a personal network or lie in the collective power of an important constituency one represents.

Power Dynamics

So far power is portrayed as a relatively static phenomenon—a function of current position, control over information, resources, etc. But principals need to look at power as a dynamic, changing, and malleable phenomenon that is used by organizational members throughout the school system and in relations with external entities. Power (and interests) often evolves as relationships develop and mature.

A principal must understand that power is not a fixed commodity. At best its ambiguous at any point in time, and often the relative power of different stakeholders changes over time as events or decision-making during change processes unfold. Thus, one of the biggest tactical mistakes a principal can make is to over-analyze the power relations prior to a change event or effort. If, for example, a principal believes that he or she enters into a school system change in a relatively low power position, the principal may behave in a way that makes his or her prediction a self-fulfilling prophecy! Or, if the principal believes his or her position or status should give them a power advantage and the right to control interactions with others during a change effort, he or she may be surprised and frustrated by their inability to "get things done."

Managing Resistance

Neither individuals nor stakeholder groups tend to give up power voluntarily. Thus they can and should be expected to resist actions that are interpreted as putting their bases or sources of power at risk. Yet most organizational interactions, and particularly school system change efforts, inherently change the distribution of power and enhance some sources of power while diminishing others. For example, delegating more decision-making power to teachers or giving them more power as part of school change decisions is often resisted by department heads and principals (i.e., middle managers) because it involves sharing some of the their power with the teachers.

These are realities that must be anticipated and taken into account by principals and other administrators in managing school or school system change. A political perspective however, shifts the responsibility for addressing resistance to change from the resisters to the principal or other administrative change agents in a school system. That is, rather than view resistance as an illegitimate or irrational response, a political perspective not only views it as a natural resource but, anticipates it as a normal and legitimate part of organizational life. (See Chapter 9 for a more detailed discussion on employee reactions or resistance to school system change). It becomes the principal's job to deal with this reality rather than ignoring it or leaving it to the individuals or stakeholders to cope with their diminished power regardless of whether it is real or perceived during a school change initiative.

Power Contests

Because power has value to individuals and stakeholder groups, it is often sought after and contested inside a school system and in relations with external entities. Increasing one's power allows one to claim a greater portion of an organization's resources and rewards, individually or for one's stakeholder group. As power dynamics are played out interests and stakeholders get redefined. Consider the fact that a principal must realize that school support staff (i.e., teachers' aides, etc.) for example, represents a key stakeholder group that they need to contend with during a school change effort.

Given the changing and uncertain demands on education in general and school systems in particular, both internally and externally, what is at stake for most of the stakeholders is always at risk (i.e., will the current bases of power remain essential, critical, or non-substitutable). To have power in the future in a school system or school is simultaneously a stake that one individual or stakeholder group wants to preserve or a stake that one individual or stakeholder group wants to transform. Transforming the stakes is about redistributing the critical resources, skills, and knowledge within a school or school system.

SCHOOL SYSTEM STAKEHOLDER MATRIX MAPPING

As articulated in our discussion to this point, the identification of stake-holders is an important step in any school system change initiative, but equally important is the interpretation of the relationships between the school system and its stakeholders. As stakeholder theory has progressed in recent years there are now several methodologies or models that can be used by administrators to understand or interpret the influence stakehold-ers have on the school system and/or the influence the school system has on the stakeholders at anytime during a change initiative.

At the minimum school administrators should complete a stakeholder analysis worksheet for each stakeholder, like the one in Table 4.2. Note that the two parts exist in the lower portion of the worksheet for stake-holders that influence the school system and for those that are influenced by the school system. Of course, some stakeholders are one or the other, while others may be both. There are more comprehensive approaches available to administrators involved in school system change and three are described below.

Table 4.2.   Stakeholder Analysis Worksheet

Definition

Stakeholder—Any group or individual who can influence, or is influenced by, the operations (or activities) of a school system.

Stakeholder Identification

Stakeholder_____

Sub-categories_____

Stakeholder Analysis _____

Influences the School System_____

How? _____

School system's response_____

How satisfactory is the response? _____

Influenced by the School System _____

How? _____

Stakeholders' response _____

How successful is the influence? _____

Through the use of instruments like a stakeholder analysis worksheet maps or diagrams can be developed for the school system that outline the relevant stakeholders in general terms at a particular time. Administrators should remember that as time passes, the composition of the map or diagram could change as stakeholder influence shifts. Stakeholder influence will also vary by the issue (or issues) confronting the school system.

Our discussion to this point have established the background for another approach to understanding stakeholders, matrix mapping. Administrators must manage a variety of things during a school system change effort and they must do this while being confronted by various issues affecting the whole system or some part of it. For each issue, a different set of stakeholders will be relevant. Administrators need some form of stakeholder management capability that emerges as a function of stakeholder mapping, organizational processes, and interactions, and stakeholder transactions.

School administrators need a methodology for assessing the importance or power of stakeholders' to achieve their change agendas and whether or not they have the means or resources to influence the various stakeholders. Through a "matrix" mapping process, administrators can ascertain the likely impact of the stakeholders on the school system's strategies and identify appropriate courses of action to counter or influence stakeholder demands as part of change efforts. The remainder of this section presents three approaches to stakeholder matrix mapping, issue position/importance matrix, power/dynamism matrix, and power/interest matrix school administrators can use to better understand the various stakeholders who are involved in school system change.

Stakeholder Issue Position/Importance Matrix

The following matrix (Figure 4.2) illustrates one methodology in which school system change stakeholders can be categorized according to their position on a particular issue or proposal and their importance. The stakeholders are identified and assessed whether they oppose the issue or support it on the vertical axis. A numerical value of 0 to –5 is assigned to those stakeholders opposing and a value of 0 to +5 to those supporting. The importance of stakeholders is measured on a horizontal axis and varies from least at a value of zero to most with a value of 10. After the two values are agreed upon, the location of the stakeholder on the matrix is plotted.

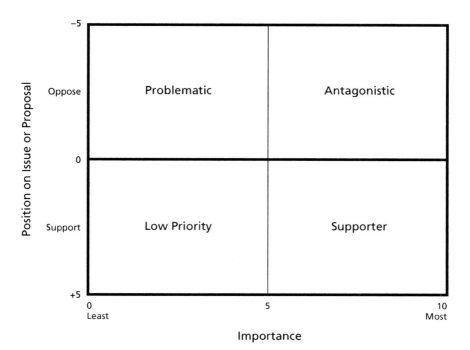

Figure 4.2.   The stakeholder position/importance matrix.

Four categories of stakeholders result from this analysis:

- "Problematic" Stakeholders—Those who would oppose the school system's course of action, and are relatively unimportant to the school system.
- "Antagonistic" Stakeholders—Those who would oppose or be hostile to the school system's course of action, and are very important to the school system.
- "Low Priority" Stakeholders—Those who support the school system's course of action, and are relatively unimportant to the school system.
- "Supporter" Stakeholders—Those who would support the school system's course of action, and are important to the school system.

After the categorization is completed, administrators can develop tactics or strategies to most appropriately deal with each stakeholder. The following are examples:

- Strategies for "Problematic" Stakeholders—target moderate stakeholders with educational programs, adjust school system change plans to accommodate stakeholder, and preparing defensive plans if coalitions of stakeholders form.
- Strategies for "Antagonistic" Stakeholders—identify potential coalitions and take defensive action, prepare from undermining supporters, anticipate nature of objections and develop counterarguments, and engage selected stakeholders in bargaining, and determining plan changes to gain support.
- Strategies for "Low Priority" Stakeholders—provide educational programs and promote involvement with supporters.
- Strategies for "Supporter" Stakeholders—provide information to reinforce position, and ask supporters to influence indifferent stakeholders.

Stakeholder Power/Dynamism Matrix

As noted previously, administrators responsible for school system change must understand the power held by stakeholders and their dynamism that is, predictability. These are variables that can be used to map and determine as part of a power/dynamism matrix the type of stakeholders who can influence a school system change effort. The power variable is measured from 0, Low, to 10, High, on the vertical axis, and the dynamism or predictability variable is measure of from 0, Low, to 10, High, on the horizontal axis. After the values for each variable have been determined for each relevant stakeholder, the stakeholders are categorized into the

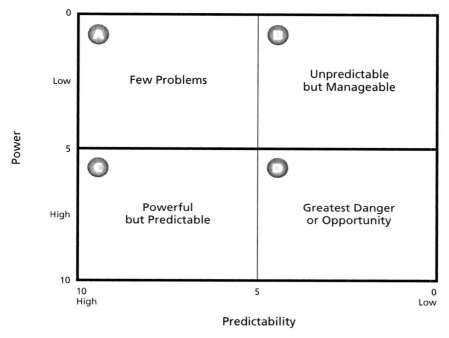

Figure 4.3.   The stakeholder power/dynamism matrix.

four quadrants. The values would also allow for positioning of the stake-holders within the quadrant. The power/dynamism matrix is presented in Figure 4.3.

There are four possible types of stakeholders:

- Highly predictable stakeholders with low power that present few problems (Quadrant A).
- Unpredictable stakeholders with low power that are manageable (Quadrant B).
- Powerful stakeholders that are predictable (Quadrant C).
- Powerful stakeholders with low predictability that present the great-est danger or opportunity for the school system (Quadrant D).

As with the Stakeholder Issue Position/Importance Matrix, administra-tors should develop strategies to influence the stakeholders or to counter the power of stakeholders. Stakeholders in close proximity to other quad-rants might be persuaded somehow to move to another quadrant. Stake-holders in Quadrant D are the most difficult as they are in a position to block or support new strategies or programs. Administrators should test out initiatives with this group of stakeholders prior to establishing an irrevocable position. Stakeholders in Quadrant C are problematic but administrators should attempt to influence their stance by formulating strategies that will address their expectations or demands. Stakeholders in Quadrants A and B are less critical but should not be ignored as they might have an influence on the attitude of the more powerful stakeholders.

Stakeholder Power/Interest Matrix

A third mapping matrix available to school administrators is based upon the power stakeholders have and the extent to which they are likely to show interest in the school system's change activities, and can be seen in Figure 4.4. Numerical estimations of the two variables are made and the location of the stakeholders plotted on the matrix.

After the stakeholders are assessed and categorized, school administrators must formulate appropriate relationship strategies. In particular, the reaction or position of "key stakeholders" (Quadrant D) towards the school system's initiatives must be given key consideration. Stakeholders in Quadrant C are the most challenging to maintain relationships with as

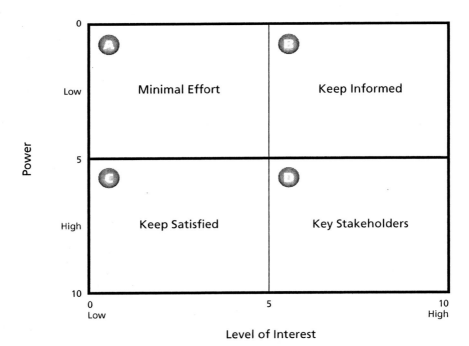

Figure 4.4.   The stakeholder power/interest matrix.

despite their lack of interest in general, such a stakeholder might exercise its power in reaction to a particular event or school system change activity. Administrators should also be sensitive to the repositioning of stakeholders from one quadrant to another that may be to the school system's advantage or disadvantage.

STAKEHOLDER MAPPING QUESTIONS FOR SCHOOL SYSTEM CHANGE

As suggested earlier, a principal or administrator must first make every effort to map the interests at stake in their school system change efforts. Who are the key stakeholders and what is most important to each of them? How fixed or malleable are these interests? How compatible are these interests? Can the goals of the change effort be redefined to increase the potential for joint gains to the stakeholders? Is the social setting or history of the relations among the stakeholders amenable to effective negotiations, conflict resolution, and problem solving, or should one first take steps to alter the climate or social norms that dominate?

Another way to analyze the key stakeholders with which a principal must interact is to identify what source of power the stakeholders bring to the situation (i.e., formal authority, contacts to or alliances with individuals or groups with higher power, the control of sanctions and rewards, specialized or technical knowledge, type of associations or referent groups, and access to critical information). What source of power do the various stakeholders bring to the situation? How much power do you have? How evenly or unevenly is power distributed among the stakeholders? Can this be changed in some way?

A principal must also find out how skilled are the various stakeholder to the type of mixed-interest compromise of decision making that is likely to be needed to reach successful change results. Can those skills be enhanced or should skilled third parties be brought in to assist in the change process? In short, will the principal need the help of outsiders to resolve differences among the stakeholders that may impede progress during the change effort?

A principal must also determine whether or not the needed policies or systems are in place to support effective negotiations, problem solving, and if necessary, conflict resolution. Are the adequate safeguards to protect the interests of the least powerful stakeholders involved? Are there interests excluded or not being heard in the process?

A principal must also answer the question of whether or not the planned change will add value or be dysfunctional or likely to leave one or all stakeholders worse off than before? Not all conflicts need to be fought nor are all differences in interests resolvable. An effective change leader knows how to tell when this is the case and move on to more fruitful endeavors.

Finally, it is important that a principal not overdo their political analysis of the change situation. People often look beyond their self-interests and act for the common good and welfare. Constantly looking for the self-interests motive or the "hidden agendas" that may be behind individual or stakeholder group action breeds an overly cynical view of a school or school system and one that may fail to appreciate the innate need and willingness of most people to try to help others achieve what is important to them, regardless of its impact on themselves. Especially given the reality that most school or school system stakeholders are committed to student growth and learning despite the very different issues and interests brought to a change effort.

CONCLUSION

Administrators must be clear about who is or should be involved in a school system change initiative. Who has a vested interest in its success? Who is going to be seriously impacted by it? Whose voice has to be heard as the change is being planned? It is essential at the start-up of any school system change effort to identify everyone internally and externally who has a stake in the change effort and is involved in or affected by it. This identification will provide administrators with an easy reference for thinking through various stakeholder needs as they work to shape a school system change strategy and process plan. It will also help identify the critical mass of support required for the school system change to succeed.

The intention of stakeholder analysis and mapping is for the key stakeholders in a school system change effort to share a common vision of the change and to work together for the collective good of the school system. When administrators map their stakeholders in detail they can also begin the process of specifying the various roles of each stakeholder. For example, the superintendent of a school system may be the change visionary or future shaper, lead the senior administrative team, and be a member of the change administrative team as well.

The stakeholder map should graphically reveal the relationships among its members. This will enable administrators to leverage these relationships strategically throughout the change process. Administrators may also want to identify any relationships within the school system that need improvement, because they will be counting on these relationships to function effectively to support the overall change.

Administrators can work with their stakeholder maps in many ways—in person, by memo, or electronically. The administrator's primary intention for the stakeholders is to create the conditions among all of them to support the change actively as it unfolds. We are not advocating that administrators make the stakeholder groups into a formal structure. They will likely have greater impact by allowing it to operate organically, working with parts of it as the school system change process requires. The administrator's strategies for the stakeholder groups as a whole may include:

- Publishing who these individuals and groups are as key players in the change;
- Keeping them informed of the status of the change effort;
- Interviewing them to gather pertinent input or using them as sounding board advisors on various strategic or operational choice points during the change;
- Assigning them key roles in major change activities or events;
- Establishing shared expectations for how they can add value to the effort;
- Working with them to create a critical mass of support for the vision and desired state; and
- Positioning them as change advocates, models of the new mindsets and behavior, information generators, and so on.

Stakeholder analysis and mapping are not new concepts. It is no big problem to identify the stakeholders in school system change, but the difficulty is to find out what their expectations are. Additionally, stakeholder maps will not stay as they are as the stakeholder environment is very dynamic. Thus, it is important for administrators to regularly reassess stakeholders and their expectations before, during and after any school system change effort.

Given this discussion about multiple stakeholders, interests, and power principals or other administrators responsible for bringing about change are left with a personal dilemma. As the administrator with change management responsibilities, how does she or he decide upon the proper means of dealing with stakeholders' expectations to expand the pie of power during school system' change efforts. The purpose of shining the light on this dilemma is not to provide an answer on a way out, but to underscore that the principal or administrators will potentially face this problem, whether recognized or unrecognized, each time he or she tries to take action and change the school or school system. What is required in the "proper management" of school system change is to think about interests and power across the entire system, both internally and externally to the school system to help insure their effective utilization. This might include the overlooked concerns of a particular department, the unheard feedback from parents, or the limited supply of a well-trained group of teachers.

The complexity of school system inputs, outputs, and interests should naturally encourage principals or administrators to not just maximize their own immediate interests, but more systematically expand their view of "interests" during a school system change effort, the alternatives we propose, and the stakeholder negotiation or cooperation strategies that bridge these interests.

CHAPTER 5

BUILDING AND COMMUNICATING THE CASE FOR SCHOOL SYSTEM CHANGE

INTRODUCTION

No one, administrator or employee, will give heart and soul to such a complex and challenging effort as school system change unless she or he understands why the change is necessary and what benefit it promises—personally and systemically. This chapter discusses the need to for administrators to create the case for school system change and answers such basic questions as: "Why change?" "What needs to change?" "What outcomes do we want from this change?" and "Why should we include others in the change process?" The chapter also discusses how administrators can use the "force-field" analysis model to assess the forces for and against change to provide them with critical information to communicate the need for school system change to key stakeholders. A framework for selling the case for school change is also discussed before concluding the chapter with a brief overview of a process for communicating school change.

Managing School System Change: Charting a Course for Renewal, pages 87–108
Copyright © 2004 by Information Age Publishing, Inc.

THE CASE FOR SCHOOL SYSTEM CHANGE

As noted in our discussion of stakeholder theory and analysis in Chapter 4, frequently, individuals and stakeholder groups have many different views of why change is needed, what is driving it, and how big it is. Until the desired school system change outcomes are clear, people will not know why they should invest in the effort it will take. Creating the case for change and the administrator's objectives for it creates a common view of the school system change leaders and gives their efforts meaning, direction, and energy for aligned action. Without a clear case for change, the change will lack relevance for school system employees, causing resistance, confusion, and insecurity.

The case for school system change includes the following:

- Why the change is needed;
- What needs to change about the school system;
- Leverage points for changing the system dynamics of the school system in support of the change;
- Impacts on the school system and various stakeholders;
- Scope of change;
- Types of change;
- Urgency for the change;
- Initial desired outcomes for the change; and
- Communicating and selling the need for change.

Preparing for change is the responsibility of administrators and many other individuals who may be involved in shaping the case for change and its outcomes. The drivers for school system change, whether internal or external, dictate the content of the case for change. Environmental requirements for success can be sought by anyone who has a perspective on what the school systems customers and sponsors are doing. When front-line school employees, curriculum leaders, and other key stakeholders participate in creating the case for change, they add credibility to the assessment of need, leverage points for change, and stakeholder impacts. As noted in Chapter 4, their participation is an enormous catalyst for their understanding and commitment. No matter who generates the data for the case, we believe school administrators are responsible for putting all of the information into a clear picture that they agree with and will communicate to the school system.

The information for the case for change may already have been generated through the school system's strategic planning efforts. If so, the administrator should take the exploration of the school system's strategic planning to the next level of specificity: How does the school system strategy require the school system to change? The administrator should use the strategy as input to ensure that they have a complete picture and that the case for change and the school system's strategy are aligned.

The administrator's decision on who builds the case for school system change and how it is accomplished should include the following:

1. Stakeholders who have a big picture understanding of the systemic and environmental dynamics creating the need for the school system change;
2. stakeholders who model the desired mindset and culture;
3. the level of urgency the administrator's face;
4. the degree to which the case has already been formulated by the school system's strategy; and
5. people's expertise in the areas defined by the predicated scope of the school system change.

The school administrator should design the process for creating the case for reviewing all of the activities for school system change and then determine how to accomplish them in a way that reflects the school system's desired culture.

ASSESSING THE FORCES FOR AND AGAINST CHANGE

One of the first things an administrator must do to build the case for school system change is to complete a force-field analysis. The force-field analysis derived from Kurt Lewin's three-step model of change discussed in Chapter 2, allows administrators to organize information pertaining to school system change into two major categories: forces for change (drivers of chance) and forces for maintaining the status quo or resisting change (Lewin, 1951). If the forces for change and the forces against change are equal, the result is organizational equilibrium. The technique assumes that at any given moment an organization is in a state of equilibrium, that is, it is balanced.

Using data collected through interviews, observation, or unobtrusive measures, the first step in conducting a force-field analysis is for administrators to develop a list of all the forces promoting and resisting school system change. Then, based on either personal belief and hopefully from several school system stakeholders, a determination is made of which of the positive and which of the negative forces are more powerful. Administrators can either rank order or rate the different forces in terms of their strength.

Change takes place when there is an imbalance between the two forces (restraining and driving) and continues until the opposing forces are brought into equilibrium. The imbalance can be planned and specifically brought about by increasing the strength of any one of the forces, by adding a new force, by decreasing the strength of any one of the forces, or by a combination of these methods. The typical steps in a force-field analysis are:

1. Identify the forces for change.
2. Identify the forces against change.
3. Brainstorm actions to reduce forces against change.
4. Brainstorm actions to enhance forces for change.
5. Assess feasibility of each action specified.
6. Prioritize actions.
7. Build a change action plan from ranking actions, and
8. Develop timetable and budget for change action plan.

Figure 5.1 illustrates a force-field analysis of the performance of a work group. The arrows represent the forces, and the length of the arrows corresponds to the strength of the forces. The information could have been collected in a group interview in which members were asked to list those factors maintaining the current level of group performance and those factors pushing for a higher level. Members also could have been asked to judge the strength of each force, with the average judgment shown by the length of the arrows.

This analysis reveals two strong forces pushing for higher performance: pressures from the supervisor of the group and competition from other

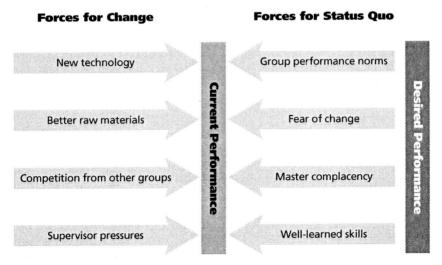

Figure 5.1.   Force-field analysis of work group performance.

work groups performing similar work. These forces for change are offset by two strong forces for maintaining the status quo: group norms supporting present levels of performance and well-learned skills that are resistance to change. According to Lewin, efforts to change to a higher level of group performance, shown by the darker band in Figure 5.1, should focus on reducing the forces for maintaining the status quo. This might entail changing the group's performance norms and helping members to learn new skills. The reduction of forces maintaining the status quo is likely to result in organizational change with little of the tension or conflict typically accompanying change caused by increasing the forces for change.

Forces for and Against School System Change

The drivers of change are the essential triggers for the scope of change facing the school system. The drivers for change include: environmental forces (the dynamics of the larger context within which the school system operates); stakeholder or customer requirements (the aggregate of stakeholder requirements that determine what it takes for a school system to succeed); strategic imperatives (strategic imperatives outline what the school system must do strategically to be successful, given its stakeholders' changing requirements); school system imperatives (school system imperatives specify what must change in the school system's structure, systems, processes, technology, resources, knowledge, and skill base, or staffing to realized its strategic imperatives); cultural imperatives (cultural imperatives denote how the norms, or collective way of being, working, and relating in the school system, must change to support and drive the school system's new design, strategy, and operations); administrator, employee, and other stakeholder behavior (collective behavior creates and expresses a school system's culture); and stakeholder mindset (encompasses stakeholder views, assumptions, beliefs, and mental models).

Each driver provides essential data for the determination of what must change in the school system and why. For example, collective behavior speaks to more than just overt actions as it describes the style, tone, or character that permeates what people do and how their way of being must change to create the new culture. Administrators and other school employees and stakeholders must choose to behave differently to change the school system's culture. School system culture is discussed in detail in Chapter 7. In addition, mindset causes people to behave in the ways in which they do; it underlies behavior. Mindset change is often required to catalyze and sustain change. Strategic imperative is often required for school system leaders to recognize changes in the environmental forces and stakeholder requirements, thereby being able to determine the best new strategic direction, structure, or operation for the school system. Stakeholder mindset change, for example in school system employees like teachers, is often required for them to understand the rationale for the changes being asked of them.

Figure 5.2 illustrates a force-field analysis of a school system. As was the case in our force-field analysis of the work group performance the arrows represent the forces, and the length of the arrows corresponds to the strength of the forces.

This analysis reveals two strong forces pushing for a change in the school system: expansion of knowledge base and economic trends. These forces for change are offset by two strong forces for maintaining the status quo: school system's history and change cost considerations. To change the school system, shown by the darker band in Figure 5.2, administrators should focus on reducing the forces for maintaining the status quo. This might entail changing the school's culture or norms and finding the resources to support making the change happen. The reduction of forces maintaining the status quo is likely to result in school system change with little of the tension or conflict typically accompanying change caused by increasing the forces for change.

Administrators must recognize the importance of using a tool like force-field analysis to gather information on the forces for and against change in their efforts to build and communicate the need for school system change. Information gathered from such a diagnosis better specifies the nature of the need for change by identifying underlying forces and multiple causality.

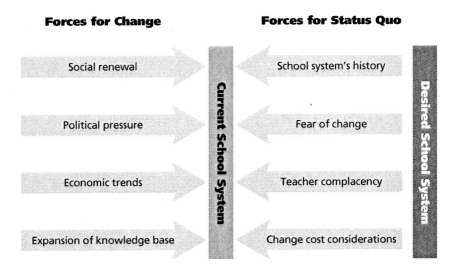

Figure 5.2.   Force-field analysis of a school system.

Although various stakeholders may have been involved in collecting and analyzing the data gathered from the force-field analysis with the help of the administrators, the administrators will undoubtedly rely on the information in their efforts to sell the need for change to various stakeholders. Additionally, properly analyzed and meaningful data on the forces for and against change can have an impact on school system change only if the administrator is able to help the various stakeholders understand and use the information to devise appropriate change actions plans.

Identifying the Leverage Points for School System Change

School systems are extremely complex. They are multi-dimensional systems comprised of an enormous number of variables. For example, school systems have strategies, structures, management systems, and organizational processes. They have cultural expectations and people who are all unique. They are affected by environmental dynamics, pressures to serve many masters, and employee morale. They may have excellent teamwork or hostile internal role conflicts. The list of elements within school systems is virtually endless. All of these variables are interdependent. Change in one factor may have either immediate or distant impacts on other variables. The dynamic interactions of all of these variables comprise the school system's "system dynamics."

Leverage points are places in the school system where small, focused action can produce larger positive changes. In other words, by altering the dynamic interactions between certain variables, positive results occur across larger domains of the overall school system. Or in Lewin's force field analysis change model, change and movement occurs.

Administrators at this point must map the school system's dynamics that are relevant to the change to reveal the underlying structures that are causing its current behavior and performance. Using this information, administrators can gain insight about what needs to change in the school system and where the leverage points are for producing that change.

Once the administrator has identified the underlying structure and leverage points, they become inputs to the case for school system change. Both are central forces for why the school system needs to change and what needs to change. Unless the administrator understands them, their effort may never affect the kinds of shifts required for the school system to achieve its desired outcomes.

Developing Stakeholder Impact Analysis

As it becomes clearer about what the school system change entails it is important for the administrator to clarify the types of stakeholder impacts it will create throughout the school system. Like the stakeholder mapping process discussed in Chapter 4 the administrator should complete a stakeholder impact analysis audit. The audit requires that the administrator list the stakeholder impact areas affected by change in the school system. These areas tell the administrator how broad and how deep the impact of making the school system change will go. Some of the stakeholder impact areas are: (1) school system (vision/mission, school system strategy, school structure, administrative systems and processes, technology, people—number/skills/systems, policies/procedures, resources needed/resources available, image—how are we perceived by others, identity—who we are and how we see ourselves, response to government regulations, governance and decision making, communication systems; (2) personal/cultural impacts (resistance and anxiety, motivation and commitment, inclusion/exclusion issues, politics and power plays, values, expectations, employee/stakeholder mindset, norms, changes in relationships, leadership style/administrative behavior, willingness to let go of old ways). This information, in addition to the assessment of the forces for change and the administrators system dynamics and leverage points, is critical to understanding what the change strategy needs to include for the change to succeed. This information is used as an input to determine the scope of the school system change.

The administrator should determine whether or not the change effort will impact the different areas directly (D) or indirectly (I) when the school system change is successfully completed. Each item, "D" or "I" requires more detailed planning and attention by the administrator as part of the change planning process. The stakeholder impact analysis is a powerful way to expand the administrator's view of the amount of attention, planning, and resources the change will require. It is designed to create a systems view of the school system and the change.

Although the administrator may have multiple types of change present within their overall effort or initial composite initiatives, one type is always primary. That is the one that will most influence the design of the school system change strategy. For instance, the administrator may need to develop better curriculums and systems, and they may need to consolidate several curriculum teams or programs to improve efficiencies, but the primary change is a radical transformation of the school system. Such a change is transformational because it calls for a significant shift in direction and requires major behavior and mindset change in school system personnel.

Identifying the Scope and Targets of the School System Change

One of the most common mistakes administrators make in change is to misdiagnose its scope, typically making it too narrow. Scope determines what the administrator will pay attention to and plan for. If it is too limited, repercussions will be occurring outside of their view of things, creating all kinds of unpleasant surprises. If the change scope is not accurate, the administrator may be missing key leverage points for getting the change to happen or expending energy on the wrong things.

Inaccurate identification of scope is one of the leading causes of failure in school system change efforts. School system change efforts should focus on changing processes, structure, job definition, internal system dynamics of people's behavior, communications, and working relationships, which are cultural, behavioral, and mindset drivers. For successful school system change, scope must attend to all of the forces, both external and internal.

The administrative case for change must accurately identify the scope of change required in the school system as well as the targets of the change. Scope is the breadth and depth of the change effort. Targets (or stakeholders) are the groups and people who will be directly impacted by the change or who are essential in carrying it out.

Identifying the Degree of Urgency

Administrators must also take the time to determine the degree of urgency for making the school system change. A common error in leading change is the automatic assumption that the change needs to occur faster than is humanly possible. Urgency, in and of itself, is not a bad thing. It is an important motivator for focused action. However, when leading school system change, a realistic sense of urgency is essential. It is one of the key determinants of how well the school system will respond to the change.

Employees will disregard fabricated urgency and label it one more reason administrators cannot be trusted to tell the truth. Administrators should not make this mistake. Administrators who push change into unrealistic timetables, without thinking through their internal motivations or the state of their people, usually cost the school system in damaged morale, lost productivity, or impaired quality, all of which inevitably take more time to repair.

Identifying the Desired Change Outcomes and Compiling the Case for Change

The information gathered by the school administrator to this point helps to articulate what they want the school system change to produce. The administrator may have outcomes for any of the forces of change as well as one central objective for the overall school system. This determination begins to shape the vision for the change. It is used to provide motivation, rationale, and inspiration for the school system to take on the change effort. The administrators responsible for change can use the desired outcomes they identify here to craft their vision for the change or provide them as input to stakeholders of the school system engaging in the visioning process.

All of the information generated by the administrator to this point forms the basis of the case for change. The information helps the administrator list all of the elements of their case for change. The administrator should review them, refine the results of their data gathering activities, and write their case for change.

By undertaking the activities discussed in this section the administrator has formed a realistic picture of the current status of the school system change effort. They understand who all of the stakeholders are and have begun to align all of these key players to support the change. In addition, they are in a position to clarify their initial assumptions about the case for change, desired outcomes, scope, and pace of the change.

Building the Infrastructure to Support School System Change

Some of the most powerful forces occurring in school system change is the political dynamics created by the introduction of a new direction. People naturally want things to go their own way, to be viewed as "winners" in the change, and they act to benefit their own interests. However, political maneuvering is rarely focused solely on their own interests or on the interest of the larger school system. Long before a major change is announced, personally motivated political behavior escalates. Individuals and stakeholder factions exert influence over others for their own agendas. Uncertainty, risk, and opportunity for power suddenly increase, especially when decision-making and authority may not be clear. In some cases, both covert and explicit power dynamics mushroom, leading to chaos, competition, and even malicious behavior.

An intriguing aspect of politics is that most people assume their efforts to influence others are invisible, with most political maneuvering occurring behind closed doors. Yet in reality, people see it clearly, discuss it actively, and can even predict it. Political behavior is far more obvious than its perpetrators would like to believe. As long as people collude with the unconscious norm of never discussing negative political realities overtly with the main players, they are allowing its consequences to run rampant, which does not support the overall change.

Depending on the school system's culture and the breadth of the change, politics can have a damaging effect on the success. It is our bias that political dynamics can be addressed and dealt with openly and consciously. Unless they are worked out through open dialogue, they can derail even the best of changes. As uncomfortable as it may be to unravel political behavior, administrators need to deal with their own power struggles impacting the change, as well as those within the change community and across the school system. Therefore, staying on top of the political terrain is critical to shaping a sound and conscious school system change strategy.

It is essential to create a positive climate within the stakeholder change team—and across the school system—for addressing difficult political realities. Mapping stakeholders and using the political lens discussed in Chapter 4 helps the administrator begin the process of identifying and addressing the political realities involved with multiple stakeholders who are part of a school system change effort. Relationship, team, and personal development work is invaluable in supporting the constructive resolution of potentially damaging politics and for preventing further political disruptions. In particular, building commitment and alignment to the larger school system outcomes of the change and creating a solid case for change and shared vision help immensely.

This task ensures that the administrator creates specific ground rules for how to deal with negative political behavior when it arises. At this early stage of the change process, it is helpful for the administrator to scan the existing political dynamics to identify the patterns currently at play, assess their impact on the change, and then devise positive strategies for dealing with them.

Another powerful influence strategy is for the administrator to create a "critical mass of support" for the change by identifying top administrators, community leaders, important stakeholders, and grassroots representatives throughout the school system and mobilizing their advocacy for the new directions. Various key stakeholders can serve as the basis for the school system change critical mass. They can be tasked with influencing others, including resistors and "fence-sitters," to back the effort and spread the word. Eventually, when enough people support the change, critical mass will actually be attained, and the change will take on a life of its own. When this occurs, administrators can guide the process toward the desired outcome and let go of any notion of forcing it forward through political manipulation.

Creating the Conditions for Change Success

It is safe to assume that all change administrators want their changes to be successful. However, to increase the probability of success, they must establish practices, circumstances, and resources that will enable it to flourish. This activity identifies the factors and conditions that change administrators believe are required for their particular change to succeed. These are conditions for change success.

Conditions for change success are requirements essential to the achievement of the school systems desired outcome(s), such as adequate resources, sufficient time to do a top-notch job, or quality communications that keep everyone engaged. Conditions for change success may also refer to a particular state of being that enables the change to occur more smoothly, such as the principals taking a conscious approach, the senior administrators presenting a unified front in support of the change, and people realizing that their needs are actually being considered as the change is planned and executed. Conditions for change success can also support the personal change work required by the change, such as creating a safe environment for truth-telling, supporting personal breakthrough, and encouraging cross-boundary conflict resolution, communication, and collaboration.

Conditions for change success include:

- Total school system (administration and key stakeholders) shares a common vision for what the desired state has to be and how to get there.
- Administration presents a unified front in support of the desired state.
- A learning-oriented, feedback-seeking climate is encouraged.
- A collaborative relationship exists between those responsible for executing the change (visionaries and executioners) and those who are expected to change (beneficiaries).
- Sufficient time and resources are allocated to the change effort.
- The reward system directly reinforces support for the change process and the desired state.
- People impacted by the change (beneficiaries) have timely input to the design, stakeholder impact analysis, and course corrections affecting them.
- Communication is frequent, accurate, and complete.

- Administrators consistently and visibly support efforts to achieve the desired state. They are models of the mindset and behavioral changes required by the desired outcomes.
- Administrators and consultants are sufficiently trained to be able to succeed in the change.
- Mindset and behavioral change are supported and expected from all stakeholders in the change.

Administrators should reflect on their own experience and the situation they face and identify their unique list of change conditions. They must agree on how to establish them in the school system, identify who will oversee and monitor them, and determine how the conditions will be used to have the greatest impact on the change experience.

EFFECTIVELY COMMUNICATING OR SELLING CHANGE

Communication is the life force of the school system, especially in times of change. In the early days of the effort, as soon as people begin to hear about the change, their needs for information and attention escalate significantly. They want to know what will happen to them and whether their position in the school system is secure. In the worst case, administrators keep people in the dark or only inform them of decisions without any opportunity to influence or respond—just when people's need to do both is the highest. Before going into more detail about communicating about the school system change it is important for the administrator to get stakeholder buy-in. And, one way of doing this is by selling the change to the stakeholders as discussed in the next section.

Selling School System Change

Effective communication is important to the success of any school system change effort. For the administrator responsible for school system change, selling or getting buy-in for a change idea or plan is an important activity and skill. Administrators need to be able to sell their ideas within the school system (and sometimes outside) if they are going to be successful. Administrators who can articulate why the school system ought to attend to ideas or issues that they think are critical to the system's survival (change) will be seen as having the leadership skills necessary to fill the important change leader role in a school system. Selling their change ideas often means administrators must manage up, laterally, and downward. Individual careers can be "made" or "broken" by associations with certain ideas or issues. For example, an administrator who brought a school systems attention to the need for an important and radical curriculum change would likely be seen in a very positive light due to their association with the idea. At the same time, bringing issues that are perceived as unimportant or inappropriate to the attention of key stakeholders can have derailing effects, hurting rather than helping both an administrator's credibility and career.

Tactical Choices for Selling Change Ideas

The question for the top administrative team (TAT) in school systems is not how to promote change idea selling, but how to engage in it successfully. There are two aspects of success for administrators. First, they must actually get the key stakeholders to give some time and attention to the ideas raised. Second, administrators must proceed in such a way that they "live to sell another day." That is, their images can't be so badly damaged in this selling effort that they lose all credibility for subsequent efforts. Administrators have a variety of choices to make regarding how to sell a change idea or plan. These choices have to do with how the idea is bundled, framed, and moved throughout the school system. Table 5.1 identifies critical change idea selling choices.

Table 5.1.   Change Selling Process Choices

Connect change idea/issue to other ideas/issues	**Bundling**	Sell change idea/issue as an isolated concern

Business frame
   No implied TAT/Other stakeholder responsibility
	Framing	Moral frame
		   Implied TAT/Other stakeholder responsibility

Universal	**Language**	Particularistic
Go solo	**Involvement**	Involve other as co-sellers
Formal Public	**Approach**	Informal Private
Early Connected to waves of change	**Timing**	Late

Bundling

The first basic change selling choice is whether to try to tie a new idea (or issue or plan or project) to other ideas or issues currently circulating within the school system. An administrator might, for example, propose that a new teaching technology idea is really a part of a bigger idea considered previously or another idea currently on the agenda. The advantages of bundling a new idea with others are several. By doing so, an administrator taps into resources and communication currency the other idea may have. If the new idea is linked to an idea that is seen as important by others, then the new idea gains by association. There may also be some established routines or mechanisms for talking about the other idea from which the new idea might benefit. For example, if a new teaching technology idea becomes linked to a larger school system technology issue, then there may exist a cross-functional team of stakeholders (e.g., teachers, parents, students, etc.) designated to address the school system's technology problem or concern. The administrator's new teaching technology idea can then be channeled through this structure as a means of getting this idea a hearing.

Of course, there is also a potential cost of bundling an idea with other ideas. If the old idea comes to be seen in a negative way, for example, the new idea that the administrator has carefully linked to it may be tainted with the same brush. It will be seen negatively as well. Ties to an "old" idea that has political enemies may activate conditions or political resistance that dampen enthusiasm for the new idea. In addition, links to an old idea may limit the range of solutions and participants connected to the neighborhood of the old ideas. Thus, bundling needs to be a measured tactic used with care in the selling process.

Framing

Administrators implicitly or explicitly choose a framing for their idea by the ways that they describe and present an idea. For example, they can choose to frame a change idea as an opportunity, this frame may induce greater participation in the idea, more commitment to taking action, and changes of lesser magnitude, than if the idea is framed as a threat. To frame an idea effectively as an opportunity, administrators must work hard to help others to see the change idea as controllable, involving gain, and as positive in impact.

Another basic choice that any administrator has to make is whether to frame the change idea to imply that the top administrator team or other stakeholders has a responsibility or obligation to address it. For example, stakeholders interested in having their schools become more diverse (e.g., teachers and students) can push this idea as a moral obligation for the school. In this approach, stakeholders would emphasize the moral obligation of all stakeholders and the morality of an affirmative response. Such framing makes getting the attention of top school administration (or other key stakeholders like parents) more likely (in that they exert more pressure on this group). However, it may have attendant image costs. Key stakeholders may not like feeling pushed and may think poorly of principals who take this kind of stand. Most successful change sellers appear to prefer a business frame to such a "hard sell" approach. With a business frame, administrators use facts and figures to suggest the financial costs of, for example, not working to improve the diversity of a school. With this framing, administrators appeal to their target's "heads" and a concern for their instrumental outcomes. With a moral appeal, an administrator appeals to their targets "hearts" and their sense of what is right. Both frames are powerful and each may be useful in certain situations.

Language

Closely tied to tactics surrounding issue framing are choices regarding the use of language to describe an issue. Administrators make language choices in their change idea-selling attempts. For example, choosing a business frame for an idea requires one kind of language and a moral frame implies another. In choosing language to use, administrators need to be mindful of what a particular target is interested in hearing. Administrators choose whether to speak similarly about their ideas to everyone or whether to customize language use to a specific target. Successful administrators attempt to communicate flexibly about their ideas. As effective sellers or persuaders, administrators are able to speak "numbers to the numbers person and morality with the idealists." In a sense, they become multi-lingual! By tailoring their approaches to particular targets, effective administrators appeal to the targets' different zones of acceptance for an idea, making them more likely to be effective.

A second language choice involves administrators' attempts to link a change idea or issue to important goals (e.g., this idea fits well with our plans to...). Administrators can also cast the change idea as a solution to current organizational ideas and problems. For example, closely aligning a potential change idea with a school system's strategic targets of increasing parent satisfaction, increasing student achievement, or reducing waste may motivate targets to invest more attention in an idea. Both connecting strategies make the language used consistent with what some stakeholders (e.g., decision makers) are ready to hear and to what has already been collectively affirmed as important to the school system. Administrators can thus more easily get an ear for their change ideas or issues.

Involvement

Administrators must decide whether to push their issues alone or to involve other individuals or stakeholder groups in any change selling effort. Though sometimes administrators have little choice (e.g., when no one wants to get involved with the idea or issue), they must decide whom to involve. Administrators should involve others who have a stake in the idea or issue. Administrators would do well to consider those who might be affected by their change idea or issue and try to include them in the selling attempt. This strategy co-opts stakeholders who might object to the idea or issue being raised or who might have a stake in how it gets implemented. The advantage here is that it gets these voices working "for" the idea rather than, potentially, speaking out against it. The disadvantage is that by including those with additional and perhaps unique concerns, it can dilute the selling effort as the administrator adds sub-issues or deletes central messages to appease the new "co-sellers."

A second group to be targeted for involvement is those stakeholders who stand to gain from the idea or issue being raised (benefactors). Here the administrator invites additional idea champions on board his or her change selling effort. The advantages of such an invitation are two-fold. First, more change sellers mean a greater potential of being heard, as there is strength in numbers. Second, if the idea is badly received, the administrator who has involved others in his or her change selling effort risks less image damage. Any negative reactions may be attributed to the group. However, there is a cost to a high involvement strategy too. If the idea is welcomed, no one particular seller stands out as the champion.

Approach

Administrators also have to make choices about their selling approach. Here two decisions stand out. First, administrators have to decide whether to make a formal or informal appeal and second whether to make these selling choices independently, administrators tend to follow the dominant school system recipe for this activity. For example, if people tend to raise ideas or issues in private forums using informal means, then administrators would be better off if they sold the idea using a similar approach. In contrast, if a school system had a formal presentation norm, then principals would be better off customizing their efforts to this type of approach. By following the prescriptive routines, administrators would be more likely to get a hearing for their idea. This "recipe following" tendency suggests that school systems might want to take a look at the prescribed routines in their settings.

Timing

There are various views on how ideas can be raised effectively. For example, one administrator might emphasize the importance of being opportunistic about timing. Another administrator, for example, might follow an approach where they keep ideas in their "desk drawer," ready to raise when the time is right. More effective administrators may pay attention to "waves" of thought, opinion, and political momentum when deciding whether to sell a particular idea or issue. Researchers who have studied politicians who effectively get issues on the congressional docket liken them to surfers. Good docket setters (or good idea sellers) are able to sense the waves of changing sentiment in an organization. They capitalize on the momentum created by the changing tides of openness and opportunity that exist in an organization. Getting in front of one of those waves with one's idea may help to propel that idea onto the agenda. On the other hand, a change selling attempt that is poorly timed may have little chance of getting on the agenda given the existing currents in the organization no matter how meritorious it is! Savvy administrators learn how to read the context effectively and to initiate their selling at the right time.

Other Tactics

In addition, administrators who want to be successful in getting their ideas supported must recognize the importance of doing one's homework as part of the work of effective change selling. Homework has two elements. First, administrators need to become experts in the content of what they are promoting. This might involve gathering external evidence on a new teaching technology, articles from educational publications about a proposed practice or anecdotes from renowned educational experts about a new technique or curriculum innovation. The goal is to not only have one's facts straight about the idea one is promoting, but also to gather evidence that will be seen as credible by those stakeholders one is selling to. In addition to homework about the topic, there is also the need to do one's political homework. This involves assessing the school system history around a change idea. Has it been brought up before? What happened then? The administrator should also assess other stakeholders' agendas related to the idea. Who is likely to be for or against it? This knowledge will be crucial in tailoring the change selling approach.

Doing one's political homework can also include informally testing the waters by stimulating early conversations about the idea of interest. In this way the administrator can obtain valuable information about the idea and how other stakeholders might view it. From these early, informal discussions, the administrator can draw better inferences about how key stake-holders in the school system might respond and can modify his or her approach to better ensure obtaining their support. These early informal conversations are also crucial for assessing whether and how much image cost there may be in pushing this idea. This assessment can be crucial in making decisions about both whether and how to proceed.

The Challenge of the "Undiscussable" Issues

The discussion to this point has ignored the *nature* of the idea that administrators might be considering. Administrators, however, must think carefully about the content of the issue that they are selling. Certain change ideas or issues seem to be more worrisome in the minds of potential change sellers. These change ideas have a characteristic nature. Administrators are reluctant to raise them in all different contexts. We have called these issues "undiscussable." By undiscussable, we mean that the issue is tough. These are what some authors have labeled "charged" in organizations. Undiscussable or charged ideas or issues are evaluated negatively, emotion laden, politically hot in that they are seen as having a divisive quality, and complex. Gender-equity concerns (whether men and women are treated equitably) is one example of a charged issue. Other such issues might be the treatment of students with learning disabilities, the treatment of religion in the curriculum, the treatment of other socially or financially charged issues. These issues are often scary ones for some stakeholders to raise. There are several concerns. An administrator might wonder whether they will be seen as rocking the boat. They worry too about being shunned by other stakeholders for bringing up issues that cause controversy. They also worry about being labeled. For the gender-equity issue, for example, individuals often worry about being labeled a troublemaker.

How should school systems handle such ideas and issues? A typical way is that top administrators create defensive routines that reduce the likeli-hood that such ideas will be expressed. For example, aggressive statements from the top administrators regarding how wonderfully the school system is addressing the issue in question can send strong signals to various stake-holders (e.g., teachers) that messages to the contrary are not wanted. The top thereby protects itself from hearing that all is not well. It's been our experience that middle managers (principals) collude in this protection. Out of an interest in remaining accepted by the other members of a stake-holder group and maintaining their team-player image, principals or mid-dle managers restrain themselves from going out on a limb for an issue that they think will be controversial or emotional. Over time and by behav-iors such as these, certain issues become undiscussable within a school system. This setting is best described as a conflict-avoiding culture. We are sure others would agree, often in private, that an issue needed to be addressed, but there is often little support in public settings. In these environments, various stakeholders recognize that risk taking is not rewarded in their settings. Given these beliefs, employees are unlikely to raise ideas or issues that entail risk.

Should school systems care that certain change ideas and issues take on the quality of undiscussables? There is reason to believe that they should. If the idea or issue that causes concern continues, it will fester within the system. Students, teachers and others feeling inequitably treated, for example, will continue to experience this. If they have no place to talk about this issue within the organization, everyone in the school system loses. There is a cost attached to the whole school system. In addition, if looming concerns (say over the need to be more responsive to students with learning disabilities) are undiscussables, then the school system loses valuable time in formulating a response. The school system may have to respond to the concern more in a crisis mode (say when a lawsuit is brought against the school system) than it would if there had been avenues for discussion earlier.

School systems in opening up the organizational conversation to include discussion of charged issues such as the inequitable treatment of any stakeholder (in all its various guises) need to work hard to make the context supportive and to establish communication avenues that put individuals at personal risk. Administrators must take the lead in creating an environment where all stakeholders feel comfortable in surfacing more troubling concerns. If administrators can create a supportive atmosphere, undiscussable or charged issues can more easily be brought out into the open. What was undiscussable becomes discussable-and by a broad range of stakeholders simultaneously.

A Process for Communicating School Change

To minimize stress and maximize productivity, administrators must make a conscious effort to sell the need for change and increase communication whenever changes affect individuals or other stakeholders. Administrators must design competent communication plans to ensure that relevant information about the change will be shared, understood, and used to support the effort.

Administrators should consider the following process to communicate a change:

1. Call a meeting of all individuals or stakeholders affected by the change. They should describe how the change will help the school

system succeed. The administrator should give the stakeholders the same information that convinced him or her the change was necessary. This should already be available to them if they have taken the time to try to sell the change as discussed in the previous section. After explaining the big picture the administrator should describe how the stakeholders will be affected by the change.

2. If the change means significant loss, the administrator should not sugarcoat the message and pretend that it is good news. They should just deliver the message, including the support they will provide during the transition period. The administrator should be straightforward and honest about the implications of the change.

3. The administrator should welcome questions and comments. Giving employees a chance to voice their concerns and listen to the concerns of others can ultimately help them accept the change.

4. The administrator should communicate the vision of the school system change; then, whenever possible, have those affected by the change create the execution plan.

5. The administrator should use active listening skills to encourage input and show that they have heard and understood the comments and concerns raised by others.

6. Finally, the administrator should emphasize to the stakeholders (especially internal school employees) that he or she will be available and willing to answer any questions they may have. The administrator should increase their exposure through "management by walking around."

CONCLUSION

The administrator must determine and identify the most appropriate infrastructure for the school system change effort, including the conditions for change success. This work, led by the administrator, paves the way for a well-supported change effort.

One of the most important steps to building and communicating a case for school system change is for administrators and others to collect and analyze information (diagnose) that supports the need for change. Lewin's general-purpose force-field analysis model is a diagnostic technique that can assist administrators in identifying the forces for and against school system change.

Selling the idea of school system change is a skilled activity. It takes a mindset and a competence that can be developed by administrators responsible for visioning, executing, and evaluating school system change efforts. Effective administrators have a good sense of the full range of change-selling choices and they customize change-selling efforts to the contexts in which they find themselves. Over time, they learn to make these choices thoughtfully and enact them with skill. The best administrators undertake this activity as a natural part of their jobs. These are the administrators who are seen as influential and able to get things done in the school system. In this way change selling is an important political skill in fostering individual and school system change success.

CHAPTER 6

SCHOOL CHANGE

Building Stakeholder Inclusion

INTRODUCTION

As suggested earlier, administrators must ensure the inclusion of *all* relevant stakeholders in school system change. Experience has shown that inclusion of the full range of stakeholders is not only an essential pre-condition for successful school system change but also vital for promoting a desire and commitment to participate, collaboration and positive cooperation by and between stakeholders. For example, when school system change decisions are made, priorities set, and actions taken without involving those relevant stakeholders, the result is usually misguided strategies and inappropriate action plans which are badly (if at all) implemented and which have negative effects on the change beneficiaries and on the school system at large. School system change approaches, which fail to properly involve stakeholders, prove to be unsustainable.

Stakeholder analysis and mapping encourages a far-reaching review of all potential stakeholder groups. This allows identification of representatives of these groups, so that they may be included in school system change efforts. The ultimate goal of stakeholder analysis and mapping is

Managing School System Change: Charting a Course for Renewal, pages 109–129
Copyright © 2004 by Information Age Publishing, Inc.

to maximize the role and contribution of each stakeholder during school system change.

This chapter first discusses the advantages and disadvantages of stakeholder participation. The chapter also discusses the need to establish open lines of communication and cooperation between major stakeholder groups as change is facilitated in a school system. This aspect of the school system change emphasizes the need for schools and school systems to genuinely include multiple stakeholders who help shape decisions and the culture of a school or school system. The chapter concludes with a look at factors that are most important to building and sustaining successful stakeholder cooperation.

ADVANTAGES AND DISADVANTAGES OF STAKEHOLDER PARTICIPATION IN SCHOOL SYSTEM CHANGE

The vision of any school system change should be to ensure that all students are provided with the highest quality education that is available. Striving to reach this vision entails the participation, collaboration and positive cooperation of multiple stakeholder groups. Stakeholder groups tend to willingly participate, collaborate, and cooperate during school system change for a variety of reasons (e.g., when the job or task they face is viewed as being too big or urgent, or requires too much knowledge for one person or group to do alone or simply because they have a vested interest in the final outcomes). Once stakeholder participation is deemed as necessary it is important for school administrators to be aware of the numerous advantages and disadvantages to including stakeholders in the school system change process. The following are some of the advantages and disadvantages of stakeholder participation in school system change adapted from InterAct, a program designed to promote participative management initiatives (see: www.interactweb.org.uk/stakeholder.htm).

Advantages of Stakeholder Participation

- Contributes to Real, Relevant, and Lasting Change—When people and stakeholders most immediately affected by a decision, project, policy or program are involved in the understanding, designing, and implementation of the initiative, they take ownership of the outcomes and thus work to ensure that the benefits last.
- Promotes Understanding and Ownership—Changes and decisions are more likely to last if they are understood and a genuine sense of

ownership is encouraged. This reduces the risk of subsequent conflict, sabotage, or resistance.

- Ensures Better Quality Projects and Programs—School must seek expert advice in consultation with immediate users of programs and initiatives to design, develop, and implement policies, programs, and projects that are meant to meet identified needs, opportunities, and demands.
- Promotes Conflict Avoidance—Dialogue should be established early in the school system change process. This promotes the early identification, avoidance, and resolution of conflicts in the early stages of change policy, program, and project development; thereby, reducing the potential for costly delays at later more crucial stages of the school system change process.
- Promotes Time Management—Early conflict resolution and participative decision making techniques that are used in school system change can reduce costly delays for proposed changes.
- Promotes Cost Efficiency—The creation of an environment where stakeholders feel a sense of ownership can speed complex decisions. In addition, reductions can be maximized if legal processes can be avoided.
- Promotes Continuous Learning and Professional Growth—Numerous opportunities exist in the school system change process to promote individual training and development opportunities in the participative decision making process. This is an opportunity for others (i.e. teachers, parents, and possibly students) to practice leadership techniques that will promote their personal and professional growth.
- Promotes Positive Relationships—A well-managed school system change process can begin the healing process for stakeholder groups who have been historically opposed to the other's position. By working together to solve problems, these stakeholder groups can begin to build a foundation based on trust and mutual understanding.

Disadvantages to Stakeholder Participation

- Shortage of Skilled Facilitators—One major obstacle to school system change is the lack of trained facilitators required to conduct the participatory processes. Facilitators must have adequate experience and knowledge to ensure best practices are adhered to by all participants. The lack of a good facilitator can easily lead to inadequate practice and loss of faith by participants in the school system change process. Group facilitators must participate in training and development activities on group interaction and managing techniques.

- Under-prepared Stakeholders—Although stakeholders oftentimes have very adamant feelings regarding a subject oftentimes they do not have the knowledge, skills, or abilities to participate in formal problem solving techniques designed to address their particular problem. This could potentially lead to an outcome with little real value or influence on the identified problem. Facilitators must ensure that specific aims, parameters, and decision-making mechanisms are in place for the engagement of these stakeholders in the change initiative.

- Fatigue—Stakeholders and other participants can easily become disillusioned if they are involved in a process that leads to no action being taken, little feedback, or if they are repeatedly asked to participate on similar subjects or on subjects of little relevance or interest to them.

- Experiment Perception of Change Initiatives—Stakeholder participation in educational change decision-making will oftentimes be seen as experimental if mainstream programs, budget priorities, and decisions remain unchanged. This lack of influence reduces the willingness of stakeholders to participate, and could easily result in delays to school system change initiatives.

- Lack of Adequate Measure of Success—Oftentimes evaluation of the effectiveness of stakeholder participation in an educational system is not conducted. Consequently, there is little evidence on the effectiveness of participatory approaches that include stakeholders in the decision making process. Hence, there is little sharing of results or best practices.

The advantages to stakeholder group participation in change decision making supersedes the disadvantages, however as administrators are involved in school system change efforts, it is important to understand the multiple barriers or disadvantages that might be encountered.

Like the stakeholder worksheet presented in Chapter 4, Figure 6.1 offers a number of questions and a process for administrators to complete a stakeholder analysis for participation assessment. The assessment allows administrators to identify various stakeholders, roles that they play, what contributions they make, capacity, interest, and strategies to generate stakeholder interest and build capacity. This form of stakeholder participatory mapping provides administrators with information that will assist them in acquiring knowledge of stakeholder differences which will allow systematic exploitation of positive attributes, identify areas where capacity building is necessary for effective stakeholder participation, and highlight possible "gaps" in the array of stakeholders.

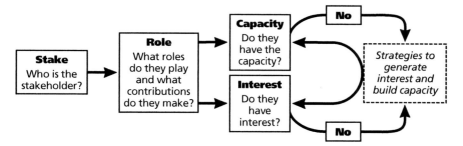

Figure 6.1.   Stakeholder analysis for participation.

Administrators can also make use of the following group technique to achieve a shared view of stakeholders, their relations to change issues and their relative importance as part of determining those stakeholders that should participate in a school system change effort.

The technique is as follows:

1. The participants put the name of each stakeholder on white, circular cards of approximately 10 cm in diameter, and then put them on a big table, or the floor or a wall (with removable adhesive).

2. When no more suggestions for stakeholders are presented, the main interests of each stakeholder are identified in relation to the change focus questions.

3. The cards are organized in clusters of related interests. When agreement has been reached, the white cards are replaced with colored cards, one color for each cluster. The name of the stakeholder is transferred to the colored card, and the main interests are written on the card below the name.

4. The colored cards are organized in starlike fashion along a line for each cluster where the center of the star is the project or the initial focus question. Using group judgments, the cards are placed at a distance from the center corresponding to the importance of the stakeholder for the project. The cards must be fixed with removable adhesive, allowing later modifications of the visual presentation.

Administrators should verify and assess stakeholders' availability and commitment. Perhaps by utilizing additional informants and information sources, the initial analysis to ensure that no key and relevant stakeholders are omitted. Administrators should also assess the identified stakeholders availability and degree of commitment to meaningful participation in the school system change process. In addition to the group card technique another way administrators can assess stakeholder commitment is by completing a stakeholder commitment chart as shown in Figure 6.2.

Key Stakeholders	No Commitment	Let It Happen	Help It Happen	Make It Happen
1. Teachers		O ←→	← →	←X
2. Parents			O →	←X
3. Superintendent				X O
4. Students	O →	←X		
5.				
6.				
7.				
8.				
9.				

Figure 6.2.   Stakeholder Commitment Chart

To make a commitment chart, administrators should list all the key stakeholders who are part of the critical change mass—those whose commitment is absolutely essential—on the vertical axis of the chart. Across the top, they should list the degrees of commitment: "No Commitment," "Let It Happen," "Help It Happen," and "Make It Happen," and draw vertical lines to make columns.

For each stakeholder in the left-hand column, administrators should place an "O" in the box that indicates the minimum commitment they must have for the school system change to occur. Administrators should not try to get as much as they can; but instead should settle for the least they need.

Administrators should then study each of the stakeholders as they are *now* and, using their best judgment, put an "X" in the box that represents their *present* degree of commitment.

Where the "O" and "X" are in the same box, administrators should circle or underline them and breathe a sigh of relief since in our experience there is not much work to do to get the necessary commitment. When the "O" and "X" are *not* in the same box, administrators should draw an arrow connecting them. This gives administrators a map of the work to be done (though not how to do it) to get the necessary commitment. Like the stakeholder matrix mapping discussed in Chapter 4, completing a stakeholder commitment chart increases the likelihood that administrators will be sensitive to those stakeholders whose commitment to the school system change is absolutely essential.

Finally, administrators must devise strategies for mobilizing and sustaining effective participation of stakeholders. Such strategies should be tailored to the different groups of stakeholders as analyzed and classified above. For example, empowerment strategies could be applied to those stakeholders with high stake but little power or influence. Undertaking efforts to increase stakeholder participation and commitment can begin with understanding the advantages and disadvantages of stakeholder participation and attending to a process like participatory stakeholder and commitment mapping. However, in our experience the real work for administrators interested in successful school system change takes place in increasing stakeholder involvement and creating an atmosphere of collaboration, trust, and positive cooperation between the various stakeholders. The remainder of this chapter discusses this process in more detail.

Stakeholder Involvement and School Change

A brief review of the literature on why change efforts often do not live up to their initial promises, invariably results in answers that run the gamut from the change champion or change agent team got the strategy wrong to the inability to develop sufficient employee (or organizational) support for the intended changes. In a number of these instances it appears that what those responsible for change often failed to recognize is that the way they were trying to bring about change (i.e., the process they employed) was the root cause of the problem. Too often, rather than involving the key stakeholders in the supposed "needed change," those responsible for change fail to fully involve the very people whose support is essential to success. Unfortunately, it has been our experience that many administrators, failing to recognize that the change process (or paradigms) they are using is the problem, redouble their efforts to make it work, resulting in increased frustration on their part and increased alienation on the part of most of the school or school system's stakeholders. In order to change the way administrators lead and manage change as internal and external change agents they need to recognize and address the frustration of other stakeholders, who on more than one change effort occasion don't believe that their voices count.

It has been our experience that school administrators in their roles as change agents do not intentionally go about creating more frustration for other stakeholders. They desperately want to involve them in the increasing number of change issues that are vital to a school or school system's success. They want other stakeholders to be willing partners. They want stakeholders who are willingly involved rather than resistant or cynical, stakeholders who are ready to put their wholehearted selves into helping bring about the required school system changes, rather than employees who readily sit back or on the sidelines and take the attitude of "this too shall pass."

We all have participated in change situations where individuals or stakeholder groups describe their experience by saying "Wouldn't it be good if every other stakeholder in the school or school system could have this same kind of positive change experience?" or "Wouldn't it be great if everyone could have learned what we learned about successful change?" These comments provide some key insights into how administrators can begin to lay the foundation for successful stakeholder involvement and cooperation during a change initiative. They must manage change in a way that decreases the likelihood of change failure, stakeholder resistance and cynicism. This involves the application of the following principles:

1. Establish the extent of stakeholder involvement in change efforts as a measure of change success;
2. Link stakeholders to each other;
3. Create change communities; and
4. Embrace open dialogue;

Establish Stakeholder Involvement as a Measure of Change Success

Simply getting stakeholder buy-in is the keystone of most school change efforts to date. Administrators must move toward deeply involving stakeholders in the change process itself, creating a critical mass of highly, energetic stakeholders who help design, sell, execute, evaluate and resell and support change in the school or school system. Increasing stakeholder involvement means going beyond the one or two handful of individuals or stakeholder groups that are typically involved as change agents in school or school system change and involving hundreds, even thousands of individuals and stakeholder groups, and so on. In practical terms, increasing stakeholder involvement means expanding who is expected (and actually gets) to participate in every phase of the change process. One way of increasing involvement is to make an informed, upfront effort to include new and different voices. Another way is by expanding the number of stakeholders in order to create a critical mass for change so that the few administrators or other change agents are no longer left in the position of deciding for the many which is what typically still happens in too many change efforts. In addition to creating a critical mass for change, achieving "maximum" stakeholder involvement also enhances innovation, adaptation, learning and a change agent "mindset" within the school system's stakeholders. In the end, by inviting and building in stakeholder involvement stakeholders are able to influence the needed changes and make things happen.

Link Stakeholders to Each Other

When stakeholders link to each other and to school or school system change ideas, creativity, and action are ensured. Barriers to the flow of information important to change and school system success and new ideas are lowered as stakeholders forge links with others. Work that is dependent upon ongoing change flows more smoothly, because stakeholders are more open to and learn how what they do fits into the larger whole, and how to draw upon the needed resources for successful individual, group, and school system change.

When stakeholders feel linked with each other, they move beyond just the familiar to really learning to trust and know each other. They stop being roles, functions, or just "differents" and become colleagues who share the same issues and concerns. Stakeholders who are doing the best they can to get the job done together. Fellow stakeholders with unique talents that recognize the value of each other and the collective and shared work to their own and the school system's success during times of rapid change. Fellow stakeholders who are trying to get to know each other as co-collaborators who have joint responsibility as change agents in helping their school system meet the challenges posed by ongoing demands for change. Building positive stakeholder cooperation is critical to creating trust among various stakeholders and will be discussed in more detail later in this chapter.

Create Change Communities

As has always been the case, successfully addressing organizational challenges cannot be accomplished by any one individual or stakeholder group single-handedly. Administrators responsible for school system change need a change community of stakeholders who willingly provide their talents and insights to address increasingly complex issues. A change community is important because one person no longer has or ever had the answers. Answers reside in all of a school system's stakeholders.

When administrators create a change community, they move beyond a group of individual stakeholders who may have personal links with each other to developing a group of linked stakeholders who have both the will and willingness to work together to accomplish a change goal that has meaning for them. Creating a sense of change community in schools or school systems is not an easy task because the requirements of rigid, bureaucratic, or mechanistic structures run contrary to what it takes to build a change community. Nevertheless, administrators cannot ignore this task.

Embrace Open Dialogue

Open dialogue is the best way to get stakeholders to come together, discuss and resolve issues, and act. It is through open dialogue that issues of self-interest versus the common good and minority versus majority opinion are dealt with in a way that ensures support and follow-through for any school system course of action. Given the increased demand for school system change today, there is more of a need for interaction, information sharing, and more need for expression than there has ever been. In this ever changing education world, imposed change is no longer acceptable. Change grounded in open dialogue has the best chance for success.

Open dialogue provides an ethical foundation and a moral fiber for any change effort. Open dialogue produces trust and confidence in both the change process and those responsible for managing and leading the change. Open dialogue, the desire to involve all, the desire to have a say, and the desire to be an active participant in shaping one's own and the school or school system's destiny is key to changing the way we manage change.

The principles offered above are important to successfully managing school or school system change. While building on the wisdom of the traditional approach to managing change, the increased emphasis on involving stakeholders in the change process provides a framework for developing not only the stakeholder support but also the enthusiastic involvement of the entire school or school system. The following offers what we believe administrators can expect when they incorporate the principles into their change initiatives:

- Stakeholders increasingly grasp the issues, become aligned around a common purpose, and collectively create new change directions because they understand both the opportunities and challenges.
- Collective school or school system urgency and energy are produced to create a new future.
- Open-dialogue, free-flowing information, and cooperation versus school or school system barriers because stakeholders are linked to the change issues and to each other.
- Improved stakeholder input and stakeholder (customer) satisfaction resulting from broad stakeholder participation which quickly identifies performance gaps and change solutions.

- Increased contribution of creative and quality ideas from stakeholders.
- Increased change capacity as stakeholders continuously develop the skills and processes to meet not just current challenges, but the increasingly demanding challenges being placed on school and school systems.

So how do administrators do a better job of incorporating these principles into school or school system change initiatives? We believe the place to start is with some of the misconceptions of stakeholder involvement as discussed in the next section.

Misconceptions of Stakeholder Involvement

There appear to be a consistent set of misconceptions of stakeholder involvement in school or school system change management efforts. These misconceptions keep administrators holding on to the familiar ways of managing change and prevent them and their schools or school systems from moving to maximum stakeholder involvement.

The first misconception is that increasing stakeholder involvement requires administrators to trust and let go more than they appear to be comfortable with. As administrators contemplate increasing stakeholder involvement and embracing open dialogue, they sometimes believe that these principles will require them to abdicate their responsibility, authority, and ability to provide and control input based on their change knowledge and experience. Nothing could be further from the truth. Striving for maximum stakeholder involvement is critical to change success. Paradoxically, increasing stakeholder involvement requires more involvement from other stakeholders. In our view, stakeholders from all levels of the school or school system must play crucial roles throughout the change process.

What shifts is the administrator's role as a change agent. Instead of being responsible for identifying the change challenge, problem and the solution, they are now expected to be jointly responsible for identifying the issues, purposes, and boundary constraints, and applying the principles of increased employee involvement to better engage stakeholders in this dialogue. Throughout the change process, administrators should concern themselves with the following questions:

- What needs to change and why?
- What needs to be different in the school or school system, each stakeholder group and individual as a result of the school or school system's mission or goals and the demands of key internal and external stakeholders?

- What boundaries or barriers must we be cognizant of?
- Whose voice (and why) needs to be heard?
- Who else must be heard and why? How do we build the necessary links between stakeholders and change ideas?
- How will we create a change community of stakeholders who are ready and willing to proactively act?
- How will we ensure open dialogue throughout the change process?

One of the challenges often confronting many administrators at the inception of change efforts is the reality that they are often concerned that if they fully and visibly participate in a change process, some stakeholders (e.g., staff) will not speak out or will blindly accept what the administrators have to say. Similarly, stakeholders are often concerned that if administrators have already laid down the change gauntlet they will not listen to their concerns. We believe this is an important situation that must be addressed. As is always the case in any change effort administrators must get other stakeholders to learn to work in an atmosphere where there is give-and-take and ideas can be freely exchanged.

Old and new demands for school system change requires that administrators get stakeholders to work together in addressing issues, because each group has vital information the other does not have. The boundaries of information sources have blurred. In any case, sets of various stakeholders' information are necessary to address today's systemic school system change issues. When school systems and their administrators are committed to maximum stakeholder involvement, they create situations where this kind of information sharing is possible. Information that is indeed necessary for successful change based on the ideas of many versus those of the few.

Administrators must continuously strive to eliminate boundaries or barriers between themselves and other stakeholders. And this means that they must increasingly be sensitive to the reality that the stakeholders will care about the way they do their change work. Accompanying the stakeholder involvement misconception is often the fear that if others, for example, those outside a particular school are included in the schools' need to change, or the change process, they will be airing their dirty laundry in public, thus alienating some of the very people who are necessary to their success. Like others in the change management arena our experience is just the opposite.

Including those affected by a change builds ownership and commitment within any organization, and this is especially important in school systems given the increasing number of stakeholders who today believe they have a stake in many instances in a school system's efforts to continuously change. All stakeholders must be involved with a school system's efforts to build a future. Administrators must see stakeholder involvement as a given thus meaning they will need to be involved before, during and after any school or school system change effort.

The next misconception is that the performance of the change team or group will suffer if larger numbers of stakeholders are involved in the change process. It is our experience that it is better for a school or school system to rely on a larger number of stakeholders than to still rely on the same five individuals when they go off site for two or three days at a time to plan the "next" change. Contrary to the belief that the change group or team's performance suffers when there is an increase in the number of stakeholder involved in school or school system change efforts it has been our experience that performance does not suffer. In fact, many times it actually improves and is well worth the cost of involving the maximum number of stakeholders in such change steps as off site retreats, for example. Old or new school or school system change demands, when stakeholders are involved in change processes, they put forth more effort when they believe their ideas count.

The final misconception is that it is more cost-effective to put the change process in the hands of external change agents or consultants (and pair them with the "best and brightest" from the school or school system) than to put the change process in the hands of the many. Certainly, it is costly to increase stakeholder involvement, both emotionally and financially. The entire change process instantly becomes more visible and the stakes become higher. But what is the cost of not striving for maximum stakeholder involvement? What is the cost of brilliant strategies that never get implemented? What is the cost of change processes that increase resistance and cynicism and provide new material for Scott Adam's Dilbert cartoons? What is the cost of all those stakeholders we didn't want to leave out of the school or school systems broad ranging plan that actually do because they believe that their voice does not count?

Making a real commitment to increasing stakeholder involvement in the way administrators manage change is not business as usual. It is not for the faint of heart administrators, and it is not for everyone. Maximizing stakeholder involvement in change efforts is hard work that requires courage, risk taking, and perseverance. The reward for these efforts is a school or school system that is flexible, energetic, innovative, linked, and responsive enough to meet the demands of a constantly changing and new education environment. In the end, striving for maximum stakeholder involvement which gives a "voice" to all is the first step to building positive cooperative relationships between stakeholders who are important to successful school or school system change. The next section offers more discussion on stakeholder cooperation.

STAKEHOLDER COOPERATION

Principals and others responsible for school system change must recognize that stakeholder cooperation is at the cornerstone of successful change. Further, stakeholder cooperation is multidimensional, interactional, and developmental. Also, successful stakeholder cooperation needs time and work to come to fruition. Additionally, stakeholder cooperation increases as stakeholders learn to understand each other and to work together. Given the developmental nature of successful cooperation, preplanning, and continued hard work and support are needed for it to develop during a school system change effort.

Collaborative and cooperative relationships amongst stakeholders like principals and teachers, for example, facilitate change in a school system. These relationships assist in bringing about the necessary changes and reduce dysfunctional conflict. For example, if teachers choose not to participate in collaborative relationships or decision-making, school system change initiatives will not enjoy sustained execution and eventual institutionalization. The creation and nurturance of a school culture that encourages and supports these types of cooperative relationships falls on those who lead the school system change effort.

We suggest that the best way to break the rigid boundaries that oftentimes exist between different stakeholder groups is by adamant commitment, enhanced communication, and strong leadership by principals and other school administrators. Stakeholder cooperation minimizes the impact of "competing stakeholder interests or issues. Sharing experiences regarding successful cooperation is one way of increasing the likelihood of it actually coming to fruition. That is, stakeholders learn that cooperation is a "doable."

FACTORS THAT CONTRIBUTE TO
SUCCESSFUL STAKEHOLDER COOPERATION

Learning from the mistakes of unsuccessful stakeholder cooperation can help overcome barriers that might jeopardize future stakeholder cooperation. Successful cooperation does not happen by accident.

Factors that are most important to successful stakeholder cooperation are:

- commitment,
- communication,
- understanding the culture of collaborating stakeholders,
- engaging in serious preplanning,

- providing adequate resources for collaboration, and
- minimizing turf issues.

These factors are interrelated and can be summed up into three major variables for promoting successful collaboration:

- commitment,
- communication, and
- strong leadership.

Commitment

Commitment entails the sharing of goals and visions and the establishment of a high level of trust and mutual responsibility for change goals. Commitment is a critical factor and the foundation of successful stakeholder cooperation in school system change. Our experience suggests that if stakeholders do not have a commitment to working together to bring about change the change will most likely fail. Clearly, all stakeholders involved in a school system change initiative must have a mutual commitment to the goals and visions of the change if it is going to reach its full potential. Examples of especially detrimental and trust-destroying behaviors include:

- Develping or following one's own agenda at the expense of other stakeholders.
- An unwillingness on the part of stakeholders to modify their positions which are unnecessarily inhibiting or detrimental to development of the cooperation needed for the success of a change initiative.
- Not providing incentives or consequences for cooperative and uncooperative behavior of stakeholders.

Suggestions related to building and maintaining commitment between stakeholders are as follows:

- If possible, develop a way to compromise on important differences.
- Make clear those issues that cannot be compromised.
- Keep the goals and the potential positive outcomes of the cooperation in mind at all times.

Communication

Open lines of communication are a critical component of successful stakeholder cooperation before, during, and after a school or school system change initiative. Communication is the most important solution for overcoming barriers to stakeholder cooperation. The following suggestions relate to enhancing communication between stakeholders:

- Develop a proactive approach to communication with stakeholders. Be up front with the issues, talk about the differences, and be sure that each stakeholder is aware of other stakeholder interests and issues. Most importantly, update stakeholders with necessary information in writing to minimize miscommunications. This precaution is particularly important in the early stages of a change initiative.
- Create frequent opportunities for communication through regular meetings, phone calls, mail, and e-mail.
- Develop personal connections to promote cooperative relationships and informal communication links (e.g., occasionally meet over lunch or dinner).

UNDERSTANDING THE CULTURE
OF STAKEHOLDER COOPERATION

Like any collection of individuals or groups, stakeholders participating in a school system change, develop their own culture, including language, values or priorities, rules and regulations, ways of doing business, and even definitions of cooperation. It is important for administrators like principals to understand the kind of culture (i.e., rules, values, communication patterns, structure, etc.) they want to develop within the total stakeholder group participating in the school system change. A principal who views the kind of stakeholder cooperation they would like to develop, as a culture, changes the context of the relationships. If principals adopt a cultural perspective, it is unlikely that they will mis-characterize the rules, values, communication patterns, or structures needed to build and sustain stakeholder cooperation. Rather, using a cultural view of stakeholder cooperation increase the likelihood that principals are sensitive to the unique culture of stakeholder cooperation.

Minimizing Stakeholder Conflict

Stakeholder conflict must be addressed by administrators for coopera-tion to endure. Administrators embarking on school system change must recognize that conflict between stakeholders will occur and cannot be ignored. The best way to minimize conflict is to anticipate its appearance and to develop a plan for anticipating, addressing or resolving as it emerges.

Engage in Serious Preplanning

Given the diversity of stakeholders and the interests and issues impor-tant to them there is an increased need for preplanning by administrators before undertaking any change initiative. Because stakeholder cooperation is difficult it is important that effort be directed at building a foundation that enhances the chances of successful cooperation. Some suggestions related to building stakeholder cooperation are serious preplanning where the administrator:

- Takes the time to identify potential problems, key issues, and similar-ities/differences between the various stakeholders.
- Clearly articulate the developing goals and anticipated outcomes of stakeholder cooperation.

Involve the Right Stakeholder

Striving for, measuring and monitoring stakeholder participation and cooperation, are all central to facilitating stakeholder cooperation in school system change. Administrators should ensure that the right people are involved, by assessing who is participating, in which activities, and what their concerns and contributions are. They should also regularly identify and address weaknesses in the change decision-making process in order to assess which activities are being poorly conducted and thus, take corrective actions. Finally, monitoring the extent to which stakeholders are cooperat-ing with each other during the school system change process can provide early warning on potential "derailers" to the initiative.

Facilitating Stakeholder Cooperation

The facilitation of stakeholder participation or involvement and cooper-ation is important to increase the potential success of school system change. Stakeholder participation and involvement ensures transparency, accountability, equity, efficiency, and ultimately the sustainability of a school system change effort. Transparency because information, priorities, strategies, and actions are open to all stakeholders in the school system; accountability, because by sharing in school system change decisions, stakeholders are accountable to the school system, and to each other vis-à-vis the tasks they have committed themselves to; equity, because the groups which are usually excluded from the change decision-making process have the opportunity to present their concerns and defend their interests; efficiency, because information is shared and decisions are taken in common, avoiding overlap and duplication of efforts; sustainability, because stakeholders have been heard, engaged, and bought-in to cooperation and school system change.

Administrators cannot idly wait by for stakeholder involvement and cooperation to occur. They must be proactive in facilitating and monitoring the extent of stakeholder cooperation. Facilitating and monitoring the stakeholder cooperation process itself allows administrators to judge, on a short-term basis whether negative or positive cooperation is developing amongst the stakeholders. Stakeholder cooperation only occurs when administrators properly organize, structure, focus, and support cooperation—in short, take the time to facilitate the process.

In conclusion, administrators must understand the role facilitation plays in building stakeholder cooperation. This includes an understanding of the factors that contribute to the success or failure of stakeholder cooperation. Commitment and communication are essential for successful stakeholder cooperation. In our experience, there are deliberate actions that can be undertaken by administrators that will contribute to the likelihood that stakeholder cooperation will exist during school system change. Cooperation is hard work, and it is our hope that administrators responsible for school system change will recognize the importance of stakeholder cooperation to successful change.

Tables 6.1–6.5 provide a summary look at factors important to successful and unsuccessful stakeholder cooperation.

Table 6.1.   Contributing Factors for Successful Cooperation During Change

Categories	Definition
Willingness to cooperate	Sharing responsibilities; coming to meetings on a regular basis; having a notion that cooperation is better than non-cooperation
Sharing a common vision for the school or school system change	Developing a common set of school or school system change goals
Trust	Being open to other's views; supporting other's interests and issues
Commitment	Not giving up easily; "whatever it takes to get the school change job done"
Previous cooperation	Past positive experiences with cooperative efforts
Sharing a sense of urgency	Agreement on the need for change in the school or school system; meeting change deadlines
Good communication	Being willing to compromise; support the final stakeholder group's decisions, school system change plan, etc.
No resistance to school system change	Preparing for school system change, even painful ones

Table 6.2.   Contributing Factors for Unsuccessful Cooperation

Categories	Definition
Lack of support from upper school administration	Not getting involved in school system change planning; having other commitments
Lack of commitment	Not fulfilling essential roles and responsibilities key to the success of school system change
Lack of common school system change vision and goals	Having own agenda and not looking at the whole picture
Lack of trust	Not being open to other stakeholder ideas; unwilling to compromise
Negative conflict/resistance to school system change	Defending one's position no matter what; fear of change
Lack of communication	Not sharing information; not listening
Lack of time	Insufficient time to meet change deadline; not having enough time to meet with other stakeholders
Lack of understanding of other stakeholders issues/interests	Having different interests/issues; having different priorities for what and how things should be in a school system or need to be done
No negative consequences if not cooperating during a school system change	Not held accountable if one does not cooperate; no repercussions
Change of stakeholders during the school system change initiative	Changing stakeholders/issues/interests; starting the school system change process all over again

Table 6.3.   Problems Encountered During Collaboration Process

Categories	Definition
Lack of communication during the school system change effort	Not sharing information; not knowing other stakeholders' interests/issues; not receiving or sharing information
Conflict/resistance to school system change	Not wanting to accept change, not seeing the necessity of cooperation
Lack of common school system change vision/goals	Having different school system change goals and objectives; having different opinions on which direction should be taken by the school system
Disrespect for others/ no trust	Dominance of certain stakeholders; making decisions or not listening to others; fear of losing something as a result of the school system change
Problems within broader school system change	Bureaucracy; lack of commitment to necessary cooperation; school system change mismanagement
Change of stakeholders	Changing stakeholders/interests/issues; goals; starting the process all over again
Lack of time	Insufficient time to meet the school system change deadlines; having other commitments
Poor participation of stakeholders	Difficulty getting stakeholders to participate/cooperate
Lack of preplanning	Not knowing the need for school system change issues; no thorough planning prior to the beginning of the change initiative; developing change goals
Lack of cooperation experiences	Unable to anticipate any problems during the school system change/cooperation process

Table 6.4.   Solutions for Overcoming Barriers

Categories	Definition
Enhanced communication	Talking about differences; being upfront with the issues; making other stakeholders aware of interests/issues
Commitment	Persevering; always focusing on the school system change vision; getting the change job done
Involvement of key decision makers	Getting top administrators involved in the school system change effort early (e.g., visioning and planning stage)
Forces behind cooperation	Facing the pressure from the main drivers for school system change (government, local community, etc.)— better to anticipate the need for school system change
Development of trust/respect	Not taking advantage of other stakeholders who are willing to compromise
Inter-school system support	Sharing resources; working together instead of competing with each other; providing support to other stakeholders or parts of the school system

Table 6.5. What to do to Increase the Likelihood of Stakeholder Cooperation

Categories	Definition
Enhanced communication	Talking about differences; being upfront with the issues/interests; making other stakeholders aware of interests/issues
School system change preplanning details	Defining stakeholder cooperation goals during the school system change effort in more detail; planning how to achieve objectives; anticipating problems
Involvement of key school administrators	Involving top school system administrators early in the change effort; especially during the visioning and planning stage
More stakeholder involvement	Including all key stakeholders
Understanding the school culture's view of stakeholder cooperation	Determining the kind of stakeholder cooperation you are striving for
Elimination of negative conflict	Identifying individuals who do not want to cooperate at the beginning of the school system change effort

CONCLUSION

Administrators interested in increasing the likelihood of successful school system change must ensure that no important stakeholder is omitted. They must also do everything they can to optimize the roles and contributions of stakeholders. Inclusiveness, collaboration, and positive cooperation are key elements to successful stakeholder participation. Where participation is generalized through careful analysis of the key stakeholders, time taken to build a stakeholder inclusive and cooperative environment, school system change is more likely to occur.

In order to remove barriers and facilitate change efforts to enhance student learning, principals and other administrators can support and nurture conditions that create the cooperative and change conducive climate or environment needed for successful change, especially those whose characteristics and background interact with the environment of the school to create continuous improvement and change.

CHAPTER 7

UNDERSTANDING SCHOOL CULTURE CHANGE

INTRODUCTION

Like their for-profit counterparts, employees responsible for bringing about a needed change will only be successful if they are able to influence or change the culture of the school system. Culture is one of the most influential factors contributing to a school system's willingness and ability to change. School system administrators can use organizational culture to create, stimulate, and institutionalize necessary changes based on new values that result in new behaviors or ways of doing things. In this chapter we first attempt to define and explore the nature and levels of organizational culture. Next we investigate how to create, maintain, and change a culture in organizations in general, and school systems in particular. Various definitions of school culture are then offered along with frameworks for identifying the uniqueness of a school's culture. The chapter concludes with a look at how best to reshape or change school culture.

Managing School System Change: Charting a Course for Renewal, pages 131–160
Copyright © 2004 by Information Age Publishing, Inc.
All rights of reproduction in any form reserved.

ORGANIZATIONAL CULTURE

At the outset, we can say that organizational culture is not the easiest concept to define. It is a complex and deep aspect of organizations that can strongly affect organization members. Informally, culture might be thought of as an organization's style, atmosphere, or personality. This style, atmosphere, or personality is most obvious when we contrast what it must be like to work in various for-profit organizations such as General Electric, Nordstrom's, the U.S. Marine Corps, or the New York Yankees. Even from their mention in the popular press, we can imagine that these organizations provide very different work environments. Thus, culture provides uniqueness and social identity to organizations.

More formally, organizational culture includes the values, norms, rites, rituals, ceremonies, heroes, and scoundrels in the history of the organization (Deal & Kennedy, 1982). Organizational culture defines what a new employee needs to learn to be accepted as a member of the organization. A similar definition of organizational culture is that it is the basic pattern of shared assumptions, values, and beliefs considered the correct way of thinking about and acting on problems and opportunities facing the organization. Organizational culture defines what is important and unimportant in the organization. You might think of it as the organization's DNA—invisible to the naked eye, yet a powerful template that shapes what happens in the workplace (Schein, 1991; McShane & VonGlinow, 2003).

Organizational cultures are similar to cultures of different countries. Your entry into a new organizational culture is like entering the culture of another country. Key aspects of organizational culture include a sharing of values and a structuring of experiences in an organization. Different sets of values can coexist among different groups of people throughout the organization. Although values differ from group to group, members of each group can share a set of values. The term share does not necessarily mean that members are in close agreement on these matters, although they might well be. Rather, it means that they have had uniform exposure to the values and have some minimum common understanding of them. Thus, not all people in an organization will fully agree about the dominant values and norms.

The specific content of an organization's culture develops from the experiences of a group adapting to its external environment and building a system of internal coordination. Each of the different human systems within which we interact has a culture. Our family, our employer, and any leisure-time organization such as clubs or religious groups all have their own cultures. These cultures can make different—and sometimes conflicting—demands on us.

When discussing organizational culture, we are actually referring to the dominant culture, that is, the themes shared most widely by the organization's members. However, organizations are also composed of subcultures. Some subcultures enhance the dominant culture by espousing parallel assumptions, values, and beliefs; others, called countercultures, directly oppose the organization's core values.

Each organizational culture divides into multiple subcultures. An organization's structural design creates varying subcultures and processes within the organization. Subcultures grow readily within these differentiated parts of the total organization. They also grow readily within departments, divisions, and different operating locations of an organization.

Different occupational groups within an organization often form different subcultures. Specialists in manufacturing, accounting, information systems, finance and education often have their own jargon that helps them talk to each other. That jargon becomes an integral part of an occupational subculture and often cannot be understood by those outside the subculture. An information systems specialist easily understands terms like upload, download, and token-ring networks, which often are a foreign language to people outside that occupation.

The global environment and workforce diversity also help build subcultures in organizations. Global operations often require organizations to hire people from the host country. Those employees will often bring values into the organization that differs from those of the organization's home country. People who come from different social backgrounds and have different values will infuse organizations with a variety of values and viewpoints. Effective organizations will develop an overarching culture that manages differences that might exist between the various subcultures.

Elements or Levels of Organizational Culture

Organizational cultures can be revealed at three different but related levels: artifacts, values, and basic assumptions. These levels vary in their visibility to an outsider, with the first being easiest to see and the last the most difficult. As Figure 7.1 illustrates, the assumptions, values, and beliefs that represent organizational culture operate beneath the surface of organizational behavior. They are not directly observed, yet their effects are everywhere.

Artifacts are the most visible parts of an organization's culture. They are the obvious features of an organization that are immediately visible to a new employee. Artifacts consist of the physical manifestation of an organization's culture. Artifacts include sounds, architecture, smells, behavior, attire, language, products, awards, observable rituals and ceremonies,

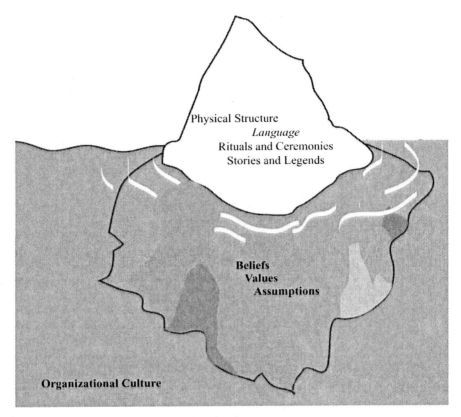

Figure 7.1.   Artifacts of organizational culture.

myths and stories told about the organization, published lists of values, special parking places, decorations, and so on.

Organizations differ in the layout of their interior space and the formality of their working relationships. Do people work in an open office space or behind closed doors? Do people dress formally or informally? Does the interior design give the impression of a cheerful or a somber work environment? Do people refer to each other by first names or do they use formal titles such as Mr., Ms., Doctor, and Captain? These factors are clues to an organization's culture. You can infer some values, norms, and required behavior from such factors. A new employee must first attend to messages from the physical characteristics of the organization and then watch the behavior of veteran organizational members.

Artifacts are easier to change than the less visible aspects of organizational culture. At the less visible level, culture reflects the values and basic assumptions shared among organizational members. These values tend to persist over time and are more resistant to change.

At the next level of awareness are the values embedded in the culture. Values tell organization members what they "ought" to do in various situations. Values are hard for the newcomer to see, but she or he can discover and learn them.

We can't determine an organization or school system's cultural values just by asking employees and other people about them. Values are socially desirable, so what people say they value (espoused values) may differ from what they truly value (enacted values). Espoused values do not represent an organization's culture. Espoused values represent the explicitly stated values and norms that are preferred by an organization. They establish the public image that organizational leaders want to display. Enacted values, on the other hand, are values in use. They are the values that guide individual decisions and behavior in the workplace. The newcomer to an organization must be aware of espoused values that guide what veteran members say in a given situation and the in-use or enacted values that really guide the behavior of organization members.

At the deepest level of cultural awareness are the taken-for-granted assumptions about how organizational problems should be solved. These basic assumptions tell members how to perceive, think, and feel about things. They are nonconfrontable and nondebatable assumptions about relating to the environment and about human nature, human activity, and human relationships. For example, a basic assumption at Nordstrom is that it is morally right to treat people with dignity and that customers treated with extraordinary service will become loyal and frequent shoppers.

Each level of culture influences the other. For example, if an organization truly values providing high-quality service, employees are more likely to adopt the behavior of responding faster to customer complaints. Similarly, causality can flow in the other direction. Employees can come to value high-quality service based on their experiences as they interact with customers.

CREATING (SHAPING) AND
MAINTAINING ORGANIZATIONAL CULTURE

Several important issues besides understanding how culture operates are: how culture is initially created (shaped) and how it is sustained—that is, what keeps it going once it is created. Another important issue, how it is changed will be discussed later in this chapter. Since our knowledge of organizational culture is limited, it is difficult to state with firm confidence, detailed prescriptions for creating and maintaining organizational cultures.

How is Organizational Culture Created?

Can a culture be created that influences behavior in the direction school administration desires? This is an intriguing question. Consider the following hypothetical situation: An experiment to create a positive, student learning school culture was conducted in one new school system. Top administrators regularly met to establish the core values of the school system. A document was developed to express the core values as: "emphasis on individualized student learning where all students could reach their full potential," "collegiality in decision making and a shared sense of responsibility for student learning," and "open dialogue among all stakeholders." The document of core values was circulated to principals who refined the statements. Then the refined document was circulated to all employees as the set of guiding principles of the school system.

An anthropologist was brought into the school system three months into the process as a consultant to central office administrators responsible for getting the new school system up and running. She insightfully analyzed what actually occurred in the school system. There was a gap between the administrative-stated culture and the school system's actual working conditions and practices. Goal conflict and communication problems existed throughout the school system. There was also a strictly enforced chain of command and a top-down only communication system. One teacher commented on the way things were done in the school system in the following way: "It's clear to me that any ideas the teachers may have on how to achieve our student learning objectives (and really any of our objectives) aren't welcome in the school system. We're frequently reminded that top administrators know what's best and that we are expected to just do what we're told." The cultural creation experiment was too artificial and was not taken seriously by employees.

The consequences of creating a culture in the school system included decreased morale, increased turnover, and a poorer student performance on state-mandated educational standards. Ultimately, a new school superintendent and several other central office administrators and at least three principals were brought in to the school system less than nineteen months after the experiment began.

The new school system case points out that artificially imposing a culture is difficult. Imposing a culture is often met with resistance. It is difficult to simply create core values. Also, when a disparity exists between reality and a stated set of values, employees become confused, irritated, and skeptical. They also usually lack enthusiasm and respect when a false image is portrayed. Creating or shaping a culture apparently just doesn't happen because a group of intelligent, well-intentioned school system administrators meet and prepares a document.

Cultures seem to evolve over a period of time, as did McDonald's and Walt Disney's. Schein (1985) describes this evolution as follows:

> The culture that eventually evolves in a particular organization is . . . a complex outcome of external pressures, internal potentials, responses to critical events, and, probably, to some unknown degree, chance factors that could not be predicted from a knowledge of either the environment or the members (pp. 83–89).

A model that illustrates the evolution of culture and its outcome is presented in Figure 7.2 (for a more detailed discussion of the model see Gross & Shichman, 1987; Gibson, Ivancevich, Donnelly, & Konopaske, 2003). The model emphasizes an array of methods and procedures that managers or school administrators can use to foster a cohesive culture. In examining this model, recall the new school system and the limited methods it used to generate a quick-fix culture. Figure 7.2 emphasizes the word HOME, which suggests the importance of history, oneness, membership, and exchange among employees.

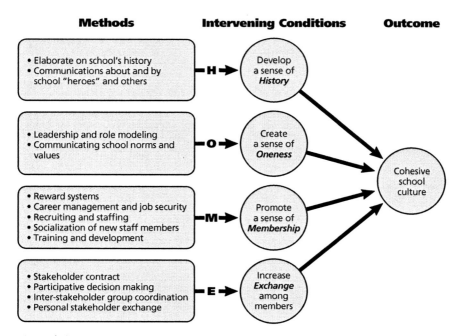

Figure 7.2.   Evolution of a positive school culture.

HOW IS CULTURE SUSTAINED?

How do employees come to learn about their organizations' cultures? Several key mechanisms are involved in the shaping, maintenance and reinforcement of organizational culture: symbols, stories, jargon, ceremonies, and statements of principle.

Symbols

Objects that say more than meets the eye. First, organizations often rely on symbols—material objects that connote meanings that extend beyond their intrinsic content. For example, some organizations use impressive buildings to convey their organization's strength and significance, signifying that it is a large, stable place. Other organizations rely on slogans to symbolize their values, including such classic examples as General Electric's "Progress is our most important product," or Ford's "Quality is job one." Corporate cars (or even jets!) also are used to convey information about certain aspects of an organization's culture, such as who wields power.

Stories

"In the old days, we used to. . ." Organizations also transmit information about culture by virtue of the stories that are told in them, both formally and informally. Stories illustrate key aspects of an organization's culture, and telling them can effectively introduce or reaffirm those values to employees (Martin, 1982). It is important to note that stories need not involve some great event, such as someone who saved the company with a single wise decision, but may be small tales that become legends because they so effectively communicate a message. For example, employees at the British confectionery firm, Cadbury, are purposefully told stories about the company's founding on Quaker traditions to get them to appreciate and accept the basic Quaker value of hard work.

Jargon

The special language that defines a culture. Even without telling stories, the everyday language used in organizations helps sustain culture. For example, the slang or jargon that is used in a company helps its members define their identities as members of an organization. For example, for many years employees at IBM referred to disk drives as "hard files" and circuit boards as "planar boards," terms that defined the insulated nature of IBM's corporate culture. Overtime, as organizations—or departments within them—develop unique language to describe their work, their terms, although strange to newcomers, serves as a common factor that brings together individuals belonging to a corporate culture or subculture.

Ceremonies

Special events that commemorate organizational values. Organizations also do a great deal to sustain their cultures by conducting various types of ceremonies. Indeed, ceremonies may be seen as celebrations of an organization's basic values and assumptions. Just as a wedding ceremony symbolizes a couple's mutual commitment and a presidential inauguration ceremony marks the beginning of a new presidential term, various organizational ceremonies also celebrate some important accomplishment. Ceremonies convey meaning to people inside and outside the organization.

Statements of Principle

Defining cultures in writing. A fifth way in which culture is reinforced is via the direct statements of principles. Some organizations have explicitly written their principles for all to see. For example, Forest Mars, the founder of the candy company M&M Mars developed his "Five Principles of Mars" which still guide his company today: quality (everyone is responsible for maintaining quality), responsibility (all employees are responsible for their own actions and decisions), mutuality (creating a situation in which everyone can win), efficiency (most of the company's 41 factories operate continuously), and freedom (giving employees opportunities to shape their future).

Shaping and maintaining organizational culture does not mean that managers passively and uncritically accept the values and basic assumptions of the present culture. Organizations must recognize that maintenance of a culture presents administrators with a dilemma. They want to hold on to the values that were successful in the past, but they also need to question whether those values are right for the environment the organization now faces.

An organization's culture is maintained, sustained or strengthened through selecting people with compatible values and socialization of new employees. Organizational socialization refers to the process by which individuals learn the values, expected behaviors, and social knowledge necessary to assume their roles in the organization. By communicating the organization's values, organizations can ensure that new hires are more likely to internalize these values quickly and deeply.

Schein (1985) suggests that "every organization is concerned about the degree to which people at all levels 'fit' into it" (p. 42). As those new to an organization learn the culture or way things are done in the organization they are socialized and the culture is internalized. The following elements affect the degree to which culture is internalized and created.

- Common language and conceptual categories. If members cannot communicate with and understand each other, a group is impossible by definition.

- Group boundaries and criteria for inclusion and exclusion. One of the most important areas of culture is the shared consensus on who is in and who is out and by what criteria one determines membership.
- Power and status. Every organization must work out its pecking order, its criteria and rules for how one gets, maintains, and loses power; consensus in this area is crucial to help members manage feelings of aggression.
- Intimacy, friendship, and love. Every organization must work out its rules of the game for peer relationships, for relationships between the sexes, and for the manner in which openness and intimacy are to be handled in the context of managing the organization's tasks.
- Rewards and punishments. Every group must know what its heroic and sinful behaviors are; what gets rewarded with property, status, and power; and what gets punished in the form of withdrawal of the rewards and, ultimately, excommunication.
- Ideology and "religion." Every organization [must reach consensus on how to manage the unmanageable and explain the unexplainable. Stories and myths about what was done in the past provide explanations and norms for managing situations that defy scientific decision making.] (p. 66)

Some of the ways organizational cultures are sustained or strengthened are by the actions of its leaders, the introduction of culturally consistent rewards, and selecting and socializing new employees. In the end, culture is really sustained if employees internalize the assumptions, values, and beliefs that make up the organization's core values.

SCHOOL CULTURE

Administrators who want to be successful in bringing about change in either a school or a school system must understand the role culture plays in such an endeavor. By identifying and being sensitive to the existing (and desired) school culture administrators responsible for leading change increase their chances of being successful. That is, a school administrator increases the likelihood that they will be able to re-shape the values, beliefs, and attitudes necessary to promote and institutionalize the requisite change.

Culture is to an organization what personality is to a human being. Culture is the personality of the school reflected through the values and beliefs of the members of the organization. It defines the mission and goals of the school and establishes the beliefs held in high esteem within the school. Culture is more than a school system's catchy slogan, it is the mind set of the members of the organization when they are asked to describe the basic purpose of the school and the beliefs on which that purpose is built. As noted in the previous section culture is an intangible, pervasive presence of being that is felt by members of the organization.

So, what is school culture? As early as 1932 Willard Waller wrote,

> Schools have a culture that is definitely their own. There are in the school, complex rituals of personal relationships, and a set of folkways, mores, irrational sanctions, and a moral code based on them. There are games, which simulate wars, teams, and an elaborate set of ceremonies concerning them. There are traditions and traditionalists waging their world-old battle against innovators. (p. 96)

Because culture is an evanescent force beneath the everyday activities of the school, school leaders can not afford to overlook its importance to any school change initiative.

Since Waller's early recognition of schools and their unique cultures the field of education has had no more success than their for-profit counterparts in coming to an agreement on defining culture or in this case "school culture." The term has been used synonymously with a variety of concepts, including "climate," "ethos," and "saga" (Deal, 1993). For example, climate is to an organization what attitude is to a human being. Climate is the attitude of the school being reflected through the feelings and perceptions of the members of the organization. It is a description of life in the organization (Banks, 1993). Climate is an intangible, pervasive presence of mind that is felt by members of the organization. It is, to a large degree, a product of the culture of the organization.

The more recent concept of culture came to education from the for-profit workplace with the notion that it would provide direction for a more efficient and stable learning environment. And scholars have argued about the meaning of *culture* for years as evidenced in the following views of school culture. For one scholar (Geertz, 1973) culture represents a "historically transmitted pattern of meaning." Those patterns of meaning are expressed both (explicitly) through symbols and (implicitly) in our taken-for-granted beliefs. Deal and Peterson (1990) note that the definition of culture includes "deep patterns of values, beliefs, and traditions that have been formed over the course of [the school's] history" or they (Deal & Peterson, 1993) simply state it as an "inner reality." Robbins and Alvy (1995, p. 23) expand the definition stating that "This inner reality reflects what organizational members care about, what they are willing to spend time doing, what and how they celebrate, and what they talk about. Heckman (1993) suggests that school culture lies in "the commonly held beliefs of teachers, students, and principals." These definitions go beyond the business of creating an efficient learning environment. They focus more on the core values necessary to teach and influence young minds.

For Stolp and Smith (1994) school culture can be defined as the "historically transmitted patterns of meaning that include the norms, values, beliefs, ceremonies, rituals, traditions, and myths understood, maybe in varying degrees, by members of the school community" (p. 1). This system of meaning often shapes what people think and how they act. Phillips (1993) characterizes school culture as the, "beliefs, attitudes, and behaviors that characterize a school in terms of: how people treat and feel about each other; the extent to which people feel included and appreciated; and rituals and traditions reflecting collaboration and collegiality. Culture influences everything that happens in a school.

Examples of culture in schools include how we celebrate Christmas, our leadership roles and how we treat people. Sergiovanni (1995) described school culture in general terms:

> School culture includes values, symbols, beliefs, and shared meanings of parents, students, teachers, and others conceived as a group or community. Culture governs what is of worth for this group and how members should think, feel, and behave. The 'stuff' of culture includes a school's customs and traditions; historical accounts; stated and unstated understandings, habits, norms, and expectations; common meanings; and shared assumptions. The more understood, accepted, and cohesive the culture of a school, the better able it is to move in concert toward ideals it holds and objectives it wishes to pursue. (p. 89)

This definition is broad and includes many ideas about what school culture really is.

Wagner (2000) recently conceptualized school culture as shared experiences both in school and out of school (traditions and celebrations), a sense of community, of family and team. Staff stability and common goals permeate the school. Time is set aside for school-wide recognition of all school stakeholders. Common agreement on curricular and instructional components, as well as order and discipline are established through consensus. Open and honest communication is encouraged and there is an abundance of humor and trust. Tangible support from leadership at the school and district levels is also present.

The way we do things around here demonstrates the values and beliefs to which school members generally subscribe and culture has its own mindset in relation to what occurs in a school's external environment. School culture is about understanding intentions as well as observing behavior (Stewart, 2000). Like other organizations, school culture is shaped by its' history, context, and the people in it. School culture is, thus, situationally unique (Stoll, 1999) with both concrete representation in the form of artifacts and behavioral norms, and is sustained implicitly by jargon, metaphors, and rites (Prosser, 1999).

School Culture Frameworks

Clearly, unraveling the complexities of school culture is a complicated process. However, although the literature does not reveal a single consistent definition, some researchers have agreed that school culture is multidimensional (Mok & Flynn, 1998). Doerger (2002) has suggested that it is important to consider culture as an enigmatic system in the context of schooling, for as Florio-Ruane (1989) states, "schools and classrooms are complex cultural settings" (p. 163). Like any other system this one can be broken into distinct dimensions or components. For example, according to Deal and Peterson (1999) component parts of a school culture can be seen as fitting into three main categories:

1. Values: vision and values
2. Beliefs: myths, norms, history, and stories
3. Traditions: ceremonies, rituals, symbols, and signs

Values are the conscious expressions of what a culture stands for. Values define a standard of goodness, quality, or excellence that undergirds behavior and decision-making, and what people care about (Ott, 1989). Beliefs are how we comprehend and deal with the world around us. They are consciously held, cognitive views about truth and reality. Assumptions are sometimes viewed as the pre-conscious, "systems of beliefs, perceptions, and values" that guide behavior. They are deeply embedded in the cultural tapestry and shape thoughts and actions in powerful ways. Cultural assumptions are hard to assess because they are closely aligned with myths (Deal & Peterson, 1999). Symbols, as representatives of what we stand for and wish for, play a powerful role in cultural cohesion and pride. "What is often labeled as fluff is more often the stuff of leadership and culture" (Deal & Peterson, 1999). Traditions are significant events that have a special history and meaning and that occur year in and year out. They re-invigorate the culture and symbolize it to insiders and outsiders alike (Deal & Peterson, 1999).

Each school has a different reality or mindset of school life, often captured in its most basic form, "as the way we do things around here" (Stoll, 1999; Stewart, 2000). In a more implicit sense like its for-profit counterparts, school culture manifests itself in customs, rituals, symbols, stories, and language—culture's artifacts. How these are played out in a school or school system can give an administrator a better understanding of what is of worth or value in a school. For example:

- Celebrations—how staff and student successes are celebrated and how achievements are recognized.
- Stories—how the school narrates itself—its history and myths; whose stories are told and whose are overlooked; community stories about the school and the school's stories about itself.
- Shared sayings—the school's own language about itself "We're a community school."
- Taboos—what is not allowed within the school, explicitly and implicitly, form types of behavior to how certain groups are treated.
- Ways of rewarding—intrinsic or extrinsic rewards to staff and students; acknowledgements.
- Rituals—how assemblies are run and what is emphasized at them—sporting achievement? discipline? academic community?
- Communications—how messages, positive and negative, are delivered to the school or wider community; the channels and levels of communication within the school.
- Behaviors—how students and staff treat each other; the level of respect, trust, collaboration, and sharing evident. How visitors are treated.
- Rites of exit and entry—how new staff are inducted; farewells for staff and students; how new students and parents are welcomed.
- Events—the focus of significant annual events like school plays, sports days, etc.

Understanding how things are done in a school or school system increases the administrator's ability to become aware of some of the "sacred cows" (symbols that have been in the school for a long time) to realize the "symbolic value" of the cultural behaviors. Behaviors may need special attention in any change effort. Failure to take the time to understand the foundation of a school, its core values or culture, will result in a less than successful change effort.

In order to change a school or its culture, administrators must understand the core values and beliefs that provide both direction and stability. Core values provide direction by serving as the ideals against which we measure our behavior. Core values provide stability by serving as the unchanging beliefs at the heart of a school. Some researchers have suggested various frameworks to help us better understand the core value and beliefs that underlie the distinct dimensions and components of each school's unique culture. For example, Piperato and Roy (2002) based on the work of Deal and Peterson (1999), describe the core values of a collaborative school culture as being founded on the Three Rs: restorative relationships, relevance, and responsibility. For these researchers a collaborative culture based on the Three Rs enhances individual relationships and fosters a sense of community. "A community in which teachers, administrators, parents and students pay attention to each other's feelings and demonstrate empathy for one another. A community in which young people are held accountable while being supported where they learn appropriate behavior without stigmatization" (Wachtel, 2000).

Some of the other distinct dimensions or components of school culture have been represented under such frameworks as "healthy versus unhealthy," "positive versus negative (or toxic)," or "effective versus ineffective." For example, according to Deal and Peterson (1999) positive cultures have these characteristics:

- A mission focused on student and teacher learning.
- A rich sense of history and purpose.
- Core values of collegiality, performance, and improvement and engender quality, achievement, and learning.
- Positive beliefs and assumptions about the potential of students and staff to learn and grow.
- A strong professional community that uses knowledge, experience, and research to improve practice.
- A shared sense of responsibility for student outcomes.
- A cultural network that fosters positive communication flows.
- Leadership among staff and administrators that blends continuity with improvement.
- Rituals and ceremonies that reinforce core values.
- Stories that celebrate successes and recognize heroines and heroes.
- An overall sense of interpersonal connection, meaningful purpose, and belief in the future.
- A physical environment that symbolizes joy and pride.
- A widely shared sense of respect and caring for everyone.

An underlying set of norms and values, history and stories, hopes and dreams that are productive, encouraging, and optimistic are found in positive cultures. On the other hand, toxic cultures (or subcultures) dampen enthusiasm, reduce professionalism, and depress organizational effectiveness. Characteristics found in toxic cultures include (Peterson, 2002):

- A lack of shared purpose or a splintered mission based on self-interest.
- Staff members who find most of their meaning in activities outside work, negativity, or anti-student sentiments.
- Viewing the past as a story of defeat and failure.

- Norms of radical individualism, the acceptance of mediocrity, and an avoidance of innovation.
- Little sense of community where negative beliefs about colleagues and students abound.
- Few positive traditions or ceremonies to develop a sense of community.
- A cultural network of naysayers, saboteurs, rumormongers, and anti-heroes, where communication is primarily negative.
- A dearth of leadership in the principal's office and among staff.
- Positive role models not unrecognized in the school and community.
- Social connections that have become fragmented and openly antagonist.
- Rather than hopes, dreams, and a clear vision, a sense of hopelessness, discouragement, and despair.

Other frameworks have also made it clear that there are specific characteristics one can attribute to an effective school or an effective learning culture. An effective school or learning culture (see Barth, 1990; Deal & Peterson, 1999; Fullan, 2001; Deal & Peterson, 1990):

- Demonstrates high standards of achievement in academics.
- Characterized by a well-defined set of goals that all members of the school—administration, teachers, and students value and promote.
- Maintains the image of a "professional community," similar to the fields of law or medicine.
- Teachers pursue a clear shared purpose, engage in collaborative activity, and there is a collective responsibility for student learning.
- Has a clear school mission. Teachers value the interchange of ideas with colleagues. Strong values exist that support a safe and secure environment. There are high expectations of everyone, including teachers.
- Is an environment of inquiry, encouraging teachers and others to work collaboratively and collegially to seek aspects of school improvement.
- Encourages teachers to work collaboratively with each other and with the administration to teach students so they learn more.
- Has leadership that invests in people, decentralizes decision making, trusts the judgment of others, facilitates participation, embraces the ethical implications in every decision, and recognizes the complexity of contemporary society.
- Is a place where both teachers and students learn.

Others (Phillips, 1993) have suggested that the three major indicators of the health of a school's culture are collaboration, collegiality, and efficacy. Collaboration is characterized by the degree to which people work together, share information and instructional strategies, and are encouraged to have constructive discussions and debates. Collegiality is about a sense of belonging, emotional support, and inclusion as a valued member of the organization. Efficacy tends to focus on how stakeholders' view themselves. Do they feel as if they have control of their destinies or do they view themselves as helpless victims of "the system?"

Another framework useful to portraying or contrasting a range of school cultures is as follows:

- Fragmented individualism—A culture where a teacher is isolated, takes refuge in the classroom, and is somewhat protected from outside interference. This reinforces uncertainty and discourages collaborative, external support.
- Balkanization—A culture comprised of subcultures of teachers who compete for position and supremacy. There is little collective acceptance on learning, teaching styles, discipline, or curriculum.
- Contrived collegiality—A culture where forms of collaboration are determined by the administration, not teachers. The teachers are regulated and predictable. This culture discourages true collegiality.
- Collaborative cultures—A culture where teacher development is facilitated through mutual support and broad agreement on educational values.

The task of an administrator responsible for change, be it simple improvement or radical reform, is made simpler by frameworks which better assist them in identifying a unique school culture and its corresponding dimensions or components.

INFLUENCING OR CHANGING CULTURE

The difficulty in creating a culture is made even more complex when attempting to bring about a significant change. The themes that appear in discussing change are these:

- Cultures are so elusive and hidden that they cannot be adequately diagnosed, managed, or changed.
- Because it takes difficult techniques, great skills, and considerable time to understand a culture and then additional time to change it, deliberate attempts at culture change are not really practical.
- Cultures sustain people throughout periods of difficulty and serve to wear off anxiety. One of the ways they do this is by providing continu-

ity and stability. Thus, people will naturally resist change to a new culture (Katzenbach, 2000).

These three views suggest that school administrators who are interested in attempting to produce cultural changes face a difficult task. There are, however, courageous administrators who believe that they can intervene and make changes in culture. One view from research in the for-profit sector suggests the following five intervention points for those who are interested in attempting to produce cultural change (Sathe, 1983):

1. A considerable body of knowledge suggests that one of the most effective ways of changing people's beliefs and values is to first change their behavior. However, behavior change does not necessarily produce culture change because of the process of justification. Behavioral compliance does not mean cultural commitment.

2. Those responsible for school culture change must get employees to see the inherent worth in behaving in a new way.

3. Typically, communication is the method used by those responsible for change to motivate the new behaviors. Cultural communications can include announcements, memos, rituals, stories, dress, and other forms of communications.

4. The socialization of new members.

5. The removal of existing members who deviate from the culture.

Each of these interventions must be done after careful diagnoses are performed. Although some individuals may not perfectly fit the school's culture, they may possess exceptional skills and talents. Weeding out cultural misfits might be necessary, but it should be done after weighing the costs and benefits of losing talented performers who deviate from the core cultural value system.

How Best to Change a School's Culture

Different school cultures affect school life each in their own way. Strong collaborative cultures affect school features in ways that "culture improves collegial and collaborative activities" (Deal & Peterson, 1994). Culture fosters effective change (Deal & Peterson, 1990). Culture builds commitment (Schein, 1985). Culture amplifies energy (Deal & Peterson, 1994). Cultural webs of significance (Geertz, 1973) focus attention on what is important. These comments on culture help to stress the importance of understanding culture if one intends to try to change the way things are done in a school or school system.

Deal and Peterson (1994) note that it is first necessary to understand the existing culture, "its historical patterns, the underlying purposes they serve, and how they came to be". Reading culture takes several forms: watching, sensing, listening, interpreting, using all of one's senses, and even employing intuition when necessary (Deal & Peterson, 1999). This means that administrators can use the frameworks identified earlier to read, measure or describe various school cultures or make use of frameworks like those proposed by Conley and others. For example, Conley (1993) suggests that a school's culture can be seen through a number of frames. These are as follows:

- The Structural Frame—concerns the importance of formal roles and relationships.
- The Human Resources Frame— based on the premise that schools are inhabited by individuals who have needs, feelings, and prejudices. The key to shaping culture is to shape it in a way that enables people to get the job done while feeling good about what they are doing.
- The Political Frame—looks at schools as arenas in which different interests compete for power and scarce resources.
- The Symbolic Frame—it treats organizations as tribes, theater or carnivals. In this view cultures are propelled more by rituals, ceremonies, stories, heroes, and myths than by rules, policies, and managerial authority.

Conley (1993) further suggests that an administrator can get an initial reading of the school by asking a number of questions such as:

- How long has the school existed?
- Why was it built and who were the first inhabitants?
- Who had a major influence on the school's direction?
- What critical ingredients occurred in the past and how were they resolved if at all?
- What were the preceding principals, teachers, and students like?
- What does the school's architecture convey? How was space arranged and used?
- What sub-cultures exist inside and outside the school?
- Who are the recognized and (unrecognized) heroes and villains of the school?
- What do people say and think when asked what does the school stand for? What would they miss if they left?
- What events are assigned special importance?
- How is conflict typically defined? How is it handled?
- What are the key ceremonies and stories of the school?

- What do people wish for? Are there patterns to their individual dreams? (p. 324)

In a similar vein, Deal and Peterson offer the following similar list of questions for taking an initial reading of a school:

- Who has had a major influence on the school's direction?
- What subcultures exist inside and outside the school?
- What do people say and think when asked what the school stands for?
- What events are assigned special importance?
- How is conflict typically defined and handled?
- What are the key ceremonies and stories of the school?
- What do people wish and hope for?

An administrator can also use some of the following attributes or characteristics to determine if a culture is dynamic and flourishing:

- Wide acceptance of the principles of life-long personal/professional growth.
- Being comfortable with innovation.
- Continuous reflection.
- Opportunities for the empowerment of individuals.
- High level of collegiality (professional dialogue and growth).
- Establishment of a vertical team culture that crosses over the horizontal cultures of the school (links between the stakeholders) (Smith & Stolp, 1995, p. 4).
- Awareness and commitment to schools' values and beliefs.
- Recognition that everyone in the building is a learner.
- Recognition that children are human beings first, students second.
- Commitment to learning that employs a broad range of instructional methods and formats.

We have found that the following questions are useful for assessing a school culture and its readiness for change:

- What facets of the school culture are likely to promote or impede change?
- What are the potential leverage points for promoting change in the school's culture?
- To what extent does the principal influence the current and future actions of the school?
- What features of the school shape the principal's ability to manage change?
- What role(s) do other stakeholders play in the development, execution, and evaluation of school change?

- What is the principal's role vis-à-vis other change agents in improvement or change processes?
- How does the nature of the various school stakeholders influence the principal's ability to sell the need for change?

These questions can be used by principals or other administrators along with the "Readiness for Change Assessment" questions introduced in Chapter 9 to assess a school's culture.

Regardless of how they decide to try to get a "feel" for the existing culture administrators have to take the time to understand the system's history and be prepared to deal with it. Patterns of communication and implicit assumptions and value systems must also be understood. Just as importantly, the hopes and aspirations, dreams and fears for the future must be articulated and addressed. Without an understanding of and a willingness to respond to school culture, change or reshaping of the culture will not occur.

Changing a school's culture takes time, effort, and persistence, especially in organizations with strong cultures. Older, strong culture schools have established stories, use symbols, conduct rituals, and even use their own unique language. In a strong culture school the core values are widely shared, respected, and protected. A school that is steeped in history, stories, and traditions will exert significant influence on the employees. On the other hand, new schools or ones with weak cultures do not have the tradition, real or mythical, to have a dramatic influence on its employees.

Various elements for understanding the maintenance of organizational culture can also provide insights as to how to reshape or change a school's culture. That is, culture may be best changed by altering what administrators' measure and control, changing the manner in which crises are handled, using different role models for new recruits and altering the socialization/orientation process, establishing different criteria for allocating rewards, and changing the criteria for promotion, hiring, and dismissal.

A school's culture and values are important because they provide guidance for behavior. As noted at the beginning of this chapter, school administrators responsible for bringing about system change will only succeed if in the end they are able to create a new way of doing things. And that means impacting the school's culture. Thomas J. Sergiovanni, in his book, *The Lifeworld of Leadership* states: "Most successful school leaders will tell you that getting the culture right" ... is the prerequisite to any and all school improvement efforts (1999).

Based on our discussion to this point, leaders who are interested in changing their school's culture should first try to understand the existing culture. School change in any form, whether in the form of simple improvement or radical reform, ends up altering a variety of accepted ways of doing things and relationships. These "ways of doing thing" and relationships are at the very core of any school's stability. School change should be approached with openness, trust, dialogue, concern for others, and some caution.

Administrators responsible for school change must find ways to get various stakeholders (students, teachers, and administrators for example) to work towards a common understanding or diagnosis of a school's need for change, existing culture, and future state. The idea is to come to agreement on the positive and negative aspects of a school's culture. Teachers, parents, and administrators are best able to identify areas that are in need of or would serve as obstacles to school culture change.

Likewise, school artifacts such as the routines, ceremonies, rituals, traditions, myths, or subtle difference in school language can provide clues for how to approach cultural change. School artifacts change over time. A school system may decide to shorten time between classes only later to find out that this time was important for teacher interaction and unity. Paying attention to such routines, before changing them, may provide valuable insights into how school cultures function. Changing a school culture requires that administrators give attention to the informal, subtle and symbolic aspects of school life which shape the beliefs and actions of each employee within the system.

Caught between the external demands of constituent groups and the needs of teachers and students, as well as the community and institutional contexts, administrators charged with the responsibility of school culture change have a difficult role to fulfill. Their attitudes, beliefs, and values, like those of other stakeholders (e.g., teachers, students, etc.) profoundly impact efforts to change a school's culture.

Administrators have to take risks regarding how much change the system can stand. It is they who provide support, both psychologically and through the allocation of resources, to give credence to change execution efforts. Without this support, these efforts will not succeed. Administrators demonstrate this support through power sharing and relationships with teachers and others. Establishing and nurturing a culture of shared power and decision making, with norms of open-dialogue and introspection for change is an important task for school administrators undertaking a cultural transformation. It is a task that is shaped by the community and institutional context in which administrators find themselves.

As emphasized at various points in this book, schools are complex organisms, with all parts interrelated and interdependent. The fact that the administrator is also part of this organism creates difficulty as he or she both acts on and is acted upon by the culture of the school. Administrators have to understand and learn how to work with elements of the school system, like its culture, which impacts the efforts to change schools. Policies may be established that encourage the development of a culture that supports school change. The culture of the school exerts a powerful and pervasive influence over everything in the school. A power that can derail any effort to radically change, reshape or continuously improve a school system or culture.

As emphasized in earlier discussions the interaction of various stakeholders' beliefs and the school setting powerfully impact what administrators do in change initiatives, what they see (in terms of what the problems are and what solutions can be considered), and what they are willing to change. Before an administrator can start the process of trying to change beliefs in an individual school or school system, the beliefs held by key stakeholders, as well as the administrator's own beliefs need examination. If the internally held beliefs and perceptions that truly guide behavior do not change, neither will the school, at least not for long.

Because actions reflect deeply held and often unquestioned beliefs and myths, the culture of a school most often needs alteration if change is to occur. This task requires understanding the culture, being open to criticism, and confronting those beliefs that act as barriers to the success of a change initiative. Changes in "the way we do things around here" will be made. A knowledge of factors identified by Schein (1985) briefly introduced earlier in this chapter that affect internalization can be used to help school stakeholders (administrators, teachers, students, staff, etc.) internalize the new culture.

Cultural norms of continuous improvement or change, a shared sense of purpose that includes a vision of continuous improvement and change as a major goal, and stakeholder involvement, cooperation and collegiality provide support for school culture change efforts. Norms of continuous improvement, experimentation, and change imply that administrators, teachers and others constantly seek and assess potentially better practices inside and outside their own schools. This culture of continuous introspection helps build a school community where change, collaboration, collegiality, and involvement by many groups in school improvement or change may exist. This is vital to the development of a shared school change (culture) vision that is, in turn, vital to successful execution. Not only should this shared change or culture vision include the outcomes desired by those involved, it also should include a shared vision about "how to get there," which includes the change process itself. A shared sense of purpose creates ownership of the program among all players.

All participants in any school change should be asked to rethink their beliefs, recognize unproductive patterns, and change them. Individuals required to change are primarily interested in three things when confronted with changing the rules they have become comfortable with as to how things are to be done. They are:

1. How will this change affect me and what I do personally?
2. Why do you have reason to believe this can be implemented? and
3. Once executed, why do you think it will work?

Administrators can help resolve fears and provide support both emotionally and with necessary resources, including time. The resource of time is especially important considering that changing the culture of the school is extremely time consuming and costly. The teachers and staff need to know what the new "thing" looks like when fully executed, and what modifications they can make, if needed, without sacrificing the integrity of the new "way of doing things."

Whether it is teachers, students, staff, or others they all need to believe that they are an essential ingredient in change success or culture change and they must be expected to act in ways that confirm the new ways of doing things at the school. For example, school administrators can focus attention on the need for autonomy, independence, and a sense of efficacy on the part of teachers. Administrators need to investigate past attempts to change the school and explain why change is needed or why things must be different. They also must understand that each individual and stakeholder groups may be resistant to change based in part on past experiences with change and their belief system or mental model of schools. Commitment and change cannot be mandated.

Any administrators responsible for change in a school's culture has to understand at the most basic level that commitment and change cannot be mandated. Education stakeholders have a history of and expect to be involved in any school change initiatives. And this does not matter whether they are internal or external stakeholders. This environment creates a starting point for changes in a school's culture. Sergiovanni (1995) has suggested that schools are "tightly coupled" around cultural themes. "Teachers and students are driven less by bureaucratic rules, management protocols, contingency tradeoffs and images of rational reality and more by norms, group mores, patterns of beliefs, values, the socialization process and socially-constructed reality . . . In a loosely connected world, it is culture . . . that is key to bringing about the coordination and sense of order needed for effectiveness" (p. 11).

Administrators must build on the collegiality, open dialogue, and desire to be involved that key school stakeholders bring to a change situation if they intend to change a school's culture. The school environment shapes what administrators are able to do. However, the belief that "the system won't let us" can become a self-fulfilling prophecy if the administrator falls into that trap. Support by administrators like principals is vital to either continuous improvement or change in the school's culture. Administrators, like principals, who have been called the "gatekeeper of change" are central to any school change effort. The relationship between teachers and the principal sets the standard for all other relationships in the school. Principals, in turn, need the support of the superintendent and central office.

The culture of the school reflects local community culture in many ways. Community support of the school itself and for any change effort is vital. Parents and community members can be active partners and allies, not adversaries. This will provide the resources needed and assist in changing the culture of the school.

PRACTICAL GUIDELINES
FOR SCHOOL CULTURAL CHANGE

Although knowledge about changing school culture is still in its formative stage, the following practical advice can serve as guidelines for administrators undertaking school culture change:

Understand Core Values

In order to change school culture, administrators must understand the core values and beliefs of the system that provide direction and stability. Core values are the foundation of a school culture as they articulate what a school measures employee behavior and provide insight into the beliefs at the heart of a school.

Formulate a Clear and Shared Strategic Vision

Effective cultural change should start from a clear vision of the school's new strategy and of the shared values and behaviors needed to make it work. This vision provides the purpose and direction for cultural change. It serves as a yardstick for defining the school's existing culture and for deciding whether proposed changes are consistent with core values of the school. For example, administrators at the Union City School System in New Jersey formulated a vision and strategy for restructuring the system and the Corrective Action Plan, for reforming the curriculum in 1989 (Kanter, 1998). A useful approach to providing clear and shared strategic vision is development of a statement of school purpose, listing in straightforward terms the school's core values. A shared vision results when a variety of stakeholders are given the opportunity to help create the vision, for example, students and staff share some of the responsibility for the new culture.

Display Top-Administration Commitment

Cultural change must be managed from the top of the school or school system. Principals and other top administrators have to be strongly committed to the new values and need to create constant pressures for change. They must have the staying power to see the changes through. For example, Thomas Highton, Superintendent of the Union City School System enthusiastically pushed school restructuring and reform through the system and averted state takeover. His and other administrator's efforts were rewarded when they finally succeeded in winning state certification in 1995 (Kanter, 1998). Beyond this accomplishment, Union City clearly established itself in the forefront of the school improvement movement, having achieved systemic change at two important levels—restructuring and reculturing. (Restructuring refers to change in organizational factors such as the curriculum, parent involvement, teacher training, etc. Reculturing refers to deeper change in the cultures, relationships, expectations, and values in the school system.) This top-administrative support assumes that authority and control of the change process is shared with teachers and others who also take on leadership responsibilities during the school culture change process.

Model Culture Change at the Highest Levels

Top administrators must communicate the new culture through their own actions. Their behaviors need to symbolize the kinds of values and behaviors being sought. In successful culture change, school administrators must show an almost missionary zeal for the new values; their actions must symbolize the values forcefully. Thomas Highton, Fred Carrigg, executive director for academic programs, and principal actively modeled the new values and behavior that were instrumental to the systemic reform and supported the change process at all levels and with the various stakeholders (Kanter, 1998) in their efforts to change the Union City school system culture.

Modify the Institution to Support School Change

Cultural change generally requires supporting modifications in school structure, human resources systems, information and control systems, and administrative styles. These organizational features can help to orient people's behavior to the new culture. They can make people aware of the behaviors required to get things done in the new culture and can encourage performance of those behaviors. For example, the Union City School System Corrective Action Plan required retraining teachers to institutionalize the new educational philosophy. A philosophy which, for instance, allowed for students to have more say in how they wanted to learn their subjects; relied on collaborative, interdisciplinary teaching instead of isolated, subject-specific teaching and towards the use of cross-curricular thematic units requiring teacher collaboration; and required changes in the physical layout of the classroom.

Think Systemically

As noted in our discussion earlier in Chapter 1, a systems view of the school is important to any change effort. This means that those responsible for change recognize the importance of focusing less on particulars and more on the whole. For example, in a school system this might include concentrating less on day-to-day events and more on underlying trends and forces for school system or culture change. When those responsible for school culture change think of the school as an interlocking unit, their focus is on the underlying cultural relationships. Relationships that more clearly help the change visionaries and executioners identify the particular components of the school culture that requires modifications as part of the overall change effort.

Select and Socialize Newcomers and Terminate Deviants

One of the most effective methods for changing organizational culture is to change organizational members. People can be selected and terminated in terms of their fit with the new culture. This is especially important in key leadership positions, where people's actions can significantly promote or hinder new values and behaviors. For example, Thomas Highton, in trying to bring about change at the Union City School system promoted Fred Carrigg in 1989, from his position as bilingual/English as a Second Language (ESL) supervisor to executive director for academic programs, a position that put him in charge of curriculum instruction. Carrigg, along with Highton, was responsible for socializing teachers, students, and parents to the new educational philosophy and overall reform in the school system (Kanter, 1998).

Even with the guidelines above changing a school culture is still not easy. Culture emerges out of the shared behaviors of organization members and working relationships that have developed over time. Consequently, it takes time for a cultural transformation to take effect. School culture change is about changing behavior of individuals—what they do, not what they think. Real behavior change will most likely come from:

- Explaining why the behavior change matters to the school system and the employee,
- Providing timely feedback about performance,
- Rewarding the desired behavior,
- Eliminating rewards for conflicting behavior,
- Principals and other administrators modeling the desired behavior, and
- Removing barriers to performing the desired behavior

CONCLUSION

Organizational change will not occur without reshaping or changing its culture. Thus, the need for administrators to take the time to understand that culture is the foundation of any organization. Organizational cultures include the values, norms, rites, rituals, symbols, ceremonies, heroes, and scoundrels in the history of the organization. Organizational cultures define what a new employee needs to learn for acceptance as a member of the organization.

The levels at which you see organizational culture vary from visible to almost invisible. Artifacts and other cultural symbols usually are visible to even the newest employee. Basic assumptions, a set of implicit values, are almost invisible to new employees and are learned only after a period of socialization and acceptance. Espoused values and enacted values have midlevel visibility.

An understanding of the existing and desired school culture is critical to successful change. An examination of school culture is important because, as Goodlad's study (1984) points out, "alike as schools may be in many ways, each school has an ambience (or culture) of its own and, further, its ambience may suggest to the careful observer useful approaches to making it a better school" (p. 81). It is the cultural change that supports the "new" way of doing things in the school system. The more the school administrator understands about school culture and their roles in shaping it, the better equipped they will be to successfully bring about change and reform. Deal and Peterson (1990) note that once the leadership has reflected to the point that the school's culture is understood, they can evaluate the need to shape or reinforce it.

School culture, despite its elusive nature, provides a steady stream of consciousness that affects the lives of the participants—administrators, teachers, staff, and students and a school or school systems ability to change. Culture determines the norms, values, and beliefs of a school. Successful administrators shape and change a school's culture by understanding the forces at work in the environment and taking advantage of the opportunities.

In the end, administrators must have a clear vision for creating change and a new school culture that includes a collaborative and cooperative activity among teachers, students, parents, staff, and other key stakeholders. Those administrators who are able to develop a clear vision of the future will be more successful in building or changing a school culture. However, all of this will go for naught if the school administrators have not developed and institutionalized some principles of change within the school system. These principles include:

- Promote institutional self-discovery.
- Be aware of how institutional culture affects change.
- Realize that school system change is often political.
- Lay groundwork for change.
- Focus on adaptability.
- Construct opportunities for continuous stakeholder interaction to develop new mental models.
- Be open to a disorderly process.
- Facilitate shared governance and collective decision-making.
- Articulate and seek agreement on core school values and characteristics.
- Connect the school culture change process to individual, group and institutional identity.
- Create a culture of risk and help people in changing belief systems.
- Be aware that various levels or aspects of the school system will need different change models.
- Realize that strategies for school culture change vary by change initiative.
- Consider combining change models or approaches.

These will help administrators develop a systematic and systemic process of change that works with individuals, acknowledges change as a human process, is sensitive to the distinctive characteristics of schools, is context-based, achieves balance of internal and external forces, and is open to creativity and leveraging culture and school system change through chance occurrences.

In conclusion, as we move further and further into the twenty-first century the world will continue in a constant state of change, and no administrators or school system can escape the effects of operating in a continually dynamic, evolving educational landscape. The forces of change are so great that the future success, indeed the very survival, of schools and their school systems depends on how well they respond to change or, optimally, whether they can actually stay ahead of the need to reshape or change the way they do things.

CHAPTER 8

CONTINUOUS IMPROVEMENT IN SCHOOL SYSTEMS

Applying the Balanced Scorecard Approach

INTRODUCTION

Clamors for change in education (e.g., increased accountability, etc.) over the past decade has forced many school systems to fundamentally rethink their strategies and operations as suggested throughout this book. By now, terms traditionally identified with the for-profit such as "rightsizing," "restructuring" and "reengineering" have become familiar parts of American education vocabulary. Just as businesses increasingly are scrutinizing how each product and process adds value to customers, schools are facing mounting pressure from increasingly demanding stakeholders to demonstrate or justify the value added given the resources allocated for schools to undertake their daily educational activities (e.g., educating students).

To their credit, many schools have not just sat passively on the sidelines. For example, Fredericks Middle School in Live Oak County Public School District that was established in 1963 as a research and development school began what many considered to be a progressive and innovative campaign for planned change. It had a long history of shared decision-making

Managing School System Change: Charting a Course for Renewal, pages 161–186
Copyright © 2004 by Information Age Publishing, Inc.

between administrators, teachers and parents. The faculty at Fredericks Middle School organized themselves into interdisciplinary teaching teams in the early 1970s in an effort to improve academic programs and collaboration among teachers, thus creating a template for our current middle school model programs. The school has continued innovative, shared decision-making initiatives and therefore serves as a great example for others who are just now undertaking a planned change initiative (Bondy, 1995).

In our view, stakeholder calls for educational change in the form of increased student testing for example are useful for stimulating and guiding educational reform. But they leave unanswered the question of how a school can effectively introduce and sustain the desired changes. This is an especially critical issue given the tremendous budget pressures many states are facing and the corresponding reduced funds for schools in general. The purpose of this chapter is to explain how the balanced scorecard, which has been successfully used in the for-profit sector to promote and sustain change, may be used to revitalize and change education as well. Our discussion of the balanced scorecard is structured in four sections. In the first section, we first define and then outline the nature of this approach in the for-profit sector. The second section offers a fictitious example of gathering data to design a balanced scorecard for a school based on responses from principals. In the third section, we discuss the development and implementation of a balanced scorecard in a school system. The final section discusses the need for and importance of creating SMART targets as part of the balanced scorecard approach in successful change initiatives.

THE BALANCED SCORECARD: PERFORMANCE IMPROVEMENT

Oftentimes we have heard the expression, "what gets measured, gets improved." Or as suggested by one individual: "You simply can't manage anything you can't measure" (Lingle & Schienmann, 1996, p. 56). Unfortunately, just saying this begs the question about what we should measure, how we should measure it, and what should we change to make those measures improve?

Problems with Just One Source of Measures

If you were to ask most anyone in the for-profit sector how they would measure company performance, they might give you a funny look and say, "How much money the company makes, of course! Isn't that obvious?" To a certain extent, they are right. Profitability, gross revenues, return on capital, etc. are the critical, "bottom line" kind of results that for-profit organizations must deliver to survive. Unfortunately, if senior management only focuses on the financial health of the organization, several unfortunate consequences arise. One of these is that financial measures are "lagging indicators" of success. This means that how high or low these numbers go depends on a wide variety of events that may have happened months or years before and that you have no immediate control of in the present. Being in a plane falling from the sky is a bad time to realize that you should have done routine maintenance, and oh, by the way, filled it with gasoline!

Another of the consequences of just focusing on financial measures is that they have nothing to do directly with the customers who use your organization's product or service. Decisions may be made that help your organization financially, but hurt the long-term relationships with one's customers, who may eventually reduce the purchases or leave you altogether. We all may have been on the spot of paying for car repairs that we need, but we know that we are paying too much and will never go back to that service station again.

Instead of such a short-sighted, after-the-fact view of for-profit organizational performance, we need a more comprehensive view with an equal emphasis on outcome measures (the financial measures or lagging indicators), measures that will tell us how well the organization is doing now (current indicators) and measures of how it might do in the future (leading indicators).

What is the Balanced Scorecard?

The balanced scorecard is just the remedy for this kind of problem. First of all, the balanced scorecard is a way of:

1. Measuring organizational, business unit or department success
2. Balancing long-term and short-term actions
3. Balancing different measures of success
   • Financial
   • Customer
   • Internal Operations
   • Human Resource Systems & Development (learning and growth)
4. A way of tying strategies to measures and actions

The balanced scorecard provides an organization's leaders with a crisp and clear way of communicating strategy or planned change. With balanced scorecards, a change vision or strategy reaches everyone in a language that makes sense. When change is expressed in terms of measurements and targets, each stakeholder can relate to what must happen. This leads to a much better execution of planned change which is especially important when one considers the reality that there are moving parts in today's organization and a common vision must have a "track" to follow to every corner of that organization, while allowing each individual, stakeholder group, section, division, and so on to develop their own and more importantly supporting actions to achieve the goals that will eventually realize the change vision.

Simply put, for our purposes the balanced scorecard is a customer-based planning and process improvement system aimed at focusing and driving the change process. It does this by translating strategy into an integrated set of financial and nonfinancial measures that both communicates the organizational strategy to the members and provides them with actionable feedback on attainment of objectives.

The balanced scorecard satisfies the individuals or stakeholder groups comfortable with financial or quantitative measures and serves the needs of those responsible for change that are concerned with the drivers that affect future performance. The balanced scorecard measures focus on key aspects of operations, for an organization, a sub-unit, or even an individual. For each organizational unit or level, the approach involves identifying several key components of operations, establishing goals for these, and then selecting measures to track progress toward the goals. In doing so, the measures as a whole provide a holistic view of what is happening inside and outside the unit or level so that each participant can see how his or her individual activities contributes to the overall mission. In addition, tying rewards to these measures motivates greater efforts toward their attainment.

At the organizational level, the balanced scorecard typically would include at least the following four components, though the exact number and nature would depend on the organization's specific goals and circumstances (Kaplan & Norton, 1996a):

1. Customer perspective: How do customers see us?

2. Internal business perspective: What must we excel at?

3. Innovation and learning perspective: Can we continue to improve and create value for customers?

4. Financial perspective: How do we look to providers of financial resources?

Each of the four perspectives is linked to one another and are the vehicles to aligning change strategy and realizing the vision. In Figure 8.1 we show how these components, or perspectives, interrelate to provide an integrated picture of the organization. The customer perspective tracks how well the organization is meeting the expectations of its customers, because they are

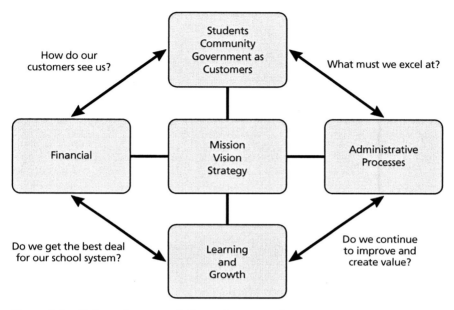

Figure 8.1.   Balanced scorecard: Strategic perspectives.

the ones who pay for its costs and provide its profit. This perspective does not end with identifying current needs, but demands anticipating what customers may require in the future. The internal business perspective focuses on the internal processes that will deliver the objectives related to satisfying current and future customer demands. This perspective expands the focus beyond just improving existing processes to defining a complete internal process value chain. The emphasis of the innovation and learning perspective is the organization's ability to sustain and increase its ability to satisfy customer demands. Finally, the financial perspective tracks how well the organization is translating its operational results into financial well-being. More will be said about these in the next section.

Over the last decade a considerable number of recent articles and books have discussed the balanced scorecard approach in the for-profit sector (see for example, Kaplan & Norton, 2000; Berkman, 2002). More generally, writers on the subject have reported that the balanced scorecard has been found to provide the following major benefits across the range of users:

1. Promoting the active formulation and implementation of organizational strategies.
2. Making organizational strategies updated and highly visible.
3. Improving communication within the organization.

4. Improving alignment among divisional and individual goals and the organization's goals and strategies.

5. Aligning annual or short-term operating plans with long-term strategies.

6. Aligning performance evaluation measurement and long-term strategies.

Though a wide variety of for-profit organizations have benefited from using the balanced scorecard, only a few applications by educational institutions have been reported to date. One company, BEST (Building Excellent Schools Together) Education Partners, offers the balanced scorecard approach as a method to enrich innovative public schools primarily in economically disadvantaged areas. This mission is achieved by developing collaborative partnerships with community, education, and technology partners (BEST, 2003).

In our view, the balanced scorecard increases the likely success of a school or school system change effort as it assists administrators and others in communicating a change strategy or plan to key stakeholders. School system change strategies or plans may in the end look nice, but they simply are worthless and will increase the likely failure of a change effort unless they impact the stakeholders who must execute the plan. A balanced scorecard provides administrators with a vehicle to counter four barriers to school system change execution:

1. Change vision barrier—No one in the school system understands the change strategies or plans.

2. Stakeholder barrier—Most stakeholders have objectives or interests that are not linked to the change strategy or plan of the school system.

3. Resource barrier—Time, energy, and money are not allocated to those things that are critical to the school system change effort. For example, budgets are not linked to school improvement or change, resulting in wasted resources.

4. Administration barriers—Administration spends too little time on change strategy or plan and too much time on short-term tactical decision-making.

Using the four perspectives in the balanced scorecard allows the administrator to take a systems view of a school or school system and avoid taking a myopic view of a planned change initiative.

DESIGNING A BALANCED SCORECARD FOR A SCHOOL:
AN IMPLEMENTATION MODEL

Assuming that one is convinced that the balanced scorecard can be useful to a school or school system, how does one go about implementing one? Answering this question requires attending to two subordinate issues: what specific items to include in the scorecard, and what development and implementation process to use. We briefly address the former (that is offer a suggested framework for undertaking such a task) in this section; consideration of the latter is deferred to the next section.

We assume that of all the stakeholders with an interest in K–12 education, principals (of course other school stakeholders like teachers could also be queried) should have thought as much as anybody about the change and other challenges to schools and strategies for meeting them. Thus, an appropriate first step would be to undertake a survey of these school leaders on the subject. We suggest developing a two-part questionnaire or survey to be completed by the principal. The first part should provide an explanation of the balanced scorecard and its four typical perspectives, or components. The second part should contain five blank tables, each with one column for goals, and another for measures. The first four tables should be named after the four typical perspectives. The fifth should be unlabeled, so respondents can introduce perspectives that they believe to be important. The respondents should also be invited to change the first four tables' labels to ones that they consider more appropriate. For each perspective, the respondent should be asked to identify up to five goals that he or she believes a school should have, and for each goal, one or more relevant performance measures. There also should be several demographic questions.

To reduce clutter once data is gathered from respondents, common terms should be used to capture responses of similar content. We recommend that these terms be developed through a process of discussion and consensus between those individuals responsible for analyzing the survey data. Tables 8.1 through 8.4 provide samples of some suggested goals and related measures for the four typical perspectives.

An important consideration in the grouping process should be preserving the richness of the responses. Items (especially goals) that seem to contain subtle differences should be kept separate (e.g., "maintain high quality programs" versus "academic excellence"). We offer only a brief overview of each of the component below since we believe the sample tables offer further explanation.

Customer Service Perspective

The customer perspective tracks how well the organization is meeting customer's expectations. In Table 8.1, we group the sample suggestions into four subsections. The first subsection focuses on the stakeholders and reveals a broad view of who the schools' "customers" are. They include students, the public (government, taxpayers, etc.), the teachers, and parents. A wide range of goals is suggested for each of these stakeholders. Relating to students, for example, suggested goals range from developing high quality students and improving student admissions to college and employment.

The remaining three subsections summarize goals and measures that apply across multiple stakeholders. For example, "academic excellence" (from the second subsection) and "reputation of school programs" from the third subsection) are potentially relevant to students and their families, as well as teachers and the community.

Table 8.1.　Sample School High School Principals' Suggested Goals and Measures for the Customer Perspective

Goals	Measures
The stakeholders: Students, public/community, teachers, and parents	
1. Students	
Student Quality	• Quality of teaching and advising
	• Pre-post tests
	• GPA over time
	• Curriculum quality
Graduate high-quality students	• Quality and appropriateness of each student's knowledge upon graduationQuality of teaching and advising
	• Quality and timeliness of placements/admissions (both employment and college
	• Outcomes assessment (1, 3, 5 years after graduation)
	• Quality and no. of colleges recruiting students
	• No. of students employed upon graduation
Admission of students in colleges/universities	• Admission rate
	• Survey of colleges/universities
	• Standardized test scores (SAT, ACT)
	• Quality of colleges/universities where admitted
	• Scholarships

Table 8.1.   Sample School High School Principals' Suggested Goals and Measures for the Customer Perspective (Cont.)

Goals	Measures
Student satisfaction	• Dropout rate as % of students
	• Student retention (nonfailing) rates
	• School academic climate
	• Number of complaints or positive sentiments reported
	• Direct current student survey of satisfaction
	• High graduate exit surveys
	• Alumni retroactive ratings of their experience
2. Teachers	
Teacher satisfaction	• Teacher ability to participate in those decisions affecting them
	• Encouragement given teachers to engage in developmental activities (e.g., relevant professional development-support to take additional courses, attendance at professional conferences)
	• Effectiveness of orientation and inculcation process, for new teachers
	• Availability of well-defined personnel policies and procedures available to teachers
	• Comfortable classroom, teachers' lounge, and technology support
	• Administrative support of teachers
3. Parents	
Parental satisfaction	• Satisfaction with student's education/learning experience
	• Response to surveys
	• Focus groups
	• Participation in school-sponsored activities
Quality programs: Quality of students and teachers, quality of teaching	
Academic excellence	• Quality of students—Standardized Testing, PSATs, etc.
	• Quality of teachers—% with masters/certifications
	• Community surveys
	• Retention rates of students
	• College admission rate of students
	• Number of graduates
	• Accreditation status
	• Self-evaluation reports
	• Awards for academic excellence

Table 8.1.   Sample School High School Principals' Suggested Goals and Measures for the Customer Perspective (Cont.)

Goals	Measures
Teaching quality	• How teaching skills are perceived by students and parents
	• Qualifications of faculty
	• Percent of certified teachers
	• Student evaluation of teachers
	• Parent evaluation of teachers
	• Focus on up-to-date teaching practices
	• Innovative teaching strategies
Curriculum	• Students' understanding of course/program objectives
	• Variety of teaching and learning methods
	• Use of technology in the classroom/learning
	• Curriculum integration across disciplines
	• Alignment of Curriculum with assessments
	• Character/Citizen development component within curriculum
A teaching focus	• Student-teacher ratios
	• Rewards for good teaching
	• Percentage of budget devoted to teacher development
Program and teaching innovations	• Quality of instruction
	• Quality of advising/counseling
	• Extracurricular activities

Public image: Value added of programs, reputation of school

Be seen as providing value for the funds allocated/per student costs	• Student and parent perceptions
	• Cost per student compared to other schools
Reputation of school	• Employment rates of high school graduates
	• State and national rankings
	• Internal survey of students
	• Accreditation
	• Reputation among peers and stakeholders
	• Acceptance of former students in colleges/universities
	• Number of students receiving scholarships
	• Discipline Reports

Table 8.1.   Sample School High School Principals' Suggested Goals and Measures for the Customer Perspective (Cont.)

Goals	Measures
Outstanding customer/ school image	• Graduation rates
	• College/university admission rates
	• Quality of colleges/universities accepting students
	• Recognition of teachers
	• Reports from key public groups
Quality service and continuous improvement	
Service to the school/ system	• Adequacy of participation in school-wide activities
	• Quality of relationships between administrators, teachers, parents, support staff, and others
Quality of support services	• Ease of communication
	• Extent of student advising/counseling and administrative processes are student-centered, effective, and efficient
	• Adequacy of library for students
	• Responsiveness of support personnel to assisting in meeting student's needs

Internal Business Perspective

The internal business perspective focuses on how well operations are satisfying customer demands (see Table 8.2). The suggested goals and measures focus on different aspects of operations and are presented under five subheadings: teaching/learning excellence; curriculum/program excellence; quality and currency of teachers; efficiency and effectiveness of service; and strategic issues. Again, the wide variety of suggested sample goals and measures indicates the scope of issues that might arise from a survey and could be considered along with the potential responses to them as part of a school change effort.

Table 8.2.   Sample School Principals' Suggested Goals and Measures for Internal Business Perspective

Goals	*Measures*
Teaching/learning experience	
Teaching excellence	• Student satisfaction
	• Teacher acquisition of competencies, skills, knowledge over time
	• Use of latest technology
	• Teaching awards
	• Student performance on assessment measures, SAT/ACT scores
	• No. of students graduating
	• College/university admission of graduates
	• Student evaluations
	• Peer review
	• Outside reviews
Excellence in developing learning and learning skills (classroom experience that prepare students for success)	• National scores on exit exams
	• Evaluations by external reviewers and employers
	• Grade point standards
	• Opportunities for writing and oral presentations
	• Improved math skills
	• Number of students going to college/universities
Develop state-of the-art teaching facilities/ classrooms	• Inventory of teaching/learning facilities/classrooms
	• Computer labs
	• Presentation capabilities
Information technology currency, usage, and applications	• Students' degree of access to technology
	• Degree of deployment of technology in learning experience
	• Currency and appropriateness of hardware/software
	• Internet access/use
Curriculum/program excellence and innovation	
Curriculum excellence and innovation	• Degree to which curriculum is up-to-date with educational, employer, and broader community trends
	• Regular feedback from employers and colleges/universities
	• Accreditation
	• Periodic review of each course/program
Introduction of new courses/innovations	• Actual versus planned
	• Number within last 3–5 years
	• Concept to implementation time

Table 8.2.   Sample School Principals' Suggested Goals and Measures for Internal Business Perspective (Cont.)

Goals	Measures
Quality and currency of teachers	
Quality teachers	• Teacher credentials
	• Teacher development plans
	• Teacher appraisals
Currency of teachers and classroom materials/experiences	• Faculty development outcomes
	• Utilization rate of multimedia in classroom
Efficiency and effectiveness of service	
Production efficiency	• Failure/drop-out rates of students
	• Teaching load management
	• Percentage of students graduating
	• Teaching costs/student
	• Administrative costs/student
	• Percentage of budget dedicated directly to learning
	• Allocation and use of equipment and supplies
	• Analysis of use space
Student services effectiveness, including advising/counseling	• Type and number of services provided
	• College and employment placement services and opportunities
	• Quality of instruction and advising/counseling
	• Effective use of Internet
Positive climate	• Degree to which staff is professional, friendly, and helpful
	• Quality of library
	• Degree of access to technology
Increased diversity	• Minority recruiting (teachers, support staff and administrators) and mentoring
	• Number of male and minority teachers
Strategic issues	
Ability to change	• Curriculum and pedagogy currency
	• Success of accepted reforms/changes
	• Number of new/revised courses/programs to meet needs and demands of various stakeholders
Shared expectations and collaborative relations	• Buy into goals and harmony in internal operations
	• Constituency/stakeholder feedback

Table 8.2. Sample School Principals' Suggested Goals and Measures for Internal Business Perspective (Cont.)

Goals	Measures
Mission updates	• Situation analysis
	• Modification methods
Positioning of school	• Match with mission
	• Establishment of image with stakeholders
	• Measures of students' knowledge

Innovation and Learning Perspective

This perspective emphasizes the organization's capacity to sustain and increase its ability to both satisfy customer demands and improve process efficiency and effectiveness. In Table 8.3, we group the sample principals' suggestions into three subsections: teaching learning excellence and innovation quality of teachers and mission-driven processes and reward system. In the first subsection the suggested goals are related to the teachers, technology, programs, and curricula as well as teaching and pedagogical improvements.

Table 8.3. Sample School Principals' Suggested Goals and Measures for Innovation and Learning Perspective

Goals	Measures
	Teaching/learning excellence and innovation
Teacher development	• Self-reports
	• Degree to which continuous teacher development is expected, encouraged, suggested, and evaluated
	• Expenditures for teaching enhancement
	• Teacher evaluations by students/administrators
	• Teaching assessment
Technology leadership (use, development, application)	• Number and types of activities
	• Student and teacher satisfaction
	• Degree to which technology is used in specific courses
	• Speed of introducing technology and technology adaptation
	• Expenditures for hardware, software, and maintenance

Table 8.3.   Sample School Principals' Suggested Goals and Measures for Innovation and Learning Perspective (Cont.)

Goals	*Measures*
Technology/learning	• Number of innovations incorporated into classroom
	• Methods update
	• Level of equipment
	• Degree of multimedia presentations
	• Teaching assessments
	• Implementation of alternatives to traditional lecture/discussion classes
	• Quality of instruction
	• Quality of advising/counseling
	• Number of ongoing instructional development initiatives
Program and curricular innovations/improvements	• Extent of curriculum revision
	• Number of new initiatives
	• Rate of change in curriculum
	• Reports of continuous improvement committees
	• Formally approved curriculum changes
	• Innovation versus competitors (e.g., other schools)
Pedagogy enhancement	• Course revision/development
	• Field trips
	• Attendance at pedagogy workshops
	• Interaction with community/business/employers
	• Development of assessment technique/device for innovation
Value-added learning	• Pre- and post-learning measures
	• Learning portfolio
Increased teacher reputation	• Rankings of teachers with peers in other schools
	• Ability to recruit top candidates
Quality service and continuous improvement	
Service to the school/system	• Adequacy of participation in school-wide activities
	• Quality of relationships between administrators, teachers, parents, support staff, and others
Quality of support services	• Ease of communication
	• Extent of student advising/counseling and administrative processes are student-centered, effective, and efficient
	• Adequacy of library for students
	• Responsiveness of support personnel to assisting in meeting student's needs

Financial Perspective

The financial perspective tracks how well the organization is translating its operational achievements into financial results. As the sample data in Table 8.4 show, our sample principals' viewed this component as investing in human capital and a school's financial viability. An examination of the suggested goals and measures reveals a wealth of ideas for schools to increase their financial viability. It also suggests areas deserving of increased effort. For example, there could be considerable emphasis on perceived and actual budget and financial accountability.

Table 8.4.   Sample School Principals' Suggested Goals and Measures for the Financial Perspective

Goals	Measures
Human capital investments	
Maintain/enhance salaries to retain and attract quality teachers	• Salaries relative to peer groups
	• Schools attended by job applicants
	• Teacher satisfaction
	• Teacher turnover rate
Provide adequate resources for teacher development	• Dollars for travel, technology support, etc.
	• Dollars/teachers
	• Program for release time and sabbaticals
Financial management	
To be financially sound	• Balanced budgets
	• Extent budget submissions cover all essential requirements
	• Efficiency and effectiveness of budget allocations spending
Be perceived as responsible stewards of the resources under our control (resource accountability)	• Effective stewards of school resources entrusted to us
	• Effectiveness of methods of monitoring our supplies and equipment
	• Degree to which expenditures are essential
	• Ability to direct resources to programmatic needs
	• Efficiency and effectiveness of use of resources given school mission
	• Graduates' track record
Succeed	• Rate of increase in number of employees to students
	• Teacher-student ratio
	• Rate of change of the survival measures

Table 8.4.   Sample School Principals' Suggested Goals and Measures for the Financial Perspective (Cont.)

Goals	Measures
Prosper	• Growth and quantity and quality of students
	• State and national ranking
	• Percentage of surplus fund balance of operating budget
	• Increased budget
	• Increased teacher lines
Survival	• Budget maintenance
	• Enrollment trend
	• Relevance preference by parents of students
	• Spending relative to budget
Stability	• Ups and downs in enrollment

DEVELOPING AND IMPLEMENTING A BALANCED SCORECARD IN A SCHOOL

Consistent with our observation that few schools have applied the balanced scorecard to date, a search of the literature reveals no real systematic study of such experiences. In the absence of such an analysis, the experiences from the for-profit sector can provide a useful point of departure. These experiences suggest that the entire design and implementation process can easily take up to 2 years or more, with the component steps illustrated in Table 8.5.

Prior to considering the details of the schedule, it is instructive to take a holistic view of the entire process. Kaplan and Norton (1996b) suggested that designing and implementing a balanced scorecard comprises four related stages:

1. translating the vision and gaining consensus;
2. communicating the objectives, setting goals, and linking strategies;
3. setting targets, allocating resources, and establishing milestones; and
4. feedback and learning.

An important component of the feedback/learning stage is post audit-ing the performance measures' continued applicability. Both the audit process and results can provide an opportunity for double-loop learning by collecting data about the strategy, reflecting on whether the strategy is working and appropriate in light of new developments, and soliciting ideas broadly about new strategic opportunities and directions in the school or school system.

Beyond attending to each stage, it is important to avoid two common mistakes (Kaplan & Norton, 1996a, pp. 284–285). First, some people regard the balanced scorecard as merely a performance measurement system. In actuality the design of performance measures is an integral part of the strategic planning process. These measures help to communicate the organization's strategies and goals, motivate actions to these, and provide guidance and feedback to their attainment. Thus, to reap the full benefits of the balanced scorecard, a school or school system needs to first define its mission, determine major program or curriculum objectives, and select strategies. And because effective implementation of strategies requires coordinated actions by all members of the school, widespread participation or involvement by stakeholders in the process of identifying missions, objectives, and strategies is crucial to ensure full and open communication of needs, concerns, and ideas, and to nurture feelings of "ownership" in the change outcomes.

The second common pitfall to avoid is simply to adopt the balanced scorecard from say, a peer school from another school district. The problem with that approach is that each school has its unique set of characteristics (e.g., size and backgrounds of students, size and mix of teachers, level of resource availability) and accordingly, its mission and associated objectives and strategies reflect these circumstances. A school that simply transplants another school's balanced scorecard not only runs the risk of trying to put a square peg in a round hole; more importantly, by omitting the scorecard's developmental process it is sure to limit the understanding and acceptance, and thus effectiveness, of the scorecard.

Shifting attention back to the schedule (Table 8.5), a retreat is a useful way to shelter the stakeholders from day-to-day concerns so they can focus on the long-run issues of school vision, mission, objectives, and strategies. Having developed a generally accepted mission statement and set of objectives and strategies, a task force can be formed, consisting of well-regarded representatives from all major stakeholder groups (e.g., administration, teachers, staff, students, and the outside community like parents). This task force can be charged with identifying more specific goals under each of the major components, or perspectives, agreed to by the school constituents as being appropriate (these can be the four components in our illustrative scorecard, a subset of those, all of them plus others, etc.). Frequent two-way communication between this task force and the various stakeholder groups is needed to ensure agreement with, and acceptance of, the final product.

Table 8.5.   A Sample Schedule for the Development and Implementation of a Balanced Scorecard for a School

Months 1–2	A strategic planning retreat involving everyone in the school is held to identify strategic issues and to discuss possible solutions. The purpose of this meeting is to form consensus regarding the vision and strategic goals and objectives. A second retreat meeting is held if necessary.
Months 3–4	A strategic planning committee (preferably including the principal) is formed with the charge to formulate objectives for each perspective in the school's balanced scorecard.
Months 5–6	Using the balanced scorecard as a communication tool, the strategic planning committee seeks comments on and acceptance of the school's balanced scorecard from school members.
Month 7	The strategic planning committee revises the balanced scorecard in response to comments from school members.
Months 8–9	The revised balanced scorecard is communicated to the school members (departments and individuals). Each member is required to develop an individual balanced scorecard that supports the school-wide goals and objectives.
Months 10–11	The strategic planning committee reviews individual and departmental balanced scorecards, suggesting possible revisions of the individuals, as well as the school's balanced scorecards.
Month 12	The school formulates a 5-year strategic plan based on finalized balanced scorecards. The 1st-year plan is expanded into the annual operating plan for the coming year.
Months 13–24	Individual departmental and school progress is reviewed quarterly to identify areas that require attention and additional effort.
Months 25–26	The school evaluation committee evaluates each member's performance, based on the individual balanced scorecards, for the last year and makes recommendations relating to retention, tenure, promotion, salary increases, or other rewards. The strategic planning committee revises the school's balanced scorecard and the 5-year strategic plan according to internal and external scanning of the school's conditions and changes in the environment. In helping to revise the strategic objectives of the balanced scorecard, the strategic planning committee identifies as many strategic issues as possible and, for each of these issues, considers possible solutions that can be employed by the school.

Next would be selection of the performance measure(s) for each specific goal. Because these measures have more immediacy to certain school members or stakeholders, it is desirable to seek even more widespread participation in this step. One possibility is to form a task force for each component, and to instruct these groups to work under three guidelines (Kaplan & Norton, 1996a, pp. 148–151, 305):

1. The performance measure(s) selected should be positively related to degree of attainment of the related goal; as the latter increase, the former also should increase.

2. The performance measures should be focused on outcomes. Outcome measures tend to be prepared only periodically and often are not sufficiently timed to alert remedial action. Performance drivers also need to be included to serve as leading indicators of outcomes. To illustrate, the ability to balance the budget can be an outcome measure for a school. But the number of teachers (or students) can be a performance driver, as it will affect both the school's budget allocation and expenditures.

3. The number of performance measures should be kept low so as not to diffuse attention and create confusion. Many instances of performance measure proliferation result from people confusing the diagnostic and strategic purposes of such measures. For example, a school's budget surplus can be a diagnostic measure, as it can indicate potential cash flow difficulties. But having an adequate budget surplus provides no indication whether the school is attaining its more fundamental or strategic goals (e.g., increased quality of instruction).

COMING FULL CIRCLE: THE BALANCED SCORECARD AND CREATING SMART TARGETS

School systems committed to being proactive in bringing about needed change would do well to make use of the balanced scorecard approach in their planning, designing, implementation, and evaluation of any change efforts. With this in mind, as a way of bringing the chapter to a conclusion we would be remiss if we did not re-emphasize the importance of the balanced scorecard while also spending some time discussing the need for and importance of SMART targets to educational reform efforts. This last section will first provide a brief review of some important components of the balanced scorecard approach and conclude with an overview of SMART targets.

As introduced earlier in this chapter the idea of the balanced scorecard is to describe the essential ingredients of organizational success. The balanced scorecard is essentially a management system (not only a measurement system) that enables organizations to clarify their vision and strategy and translate them into action. It provides feedback around both the internal business processes and external outcomes in order to continuously improve strategic performance and results. When fully deployed, the balanced scorecard transforms strategic planning from an academic exercise into the nerve center of an organization. To be effective a balanced score-card must focus on measures, context and strategy, finding the causes and drivers of success, and creating SMART targets.

Four Measures

As noted earlier, under the balanced scorecard system in the for-profit-sector, financial measures are the outcome, but do not give a good indica-tion of what is or will be going on in the organization. In a school system, measures of customer satisfaction, student growth (e.g., learning), and retention in school are indicators of school performance, and internal operations (efficiency, speed, reducing non-value added learning, mini-mizing learning problems) and human resource systems (e.g., teacher and staff development) can be leading indicators of school performance.

Context and Strategy

Just as financial measures have to be put in context, so does measure-ment itself. Without a tie to a school's strategy, more importantly, as *the mea-sure* of school strategy, the balanced scorecard is useless. A mission, strategy, and objectives must be defined, measures of that strategy (the bal-anced scorecard) must be agreed to and actions need to be performed for a measurement system to be fully effective. Otherwise, to use an American expression, the school is all dressed up but nowhere to go.

Finding the Causes and Drivers of Success

Once the school mission, strategy and measures have been defined and agreed upon, the next step is to understand fully the drivers (causes) behind movement (up and down) of a school's balanced scorecard. With-out the specific knowledge of what drivers will affect a school's scorecard, the school just might spend much time, money and effort and achieve very little. These drivers fall into four categories

- Environmental—those factors outside the influence of a school, such as governmental regulations, the economic cycle, local, national, and global politics, etc.
- Organizational—systems inside the school such as school strategy, human resource systems, policies, procedures, school structure, pay, etc.

- Group or departmental—work processes, group relationships, work responsibilities, assignments.
- Individual—personality, communication or administrative style, skills behaviors.

A good method of outlining the causes and effects among these drivers is a flowchart or affinity diagram.

Creating Smart Targets

After a full understanding of the relationships among the drivers and between the drivers and measures is reached, the next step is to create a SMART target or objective. A SMART target is:

- Specific
- Measurable
- Agreed upon
- Realistic, and
- Time-bound

In reality, though, a SMART target is not enough. A SMART project must be created as shown in the following example describing not only the target, but the methods, timetables and resources needed to accomplish the task:

- We will reduce the current cost-per-barrel of oil by 20% by the end of April 2002 by:
  - Adding a 10% bonus to all employees salaries for every 10% drop of the cost-per-barrel
  - Moving to a completely asset- or area-based organizational structure
  - Creating a team to eliminate non-value-added steps from the management and operations functions, so that only critically essential functions are kept.

The implementation plans for these steps are attached, including personnel assignments, workloads, budget assignments, sequence of implementation, etc.

Similar SMART projects can be designed for schools:

- We will reduce the number of behavior incidents from 12 per week to 3 per week by October 31st by:
  - Increasing the number of teachers patrolling the halls from 5 to 10 during major transitions to classes.
  - Increasing our counseling of students on what constitute negative behavior and how it can be avoided.

- Notifying all students and parents of the consequences of negative behaviors in the school building
- Creating a team that includes administrators, teachers, and students to assess the impact of implemented changes on negative behaviors

Problems that exist within a school and changes to address them can be managed by identifying and developing SMART targets for the agreed upon solutions. Action plans can then be generated to assist in the achievement of those targets or changes.

KEYS TO CREATING SMART CHANGE PROJECTS AND IMPLEMENTING THE BALANCED SCORECARD

The Equation

We suggest administrators and others involved in school system change look at the successful implementation of the balanced scorecard as an equation:

$$\text{Success} = \text{Measurement} \times \text{Technique} \times \text{Control} \times \text{Focused Persistence} \times \text{Consensus}$$

Measurement

First of all, success is a function of what measures you use. If you don't measure the right things and the measures don't reflect what is really going on, much will be done in a school or system, but little will be accomplished.

Techniques

Second, what Techniques or methods also have a significant bearing on success? Techniques fall into two categories:

- Large-scale, or major techniques
  - Examples include restructuring, tying teachers pay to measurements (e.g., student performance on government-mandated standardized tests), putting in added resources (dollars and people), adding or changing customers or products, re-engineering processes like curriculums, change of strategy, addition or change of teachers or administrators' core competencies, and so on.

- Small-scale, or minor techniques result in small changes in drivers
  - Motivational speeches, problem-solving teams focused on how best to integrate technology into classrooms, displaying graphs to teachers on student performance on standardized tests on bulletin boards, etc.

The key to administrators' use of these techniques are to realize that if major improvements in balanced scorecard measures are needed, then large-scale change techniques must be used. This fact usually causes great distress in a school or school system because many stakeholders think major improvements can be made only by tinkering with the school or school system, instead of making fundamental change. If school administration is willing only to use small-scale techniques, then they must expect only modest improvements in balanced scorecard measures.

Control

Another part of the equation is control. Once school administrators have brainstormed a list of possible actions that might accomplish its SMART target, these actions need to be categorized into four levels:

- Level 1 action: in control of action and effects are inside the school
- Level 2 action: in control of action, but effects are outside the school
- Level 3 action: not in control of action, but it affects the school driver(s)
- Level 4 action: not in control of action, but does not affect the school driver(s)

For school administration to be successful, they have to:

- Concentrate on level 1 & 2 actions
- Gain control of, or compensate for, level 3 actions
- And if they do not have sufficient control over the actions necessary to achieve their SMART target, then they must lower their expectations on what they can accomplish and either set a lower target, or abandon the target altogether. Otherwise, it just isn't "SMART."

Focused Persistence

Focused persistence, otherwise known as project management, is another key in the equation. Project management includes having a timetable (beginning and end) for each task, periodic reviews of accomplishments, resources and people assigned to each task and most importantly, a sincere drive to accomplish the tasks. The use of such tools as Gantt charts, PERT charts, etc. are essential tools in this process.

Consensus

The last, but just as critical factor is consensus. The best laid plans, with a thorough knowledge of measures, drivers, and with sufficient resources will fail if there is not agreement enough among those with sufficient power to block balanced scorecard school system implementation. Key stakeholders need to be involved in decision-making, and as many others in the various stages and steps outlined here. Among some opportunities for involvement include:

- Communicate with them on the importance and status of the school system change project
- As part of planning and decision-making
- Implementation of action
- Suggestions for improvement

Keeping in mind these factors when implementing the balanced scorecard will substantially increase the chances of change success in school systems. Though every factor in the equation above does not have to be perfect, and can compensate for one another, all must be present to some extent for the balanced scorecard to be successfully implemented.

Based on the preceding discussion and the illustrative sample design/implementation schedule, it is obvious that the time span between start of process and harvesting of initial results can be considerable. Given the mounting challenges to schools and education, we believe there is little time to lose in implementing the balanced scorecard or similar approaches to promote and support change.

CONCLUSION

As highlighted at various points throughout this book the environment for schools and school systems are characterized by unprecedented levels of change and escalating customer and other stakeholder' expectations. Meeting these new challenges in an era of shrinking resources will require schools to undergo fundamental changes and to continuously seek ways to create future value. In this chapter, we have provided an explanation of the balanced scorecard approach. We also presented some sample principal responses on the potential components of an effective balanced scorecard for a school.

Like the competencies needed by administrators to more effectively lead and manage change discussed in Chapter 3 increasing their skill in using tools like the balanced scorecard can do nothing but increase the likelihood of change success in schools and school systems. The balanced scorecard reflects the values of a school or school system, and therefore requires the support of all key stakeholders. One of the benefits of the balanced scorecard process is that it forces key stakeholders to sit-down and articulate the vision of the school or school system before moving to an action plan. By doing this, stakeholders can then decide on change goals that are imperative to realizing the vision. From these goals, measurements can be chosen. These measurements are the critical part of the balanced scorecard because "what gets measured gets managed."

Another important value of using the balanced scored process as part of a school or school system change effort is that consensus can be built around the school or school systems' strategic or change objectives. The balanced scorecard links actions back to the vision and strategy of the school or school system, creating an inherent change plan that will help align stakeholder behavior with strategy. In conclusion, it is our belief that because of the favorable results experienced in the for-profit sector, schools and school systems will likely find this approach to be worthy of consideration as well in their efforts to respond to stakeholder calls for school change.

CHAPTER 9

THE DYNAMICS OF SCHOOL OR SCHOOL SYSTEM CHANGE

INTRODUCTION

It is a rare school or school system today that has the luxury to operate in a stable and predictable environment. The adjective school systems and their employees are increasingly using to describe their world is chaotic. In today's education world, change is an everyday occurrence for schools and school systems. The message is clear: "Change or else!"

Clearly, the education landscape is not the same as it was just a few years ago. Change is everywhere. Today's schools and school systems cannot afford to be static, but must continually change in response to a variety of influences coming from both outside and inside. For today's administrators, the challenge is to anticipate and help implement change processes so that school or school system performance is enhanced. In this concluding chapter, we first briefly revisit the challenge of change facing today's schools and administrators. The discussion then focuses on employee and administrator reactions to change and how schools or school systems can overcome resistance to change. The chapter concludes with strategies available to administrators for building support for school or school system change.

Managing School System Change: Charting a Course for Renewal, pages 187–217
Copyright © 2004 by Information Age Publishing, Inc.

THE CHALLENGE OF SCHOOL OR
SCHOOL SYSTEM CHANGE

School or school system change is any substantive modification to some part of the school or school system. It involves movement from the present state of the school to some future state. The future state may be a new strategy for the school, changes in the school's culture, introduction of new teaching technology, and so on. Change can involve virtually any aspect of a school including work schedules, departmentalization, technology, organizational design, and employee selection. It is important to keep in mind that any particular change in a school or school system may have ripple effects. For example, when a school system installed computers to support new teaching technology in classrooms in several departments at one of its schools, teachers were required to learn to operate the new computers and change their teaching approaches, the compensation system was adjusted to reflect those newly acquired skills, team leader's span of management was altered, several related staff jobs were redesigned, the criteria for selecting new teachers and support staff was changed, and a new teacher performance system was implemented.

Understanding and managing organizational changes presents complex challenges. Planned change may not work, or it may have consequences far different from those intended. Today, school must have the capacity to adapt quickly and effectively in order to survive and meet the increased demand for change. Often the speed and complexity of change severely test the capabilities of administrators, teachers and other employees to adapt rapidly enough. However, when schools fail to change, the costs of that failure may be quite high. Hence administrators and others must understand the nature of the change needed and the likely effects of alternative approaches to bring about that change.

Because schools exist in a changing environment and are themselves constantly changing, schools that emphasize bureaucratic or mechanistic systems are increasingly ineffective. Schools or school systems with rigid hierarchies, high degrees of functional specialization, narrow and limited job descriptions, inflexible rules and procedures, and impersonal, autocratic administration can't respond adequately to demands for change. Today's schools need designs and internal operations that are flexible and adaptable. They also need systems that both require and allow greater commitment and use of talent on the part of teachers, support staff and administrators alike.

School or school system change can be difficult and costly. Despite the challenges, many schools successfully make needed changes, but at the same time, failure also is common. It is our belief that adaptive, flexible schools will survive in the years to come and have an advantage over rigid, static organizations. As a result, managing change has become a central focus of effective schools, and this focus is even creating its own vocabulary (i.e., the learning organization, reengineering, core competencies, organizational architecture, learning strategies, mission and vision statements, and strategic alliances among various schools and stakeholders). In many respects, managing change effectively requires an understanding and use of many of the ideas explored in this book.

The Process of School or School System Change

Once a school has made the decision to change, careful planning and analysis must take place. An important way to increase the likely success of such change is for administrators to attempt to anticipate the need for change and to develop creative innovations before serious problems evolve.

The Need for Anticipation

Far too frequently, administrators and their schools or school systems fail to set aside the time necessary for analyzing changing conditions and attitudes and have suddenly found themselves in the middle of severe complications. Administrators must learn to anticipate the need for change.

There is something of a paradox between the need for continuity and the necessity for change in schools. For example, customers (employers, for example) and employees (teachers and support staff) usually prefer feelings of continuity in their lives because such feelings enable them to have faith that events in the future will unfold in a predictable manner. Customers hope that a continued supply of educated students will be available. Employees want their paychecks to be secure so that they can continue to purchase the items they want and need.

However, as evidenced by our discussion on change to this point, conditions seldom remain static. Whenever possible, the need to change with the times (or even before) should be anticipated, and administrators should attempt to implement these changes before the crisis-state is reached. Otherwise, serious organizational behavior difficulties can result.

EMPLOYEE REACTIONS TO CHANGE

How employees in a school or school system perceive a change greatly affects how they react to it. While many variations are possible, there are only four basic reactions. If teachers, for example, clearly see that the change is not compatible with their needs and aspirations, they will resist the change. In this situation, the teachers, for example, are certain that the change will make things worse. If teachers cannot foresee how the change will affect them, they will resist the change or be neutral, at best. Most people shy away from the unknown. They often assume that the change may make things worse.

If teachers see that the change is going to take place regardless of their objections, they may initially resist the change and then resignedly accept it. Although their first reaction is to resist, once the change appears inevitable, they often see no other choice than to go along with it. If teachers see that the change is in their best interests, they will be motivated to accept it.

Obviously, it is critical for teachers and other school employees to feel confident that the change will make things better. It is the administrator's obligation to foster an accepting attitude. Note that three out of the four situations involve some form of resistance to change. Resistance to change is an emotional/behavioral response to real or imagined threats to an established work routine. Administrators must understand resistance to change and learn techniques to overcome it.

Understanding and Managing Resistance to Change

We tend to be creatures of habit. Many people find it difficult to try new ways of doing things. It is precisely because of this basic human characteristic that most employees are not enthusiastic about change in the workplace. This resistance is well documented. As one person once put it, "Most people hate any change that doesn't jingle in their pockets." No matter how technically or administratively perfect a proposed change may be, people make or break it.

Rare is the administrator who does not have several stories about carefully cultivated changes that died on the vine because of employee resistance. It is important for administrators to learn to manage resistance because failed change efforts are costly. These costs may include decreased employee loyalty, a lowered probability of achieving school or school system goals, a waste of money and resources, and the difficulty of fixing the failed effort.

People resist change for many reasons. Resisting change does not necessarily mean that they will never accept it. In many cases, the change may be resisted because it was introduced improperly. The administrator, by implementing drastic change, could have created feelings of insecurity in the employees. Perhaps the administrator did not inform the teachers, for example, about the change until the last minute. Sometimes the change is introduced properly but is still resisted. The administrator may use resistance to change as a means of "taking the pulse" of a school or school sysstem. If minor change meets with resistance, it could indicate that other problems exist, such as problems with morale, commitment, or trust.

Individual and group behavior following an organizational change can take many forms, ranging from extremes of acceptance to active resistance. Resistance can be as subtle as passive resignation or as overt as deliberate sabotage. Resistance can also be immediate, or deferred. It is easiest for administrators to deal with resistance when it is overt and immediate. For instance, a school proposes a change, and teachers quickly respond by voicing complaints or threatening to go on strike. Although these responses may be damaging, their cause is clearly identifiable.

It is more challenging to manage resistance that is implicit or deferred. Implicit resistance is subtle-such as loss of loyalty to the organization, loss of motivation to work, increased errors or mistakes, or increased absenteeism due to "sickness"-and hence more difficult to recognize. Similarly, deferred resistance clouds the link between the source of the resistance and the reactions to it. For example, a change may produce what appears to be only a minimal reaction at the time it is initiated, but then resistance surfaces weeks, months, or even years later. In another type of deferred resistance, a single change that in and of itself might have had little impact can become the straw that breaks the camel's back. Reactions to change can build up and then explode in a response that seems totally out of proportion to the change it follows. The resistance, or course, has merely been deferred and stockpiled. What surfaces is a response to an accumulation of previous changes.

Administrators need to learn to recognize the manifestations of resistance to change both in themselves and in others if they want to be more effective in creating, supporting, and managing change. So why do people resist change? A number of specific reasons are discussed in the next few paragraphs.

Predisposition against Change

Some people are predisposed to dislike change. This predisposition is highly personal and deeply ingrained. It is an outgrowth of how they learned to handle change and ambiguity as a child. Consider the hypothetical examples of Amy and Fred. Amy's parents were patient, flexible, and understanding. From the time Amy was weaned from a bottle, she was taught that there were positive compensations for the loss of immediate gratification. She learned that love and approval were associated with making changes. In contrast, Fred's parents were unreasonable and unyielding. They frequently forced him to comply with their wishes. They required him to take piano lessons even though he hated them. Changes were accompanied by demands for compliance. This taught Fred to be distrustful and suspicious of change. These learned predispositions ultimately affect how Amy and Fred handle change as adults.

Habits

Habit is a wonderful thing for human beings. Can you imagine how difficult life would be without habits? Imagine if you had to think consciously about every little movement needed to drive an automobile. Would you ever make it to work in the morning? When we drive by habit our mind can think about other things, secure in the knowledge that our senses will warn us when something is wrong.

We do things by habit: routine household chores, dressing ourselves, greeting one another, sorting our mail, and so forth. Habits are easy and comfortable, freeing our minds to focus on other, more important things. Furthermore, habits are often difficult to change-reflect on a time when you or a friend tried to alter your morning routine or drop a bad habit. One very important reason we resist is because we do not want to change our safe, secure, habitual way of doing things.

Lack of Trust

Trust is a characteristic, for example, of high-performance teams, in which team members believe in each other's integrity, character, and ability. Principals, for example, who trust their teachers make the change process an open, honest, and participative affair. Teachers who trust principals are more willing to expend extra effort and take chances with something different. Mutual mistrust, on the other hand, can doom an otherwise well-conceived school change or project to failure.

Surprise and Fear of the Unknown

When finding yourself in the presence of an unknown insect, many of us typically choose to kill it by swatting it or stepping on it. We typically rationalize, "Better safe than sorry." It is a natural reaction to fear the unknown. When innovative or radically different changes are introduced without warning, affected employees become fearful of the implications. Grapevine rumors fill the void created by a lack of official announcements and employees often develop negative attitudes toward the change. They may also behave dysfunctionally-complaining, purposely working more slowly, or undermining team or department morale-if required to go through with the change. In these situations, teachers, for example, let fear paralyze them into action. Administrators should therefore avoid creating situations in which teachers and other employees are surprised, and thus fear change. They can do this by keeping all affected employees adequately informed.

Poor Timing

The timing of change in relation to other events also may increase resistance to the change. The poor timing may be caused by events within the school, in relation to events outside the school, or by events occurring in someone's personal life. For example, bringing in a young principal from outside the school system at the same time that a school is undertaking a major curriculum change may increase resistance to both changes. On a personal level, changing a parent's work start time just as his or her child begins school and thus preventing the parent from driving the child to kindergarten can increase resistance to the new schedule. Administrators should consider other events that are occurring at the same time that a major change is proposed or implemented and avoid poor timing, if possible.

Poor Approach

The approach used in presenting a school change can increase resistance to the change if people dislike the approach. A poor approach to change can be caused either by the way change is communicated or by the communications channel that is selected. Sending an e-mail message or a memo to someone, for example, may not be as effective as delivering the change message in person. An approach may also be considered poor if the person delivering the change message is already disliked. Finally, the words used to explain the change may cause the approach to be poor. Telling teachers that there will be no raises this year and that everyone will have to increase productivity in order to meet the new demands of programs like "No Child Left Behind" may be a poor approach because the teachers will assume the real objective is to make the superintendent look better to the School Board. However, explaining that the change is needed so that the school can avoid takeover by the State or laying-off of teachers may generate more cooperation for the change. Communicating change is discussed in more detail later in this chapter.

Ignoring Change through Selective Perception

We are bombarded every moment with information pouring into our brains from our sensory organs—our eyes, ears, nose, taste buds, and various touch and balance sensors. We cannot possibly attend to all of the information, so we screen out much of it through a process called "selective perception." This means that we pay attention to those sensations, which we judge to be important, while ignoring the rest. Selective perception is a complex psychological process that occurs both intentionally and unconsciously.

How do we choose those messages to which we pay attention? When faced with messages signaling a change, we frequently attend to those that reinforce our belief in the status quo and maintain our present comfort level. In other words, too often we see only what we want to see, and hear only what we want to hear. Through selective perception, we frequently protect the status quo by filtering out troubling signals that a change is needed, or may be on its way.

Similarly, we often listen only to commentators or others with whom we agree or whose ideas resonate with our own. Dangerous messages, which somehow threaten our comfort level-are "tuned out" and ignored. The natural human tendency toward selective perception can harm our ability to deal with change. If we block out all information with which we do not agree, we often miss clear signals that change is on the horizon. Thus when change occurs we are surprised by it, unprepared for it, and afraid of it.

Too Much Dependence on Others

One way to deal with the bombardment of information at work is to specialize. We tend to gravitate to our own spheres of interest and depend on others for information and insights outside our scope of knowledge. For example, when a car needs repairs, you may take it to a trusted mechanic rather than attempt to repair it yourself. The point is that everyone depends on certain people for advice and guidance. This dependence may serve you well, but only if the people on whom you rely are well informed—not if they give you misinformation or poor advice. Although you should not immediately become suspicious of all your advisors, you should recognize that too much dependence on others could become dangerous. Administrators, teachers, and other employees may resist change if they are advised to resist because the change may adversely affect them. Trusting in this advice, they may fail to understand for themselves the true nature of the situation, and may be "blindsided" by the change when it occurs.

Threats to Jobs and Income

Employees often fear that change may reduce their job security or income. Hiring uncertified teachers, for instance, may be interpreted as a signal that replacement of certified teachers are imminent. When a potential change has the real possibility to cause employees harm, they are likely to resist it with all their might.

Changes in job tasks or established work routines often threaten employees. They worry that they won't be able to perform successfully, particularly where pay is closely tied to productivity. It is therefore important that administrators consider any adverse effect employees might experience as a result of a proposed change. If teachers, for example, perceive that they will lose money, influence, clout, or status as the result of a change, administrators can expect strong and active resistance. This resistance is not irrational, but is aimed at protecting employee self interest.

Revenge

Employees may resist change out of revenge. When teachers, for example, perceive that administration has wronged them in the past or that a principal has not trusted or supported them, then they may feel that resisting change is a justified payback. Here also may be the time that a person seeks a return to equity when an imbalance is perceived. Herzberg (1966) has discussed a whole "revenge psychology" whereby people feel that they have been so grievously wronged that they not only resist change (in addition to taking other measures), but the story of the perceived wrong is passed on. Sometimes none of the people who were originally "wronged" are still at work, and yet people still say things like, "Remember the time management..." Herzberg claims that some actions by managers (administrators) can create a "remembered pain" that can never be removed.

Absent Benefits

When people resist change because of absent benefits, they are really saying that there is nothing in the change for them. When a change is absent benefits, it means that the change or the change agent has provided no incentive for the people to change. In actuality, there may be benefits in the new change, but they may not be obvious, or they may not have been explained. Some people may feel this way about recycling paper or soft-drink cans at work. If no immediate benefit is seen, some may not bother.

If, however, the long-term environmental benefits are explained, then these people may comply.

INEVITABLE REACTIONS TO CHANGE

In spite of attempts to minimize the resistance to change in an organization, some reactions to change are inevitable. Negative reactions may be manifested in overt behavior, or change may be resisted more passively. People show four basic identifiable reactions to change: disengagement, disidentification, disenchantment, and disorientation. Administrators can use interventions to deal with these reactions (Woodward & Bucholz, 1987; Sims, 2002).

Disengagement is psychological withdrawal from change. An employee appears to lose initiative and interest in the job. Employees who disengage may fear the change but take on the approach of doing nothing and simply hoping for the best. Disengaged employees are physically present but mentally absent. They lack drive and commitment, and they simply comply without real psychological investment in their work. Disengagement can be recognized by behaviors such as being hard to find or doing only the basics to get the job done. Typical disengagement statements include "No problem" or "This won't affect me."

The basic administrator strategy for dealing with disengaged individuals is to confront them with their reaction and draw them out, identifying concerns that must be addressed. Disengaged employees may not be aware of the change in their behavior, and may need to be assured of the good intentions of the administrator. Helping them air their feelings can lead to productive discussions. Disengaged people seldom become cheerleaders for the change, but they can be brought closer to accepting and working with a change through open communication with an empathetic administrator who is willing to listen.

Another reaction to change is disidentification. Individuals reacting in this way feel that their identity has been threatened by the change, and they feel very vulnerable. Many times they cling to a past procedure because they had a sense of mastery over it, and it gave them a sense of security. "My job is completely changed" and "I used to..." are verbal indications of disidentification. Disidentified employees often display sadness and worry. They may appear to be sulking and dwelling on the past by reminiscing about the old ways of doing things.

Disidentified employees often feel like victims in the change process because they are so vulnerable. Administrators can help them through the transition by encouraging them to explore their feelings and helping them transfer their positive feelings into the new situation. One way to do this is to help them identify what it is they liked in the old situation, as well as to show them how it is possible to have the same positive experience in the new situation. Disidentified employees need to see that work itself and emotion are separable-that is, that they can let go of old ways and experience positive reactions to new ways of performing their jobs.

Disenchantment is also a common reaction to change. It is usually expressed as negativity or anger. Disenchanted employees realize that the past is gone, and they are mad about it. They may try to enlist the support of other employees by forming coalitions. Destructive behaviors like sabotage and back-stabbing may result. Typical verbal signs of disenchantment are "This will never work" and "I'm getting out of this school as soon as I can." The anger of a disenchanted performer may be directly expressed in organizational cultures where it is permissible to do so. This behavior tends to get the issues out in the open. More often, however, cultures view the expression of emotion at work as improper and unbusinesslike. In these cultures, the anger is suppressed and emerges in more passive-aggressive ways, such as badmouthing and starting rumors. One of the particular dangers of disenchantment is that it is quite contagious in the workplace.

It is often difficult to reason with disenchanted employees. Thus, the first step in managing this reaction is for administrators to bring these employees from their highly negative, emotionally charged state to a more neutral state. To neutralize the reaction does not mean to dismiss it; rather, it means to allow the individuals to let off the necessary steam so that they can come to terms with their anger. The second part of the strategy for dealing with disenchanted employees is for the administrator to acknowledge that their anger is normal and that as their administrator you don't hold it against them. Sometimes disenchantment is a mask for one of the other three reactions, and it must be worked through to get to the core of the employee's reaction. Employees may become cynical about change. They may lose faith in, for example, the principal and other leaders of change.

A final reaction to change is disorientation. Disoriented employees are lost and confused, and often are unsure of their feelings. They waste energy trying to figure out what to do instead of how to do things. Disoriented individuals ask a lot of questions and become very detail oriented. They may appear to need a good deal of guidance, and may leave their work undone until all of their questions have been answered. "Analysis paralysis" is characteristic of disoriented employees. They feel that they have lost touch with the priorities of the school, and they may want to analyze the change to death before acting on it. Disoriented employees may ask questions like "Now what do I do?" or "What do I do first?"

Disorientation is a common reaction among people who are used to clear goals and unambiguous directions. When change is introduced, it creates uncertainty and a lack of clarity. The administrator's strategy for dealing with this reaction is to explain the change in a way that minimizes the ambiguity that is present. The information about the change needs to be put into a framework or an overall vision so that the disoriented individual can see where he or she fits into the grand scheme of things. Once the disoriented employee sees the broader context of the change, the administrator can plan a series of steps to help this employee adjust. The employee needs a sense of priorities.

Administrators need to be able to diagnose these four reactions to change. No single universal strategy can help all employees adjust because each reaction brings with it significant and different concerns. By recognizing each reaction and applying the appropriate strategy, it is possible to help even strong resisters work through a transition successfully. It is also helpful to identify some more specific ways that employees resist change as offered in the next section.

HOW EMPLOYEES SHOW THEIR RESISTANCE TO CHANGE

Besides understanding why people resist and might emotionally respond to change, it is also important to examine how people show their resistance to change. There are a number of methods by which people demonstrate resistance: absenteeism, decreased productivity, regression, resignation, transfer, and sabotage. Note that outright refusal to change is not on the list. People do not usually openly refuse to change, probably because this would be a highly visible act that carries too much risk. Instead of refusing and taking the risk of being disciplined or fired, most people choose a less obvious and less confrontational method of protesting a change.

Absenteeism

Instead of changing, people may try to escape the change by calling in sick or arriving late to work. Through their absence, they are not trying to have the change reversed as much as they are trying to avoid the change or delay its implementation. For example, given a new principal or team leader, people may be absent or late in order to escape having to deal with or work for the new individual. Absenteeism is a more complex phenomenon. First, it has causes other than just change, some of which are related to work and others that are not. Second, absenteeism not only affects the school as the employer or the boss; it affects coworkers who must perform the extra work left by a person who is absent. By trying to escape the change rather than trying to cope with it, the resister creates stress by not facing the change. This stress can be even greater than the stress of adapting to the change.

Decreased Productivity

Decreased productivity differs from other ways people show resistance to change in that it is aimed at reversing the change and it has some chance of working. This tactic involves people who deliberately slow down so that their own or more specifically the school's productivity declines. The thinking behind this tactic is that the administrator will notice after the change that productivity is lower than productivity before the change without seeing that the decline was artificial. The underlying hope is that if the administrator notices the decline, he or she will blame the drop on the latest change, decide that the change is failing, and return conditions back to the way they were before the change. There are no statistics on how well this works because if it is done properly, administrators will never realize that it was done—and employees certainly won't admit to it.

Regression

Regression is a relatively simple method of showing resistance to change. Here, to resist change, people regress their behavior and understanding to the level of a new, untrained worker. People who display regression are essentially saying, "If things change, you [the administrator] will have to tell me how to work under this change and how to do all the rest of my job too." The behavior is not uncommon, even though it is rather childish to pretend that one change has somehow caused people to forget how to do everything. Some people, however, use regression to make the change as painful as possible, hoping the administrator will give up or return to the old ways.

Resignation

Resigning, the ultimate escape mechanism, is also a method for coping with unacceptable change. Resignation may be a poor choice for a resister because he or she may suffer more than the employer, and if the change is later rescinded, he or she will not be there. Resignation should never be used without careful consideration. A person must consider the availability of other jobs and his or her own financial needs before quitting. It can also be more difficult to go from being unemployed to employed than it is to go from being employed in one job directly to being employed in another job. On the other hand, if the change truly is unacceptable, then it may be better to leave a situation than to stay and be miserable. One might, however, be able to transfer rather than resign.

Transfer

A request for a transfer to another school in the same school system may be caused by change or some other factor. Like resignation, transferring can be an escape mechanism if the person is unwilling to confront the change, or it can be a coping mechanism when the person really cannot cope with or accept the change. Transferring carries less financial worry and risk than resignation, and a transfer can help a school system retain valuable people.

Sabotage

Sabotage can be considered the severest form of resistance to change because it is tricky, damaging, and typically illegal. Sabotage is a deliberate act to harm the organization. The sabotage can be subtle—sometimes so subtle that it goes undetected. Other times, it can cause significant damage to the organization and to innocent employees also. People who choose sabotage generally feel that they have been greatly wronged by the boss or the organization. They typically feel that they are justified in their actions, so sabotage may just be an example of equity theory taken to an extreme. Of course, sabotage can never be condoned; it can be costly, and it can negatively affect many innocent people, such as coworkers and customers. Still, incidences of sabotage are more frequent than one might initially suspect.

ADMINISTRATORS' ORIENTATION TO RESISTANCE TO CHANGE

Administrators can react to resistance to change in two ways. They can treat resistance as a problem to overcome or view it as a signal to get more information about the reasons for resistance. Administrators who view resistance as a problem to overcome may try to forcefully reduce it. Such coercive approaches often increase the resistance.

Alternatively, administrators may see resistance as a signal that those responsible for the change need more information about the intended change. Those employees who will be affected by the change may have valuable insights about its effects. An alert administrator will involve the employees in diagnosing the reasons for the resistance. This effort is no different than involving stakeholders in the change process discussed earlier in this book. In this way, administrators can use resistance to change as a tool to get needed information.

Should administrators and others see the absence of resistance to school or school system change as a stroke of good fortune? Many reasons suggest that they should not. The absence of resistance is also a signal to administrators. A change that is automatically accepted can be less effective than one that has been resisted and actively debated. The resisters play an important role by focusing administrator's attention on potentially dysfunctional aspects of the proposed change.

MANAGING THE CHANGE PROCESS TO REDUCE RESISTANCE

As suggested earlier in the book most school or school system changes are originated by middle- (principals) or senior-level administrators (superintendents). The changes are then passed down to the principal, the link between senior-administration and teachers and other employees, for successful execution. In this process, the principal is the person who must cope with employees' anxieties and fears about change. The environment created by the administrator can greatly affect employees' acceptance of change. Several suggestions for creating a positive environment for change are discussed in the following paragraphs.

Build Trust

If employees trust and have confidence in the principal, school or school system, they are much more likely to accept changes; otherwise, they are likely to resist change vigorously. Trust cannot be established overnight; it is built over a period of time. The school or school system's actions determine the degree of the employee's trust. Teachers, for example, will trust a principal they perceive to be fair, honest, and forthright. Teachers will not trust a principal who they feel is always trying to take advantage of them. Principals can go a long way toward building trust if they discuss upcoming changes with their teachers, and if they actively involve the teachers in the change process.

Openly Communicate and Discuss Changes

Communication about impending change is essential if teachers and others are to adjust effectively. The details of the change should be provided, but equally important is the rationale behind the change. Teachers and other employees want to know why change is needed. If there is no good reason for it, why should they favor the change? Fear of the unknown, one of the major barriers to change, can be greatly reduced by openly discussing any upcoming or current school changes with the affected employees. An administrator should always begin by explaining the five W's and an H to the employees—What the change is? Why it is needed? Whom it will affect? When it will take place? Where it will take place? and How it will take place? During this discussion, the administrator should be as open and honest as possible. The more background and detail the administrator can give, the more likely it is that the employees will accept the changes. The principal should also outline the impact of the changes on each of the affected employees (Remember our discussion of stakeholder impact analysis and matrix mapping). People are primarily interested in how change will affect them as individuals.

It is critical that the administrator gives employees an opportunity to ask questions. This is the major advantage of an oral discussion over a written memo. Regardless of how thorough an explanation may be, employees will usually have questions that administrators should answer to the fullest extent possible. When employees receive all the facts and get their questions answered, their resistance often fades. Improved communication is particularly effective in reducing problems resulting from unclear situations. For example, when the grapevine is active with rumors of decreased budgets, cutbacks and layoffs, honest and open communication of the true facts can be a calming force. Even if the news is bad, a clear message often wins points and helps employees accept change. When communication is ambiguous and employees feel threatened, they often imagine scenarios that are considerably worse than the actual "bad news."

Involve the Employees

Changes that are "sprung" on school employees with little or no warning will likely result in resistance-simply as a "knee-jerk" reaction-until employees can assess how the change affects them. In contrast, teachers, for example, who are involved in the change process better understand the need for change, and therefore, are less likely to resist it. Additionally, people who participate in making a decision tend to be more committed to the outcome than those who are not involved. Employee and other stakeholder participation and involvement in school system change can be extremely effective. It is difficult for individuals to resist a change when they participated in the decision and helped implement it. The psychology is simple: no one wants to oppose something that he or she has helped develop. It is useful to solicit teacher and other employee ideas and input as suggested in our discussion of stakeholder involvement earlier in this book, as early as possible in the change process. Don't wait until the last minute to ask the employees what they think about a change. When affected employees have been involved in a change at, or near, its inception, they will usually actively support the change.

Provide Rewards and Incentives

School systems can give employees rewards and incentives to help them see that supporting a change is in their best interests. One rather obvious-and quite successful-mechanism to facilitate change is rewarding people for behaving in the desired fashion. For example, teachers who are required to learn to use new computer equipment in the classroom should be praised for their successful efforts. In order to make incentives work effectively, administrators should analyze the source of the resistance, and what might overcome that resistance. For example, teachers may be afraid they won't be able to use new technology in teaching in the classroom. Administrators could provide them with new-skills training (like Thomas Highton did with the teachers in the Union City School System). A difficult change can also have positive aspects. Layoffs can be viewed as opportunities for those who remain, allowing jobs to be redesigned to provide new challenges and responsibilities. Other incentives that can help reduce resistance include a pay increase, a new title, a change in work hours, or increased job autonomy.

Make Sure the Changes Are Reasonable

The administrator should always do whatever is possible to ensure that any proposed changes are reasonable. Administrators can do this by striving to employ empathy by asking themselves, "How might my teachers and other staff view and react to this change?" This is especially important since some proposed changes that originate with senior administration are sometimes totally unreasonable. When this is the case, it is usually because upper administration is not aware of specific circumstances that make the changes unworkable. It is administrators, like principal's responsibility to intervene in such situations and communicate the problem to senior administration.

Educate the Teachers and Staff

Sometimes, people are reluctant to change because they fear what the future has in store. For example, fears about economic security may be put to rest by a few reassuring words from management. As part of educating teachers and others about what school or school system change means for them, administration must show considerable emotional sensitivity. Doing so makes it possible for people affected by a change to help make it work. It has been our experience that simply answering the question "What's in it for me?" can help to allay many fears.

Avoid Threats

The administrator who attempts to implement change through the use of threats is taking a negative approach likely to decrease employee trust. A natural reaction is: "This must be bad news if it requires a threat." Most people also dislike being threatened into accepting something. Even though threats may get results in the short term, they may be damaging to employees' morale and attitude over a longer period of time.

Follow a Sensible Time Schedule

As mentioned previously, most changes are passed down from senior administrators to the principals for implementation. The principal often has control or influence over when changes should be implemented, however. Some times are better than others. For example, the week before Christmas or the height of the summer vacation season would ordinarily not be good times to implement a major school change. Principals should rely on their valuable insights into the school and on their common sense when recommending a time schedule for implementing a change.

Implement the Changes in a Sensible Manner

The administrator often has some choice about where changes will take place. When making these decisions, administrators should rely on logic and common sense. For example, the principal usually decides what teachers will get new computers in their classrooms. It would be sensible to introduce the computers through those teachers who are naturally more adaptable and flexible than others. If the principal makes it a point to know their teachers, they usually will have a good idea as to which are more flexible. Another consideration in introducing school changes is to implement them where possible in a way that minimizes their effects on interpersonal relationships. The principal should try not to disturb smoothly working groups or teams.

Provide Empathy and Support

Another strategy for overcoming resistance is providing empathy and support to employees who have trouble dealing with the change. Active listening is an excellent tool for identifying the reasons behind resistance and for uncovering fears. An expression of concerns about the change can provide important feedback that administrators can use to improve the change process. Emotional support and encouragement can help an employee deal with the anxiety that is a natural response to change. Employees who experience severe reactions to change can benefit from talking with a counselor. Some for-profit companies provide counseling through their employee assistance plans.

BUILDING THE FOUNDATIONS
FOR SCHOOL SYSTEM CHANGE

Managing change means managing the conditions and activities that move a school or school system from its present state to some desired future state. Without careful management, a much needed change can fall by the wayside.

As suggested earlier, change failures represent a tremendous cost to organizations in terms of money, resources, and time. Failed change initiatives also take a human toll. Employees are left feeling discouraged, distrustful and reluctant to participate in the next round of failures.

As evidenced in previous discussion, one primary reason that changes fail in school systems is resistance. Those school or school system administrators who close their eyes to resistance are inviting disaster. Thus the need for administrators to manage the school change process to reduce resistance. There are several other things administrators can do to "build a foundation for managing school change" as outlined in the remainder of this chapter. More specifically, administrators should add strategies to their initial plan to build support for the change. To do so, the following steps should be part of every school change plan: conduct a change readiness assessment; plan for the inevitable; keep it alive; effectively plan, announce, execute, and communicate a change initiative; and allay employee's anxieties and get them fired up about future prospects.

Conduct a Change Readiness Assessment

A change readiness assessment answers the question, "Where are we today?" It looks at both past practices and the current situation. Answering the questions below can help a school administrator begin that assessment. The administrator should ask a cross-section of people in the school system to respond to the questions. Often, an administrator's own vantage point allows them to see a portion of the whole picture; other departments and levels within the school system will give them a more complete view of where things stand.

History of Change

What's our track record for handling change?

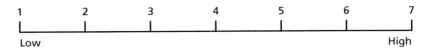

The past is the best predictor of the future. If the change ideas were met with cheers in the past, then it might be reasonable to expect that a new initiative will meet with similar applause. However, if past changes were nothing but headaches—if the administrator had to fight, manipulate, cajole, and make back room deals to push their ideas through—then expect much the same this time. Low scores indicate a strong likelihood that this change will be resisted with great force. The administrator will need to demonstrate repeatedly that they are serious—and that this change is important. People are likely to be very skeptical, thus, the administrator will need to be persistent.

Direction

Do people throughout the school system understand and accept the direction that the school system is moving and the values that fuel that vision?

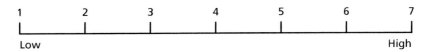

Low scores could indicate a conflict over values and overall direction. The people who must support the change may not believe they share much common ground with the administrator. This is a serious problem. It almost guarantees that any major change will be resisted. Without shared values and vision, people lack a context for the change.

On the other hand, low scores simply may indicate a communication problem. In some situations, values and visions remain secret. People don't know where the school system is going. Top school administrators hang onto these documents and ideas as if they were sacred texts or viewpoints that only they, the high priests, can interpret. This is a communication problem that can be easily resolved by getting the word out.

Cooperation and Trust

Do people share information and deal with each other openly and with respect?

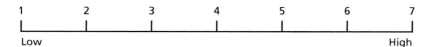

Low scores indicate very serious problems. It is difficult, if not impossible, to build support for major school change without trust. Since the opposite of trust is fear, a low score almost guarantees strong opposition. When teachers and other school staff are afraid, they will either fight or lie low: neither response will give the administrator the commitment they need for the change to be successful.

Culture

Is this a school system that supports risk taking and change?

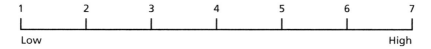

Mid-range to low scores indicates that it may be difficult for those in the school or school system to carry out the changes even if they support the school system change. The school system policies and procedures hinder change. The administrator must examine these deeper structural issues.

Resilience

Can people handle more change?

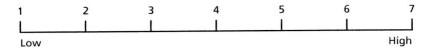

People in many school systems are simply worn out by the number of changes and transitions they've been asked to weather in recent years. No matter how worthy the change their opposition to it may stem from a lack of resilience, and not from some objection to the idea being proposed.

Low to mid-range scores probably indicate that people have lost their capacity to respond to another school change initiative. Even though employees may see the need for this change, they may have little energy to give to it.

So, administrators must keep two important questions in mind: Is this change really necessary at this time? If so, how can administration support people so that the change can be implemented with the greatest ease?

Rewards

Do people believe this change will benefit them?

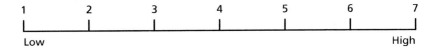

One well-used truismism: What gets rewarded gets done. Unfortunately, its counterpart doesn't get as much attention: What gets punished gets avoided. For example, school systems that say they want teamwork in the classroom but reward individual teacher achievement shouldn't be surprised when cooperation falters.

Obviously, low scores indicate strong potential resistance. After all, who would support something they think will harm them? If employees' perceptions are accurate, then the administrator has a difficult challenge: They must find a way to move forward with the change and find ways to make it rewarding for others. If the low scores indicate a misperception, then the school administrator must let people know why they are misinformed. The school administrator must remember that as anxiety increases our ability to listen diminishes. It is likely that this message will have to be communicated repeatedly (especially if trust is low as well).

Respect, Control, and Saving Face

Will people be able to maintain dignity and self-respect?

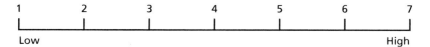

Low scores probably indicate concern over loss of respect, status or face. The school administrator must find ways to make this a situation in which all can win. Given that there are various levels of resistance to school change administrators often hope that all resistance will be at the lowest level: opposition simply because people don't have all the facts. Unfortunately, most resistance to major change is deeper: a fear of loss. School administrators must be prepared to deal with these deeper and more emotional issues. They must engage wary people in conversation. Be open and listen to their concerns.

Impact on Status Quo

How disruptive will this change be to the status quo?

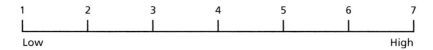

High scores indicate that people view this change as very disruptive and stressful. School administrators must get teachers and others involved because when they have some control over changes that affect them, the less likely they are to resist.

Skill at Managing Change

How adept are administrators at planning and executing change?

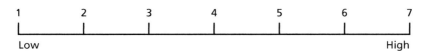

School administrators responsible for managing change need to be adept at such things as:

- creating alignment among diverse interests;
- listening: getting concerns, fears, and interests on the table;
- articulating a compelling vision (or working with others to create a shared vision);
- anticipating and responding appropriately to resistance;
- communicating: keeping people informed.

If scores are low in this category, the school administrator should consider how they can develop change management skills as they proceed with the change. There is no shortage of articles or books that cover the needed skills. Chapter 8 provided a more detailed discussion of competencies and skills important to administrators to successfully serve in the role as change agents.

Interpreting the Overall Results

High scores (Range = 6–7):
   Indicate that an administrator is in good shape for this change and suggest that his or her school system knows how to work well with its people.

Mid-range scores (Range = 3–5):
   Reveal potential danger and signify the need to look into what is behind these scores. For example, mid-range scores on a category such as Cooperation and Trust might indicate a problem that is slowly developing. Administrators should take these scores seriously. Administrators have an opportunity to tilt the balance in their favor by addressing these issues via suggestions for fostering stakeholder collaboration and cooperation.

Low scores (Range = 1–2):
   Point to serious trouble. The lower the scores, the more likely it is that the administrator will face intense resistance. But even a single low score can pose a problem. The administrator should treat any low score seriously because raising low scores helps to build stronger relationships with other individuals and stakeholders.
   In interpreting the results the administrator must remember that the actual scores are less important than the reasons people chose the scores they did. Responses to the questions should act as a springboard for conversation about school system change and resistance. Conversations should focus on the experiences and feelings that accompany these scores. For example, if the superintendent rated everything a seven (high), principals scored in the three to five range, and teachers rated everything low, there

are a lot of issues that need to be addressed. In doing so, the administrator should consider the following questions:

- What interests them about the scores?
- Where do they see patterns?
- Where are the points of greatest agreement?
- Where are the points of greatest disagreement?

PLAN FOR THE INEVITABLE

The administrator has gotten stakeholders deeply involved in the new change plan, they are cooperating with each other, and they are enthralled with its potential. And then something happens that rocks the boat. Perhaps it's a disagreement over which stakeholder will get to control the project, or perhaps someone fails to live up to an agreement. Old animosities flare.

This scenario can be avoided with a little planning for the inevitable. Asking a variety of "What if?" questions will help the administrator address things that could go wrong. It's easier to devise a solid approach to a problem before it surfaces than when it is staring you in the face. "What if?" scenarios allow the administrator to step back and calmly play with possibilities without the risk.

Here are some ideas for the administrator to consider:

A. If the stakeholders have worked together before, identify times when they were in conflict. If they are new, ask people to draw on their own experience to identify potential conflicts that might occur during the change. Do not assign blame. The goal is to identify issues that could come up during the current change, not dissect past events.

B. Form mixed stakeholder groups that contain representatives from a cross-section of the school system. Have those groups take on the issues identified in the first step above and develop strategies to address these problems should they occur.

   The administrator should consider the six principles as they develop change strategies. Stakeholder groups should address the following questions:

   - How can we keep our focus on the goal if this issue occurs? (Maintain Focus)
   - How will we summon the courage to stick with it, even if the going gets extremely tough? (Maintain Focus)
   - What can we do to ensure mutual respect in the midst of this issue? (Respect)

- What can we do to ensure that all the critical issues get out on the table? (Embrace Resistance)
- How can we stay relaxed in the midst of this conflict? (Relax)
- How can we promote the development of common values? (Join Resistance)

C. Have stakeholder subgroups report to the entire group all questions, comments, and suggested changes.

D. Encourage all of the stakeholders to decide together which of these strategies it can fully support. By addressing potential resistance before it occurs, the administrator can often preempt it. People get the critical issues out on the table and make agreements before anyone feels a need to put up a wall or attack others.

KEEP IT ALIVE

Although planning for the inevitable should reduce a significant number of problems, the unexpected will still occur. To be prepared, an effective plan should include the following:

1. A way to include those who were inadvertently left out in the early stages of the school or school system change. One school system did a fine job of getting various interested parties involved, but after the change effort was well into implementation stage, they realized that teacher aides had been omitted from the process. The administrators had never thought about the teacher aides as an important stakeholder group when they planned for this change. Those things happen. But, when they do, an administrator has two options. They can keep on moving, crying "Tough luck, Charlie" as they forge ahead. Or, they can apologize for the oversight, and try to gain the support of those that were overlooked.

2. A way to engage those who have a change of heart about the school or school system change effort. Often people will agree to a change during the early stages, only to discover that they aren't too wild about the idea later on. While it is easy to get angry with these people, this will do nothing to build support for the change plan. People often change their minds once they see how much the new program will cost in time and resources.

3. A way to monitor progress of the school or school system change initiative. The change plan will no doubt include a way to gauge progress versus deadlines and budgets. But it is equally important to have a way to monitor whether support for the change is building. Some questions to ask include:

- How will we know that support is building for the plan?
- What will support look like?
- What level of commitment will we need at each stage of the project?
- How will we measure active commitment?

4. Finally, administrators must pay attention. Unfortunately, still too many plans for school system change are linear: A leads to B, followed by C. It all seems so rational and sane. Unfortunately, support and resistance are ruled by intangibles such as enthusiasm, commitment, energy, fear and threat. These emotional issues don't lend themselves to neat A + B + C plans. The administrator should be prepared to work with resistance at every stage of planning and implementation. And, they should be prepared for support that comes as a gift out of the blue. Good things do happen. Paying attention to what's going on today is the most important thing an administrator can do.

Attending to these steps will not only help the administrator build support for change, but will enable them to begin to develop stronger working relationships with those stakeholders who must support the change. In the end, school administrators can increase the likely success of a school system change by building bridges within the school system and with key stakeholders.

PLAN, ANNOUNCE, EXECUTE, AND COMMUNICATE CHANGE

While school system change requires many things happening simultaneously administrators must keep in mind the following things when planning, announcing, implementing, and communicating a change initiative:

1. **Remember that there's no one perfect way to communicate change.** Change is uncomfortable, and adapting to change is messy. The perfect Gantt chart does not a painless change experience make. Why? Because tasks are easy to list, but behavior and long-held habits are not easy to change. Gather outside information, solicit perspectives, and adapt the approaches for the school system and its stakeholders.

2. **Start by asking yourself what exactly is changing and why.** Too many school or school system change efforts are heavy on the jargon and light on the substance of what the buzz phrases mean in the day-to-day reality of the school or school system's members. Administrators have to make that link. For example, what does it mean when admin-

istrators say the school or school system needs to be more responsive? What behaviors characterize a so-called new school or school
system culture? Administrators must go to the root of what they're
trying to achieve from an organizational behavior perspective, and
give the jargon life.

3. **Know what results you want, ideally, from both the school or school
system change initiative and the communication program or tactic.**
What's the call to action for the communication program? What's
the call to action for the specific communication tactic? What systemic or operations changes are under way that provide the framework for the desired results and behaviors?

4. **Include communication strategists at the very beginning of the discussions about the school or school system change, on the strategic
team from the start.** Too often, qualified communicators are
involved after backlash is in full force, when the leaks and rumor
mills are rampant. Administrators must understand how the members of the school or school system will respond to change and what
information they'll need.

5. **Share information with employees as soon as possible.** There's a real
dilemma in public schools or school systems, for example, where
teacher communication should be a priority, however, they hear
about impending cuts in the number of teachers on their car radio
while commuting to work. Once fear and insecurity are heightened,
administrators waste a lot of time getting back to a place of order,
understanding, and productivity, and many members of the school
or school system head for their desks to update résumés and to look
for employment elsewhere.

6. **Keep in mind that quantity is fine, but quality and consistency are
crucial.** Most of those who write about or manage school or school
system change are quoted as saying, "You can't communicate too
much," but you can communicate too much insignificant or insensitive information. Administrators can't communicate too much significant, substantial information.

7. **Longevity.** Administrators should remember that a school system
change effort starts with the announcement of a change initiative.
Many administrators underestimate the length of time required by a
change cycle. That's why numerous reports indicate poor performance following many change initiatives. Just as Rome wasn't built
in a day, neither do schools or school systems or its members change
in a week, or even a year. Administrators should think of it as changing some very ingrained habits; that's what they're doing. Remember

our discussion of school culture and its impact on "the way we do things around here."

8. **Remember to use a variety of communication pathways and vehicles.** Some schools or school systems make an enormous mistake in using only one vehicle, such as e-mail or their newsletters. Redundancy and repetition are helpful in creating an effective communication program.

9. **Don't confuse process—visioning, chartering school system change teams, planning, endless PowerPoint presentations—with communication.** While those meetings and processes can be communication vehicles if designed mindfully and handled in the context of a broader program, they aren't adequate to meet school or school system change communication needs.

10. **Give individuals and stakeholder groups multiple opportunities to share concerns, ask questions, and offer ideas, and make following up with answers and updates a top priority.** As discussed in several chapters, the more people are involved in the process, the fewer administrators will have resisting the change effort or worse, acting as internal saboteurs.

ALLAY EMPLOYEE'S ANXIETIES AND HELP GET THEM FIRED UP ABOUT FUTURE PROSPECTS

While the list of communication actions in the previous section build support for school system change administrators have to also allay employee's anxieties and help them get fired up about future prospects. For that to happen we suggest administrators use additional approaches. Three key points:

Tap into positive emotions. High-performing school systems create a strong emotional bond (or trust) with its employees. And in a time of change, positive emotions are often the best antidote to feelings such as anxiety and powerlessness. The administrator's task: connect the change with objectives that employees care about. "Identify the emotional hot buttons in the group—what teachers and other staff (and stakeholders) are going to respond to and develop some feelings about.

Manage one-to-one. To get school system members thinking about a proposed change it helps to hold individual meetings with each of them. This gets them to thinking, "this is possible" and "I have a say in it." It should be no different if there are 50 or 500 members; each individual or stakeholder group wants to know what's being planned and what it means for him or her—and most will want a chance to put in their two cents.

Administrators have to be open, they have to engage people, and they have to empower them to be part of the solution.

Lead, don't force. Far too many change initiatives are forced into schools or school systems. But force rarely works' even if people act as they're supposed to, they'll lack enthusiasm. Better to invite members of the school or school system to join in creating the change—and then to work first with the 25% or so who are likely to respond.

It is also important to make sure the school or school system lives up to its stated objectives. For example, if the school system wants certain employee behaviors or outcomes but the reward structures don't encourage the behaviors or outcomes then the administrator's role is to say, "Look, our current systems aren't encouraging this. We need to redesign the way we reward people." As the leader of school or school system change the administrator's role is to create an environment that fosters the kind of behaviors they want—and to understand what dissonances there are in the current system.

CONCLUSION: CONTINUE TO CHART THE COURSE FOR SCHOOL SYSTEM CHANGE

What is important for administrators to remember is that school systems at all levels of readiness can successfully initiate change—it is simply a matter of doing the following.

1. Identify the level of readiness and select an appropriate approach to executing change.
2. Recognize that in the real world, change usually happens from the inside out, not from the top down.
3. Remember, their school or school system is very different from any other organization; and because of that, their strategy for initiating change will be unique to their school or school system. That is why it is important to develop a change initiative or program that meets the specific needs of their school or school system, not because another school or school system had great success with it.

Each school or school system's level of readiness is different from other schools or school systems and, therefore, their approach should be different as well.

If administrators are trying to make improvements in their school or school system, it may seem as if they are trying to move a large object by tying a rope to it and pushing on the rope. It gets really frustrating, and brings to mind an apt statement: "The only good thing about banging your head against the wall is that it feels good when you stop."

So, we recommend school administrators stop banging their heads against the wall. Recognize that change is difficult. Recognize that they will not always get the level of support they want—or need. On the brighter side, administrators should recognize that step-by-step they can begin to make progress in their change efforts by understanding the capability of their school or school system to support its change initiatives.

BIBLIOGRAPHY

Anderson, D., & Anderson, L. A. (2001a). *Beyond change management.* San Francisco: Jossey-Bass/Pfeiffer.

Anderson, L. A., & Anderson, D. (2001b). *The change leader's roadmap.* San Francisco: Jossey-Bass.

Applegate, L., & Saltrick, S. (2002). *Oklahoma VISION project.* Boston, MA: Harvard Business School Publishing.

Banathy, B. H. (1991). *Systems design of education: A journey to create the future.* Englewood Cliffs, NJ: Educational Technology Publications.

Banks, J. A. (Ed.). (1993a). *Multicultural education: Issues and perspectives* (2nd ed.). Boston: Allyn and Bacon.

Banks, J. A. (1993b). *Multicultural education: Issues and perspectives* (2nd ed.). Boston: Allyn and Bacon. pp. 3–28.

Barth, R. S. (1991). Restructuring schools: Some questions for teachers and principals. *Phi Delta Kappan, 73*(2), 123–128.

Barth, R. S. (1990). *Improving schools from within.* San Francisco: Jossey-Bass.

Berkman, E. (2002). How to use the balanced scorecard. *CIO Magazine.* (May 15), 7–9.

BEST Education Partners. (2003). www.besteducationpartners.com. April 18.

Blanchard, K. (1992). Six concerns in the change process. *Quality Digest,* (June), 14, 62.

Block, P. (1992). *Stewardship.* San Francisco: Berrett-Koehler Publishers.

Bolton, R. (1986). *People skills: How to assert yourself, listen to others, and resolve conflicts.* New York: Simon & Schuster.

Bondy, E. (1995). Fredericks Middle School and the dynamics of school reform. In Ann Lieberman (Ed.), *The work of restructuring schools.* New York. Teacher College Press.

Briner, B. (1996). *The management methods of Jesus.* Nashville, TN: Thomas Nelson Inc.

Managing School System Change: Charting a Course for Renewal, pages 219–223
Copyright © 2004 by Information Age Publishing, Inc.
All rights of reproduction in any form reserved.

Conley, D. (1993). *Roadmap to restructuring: Policies, practices and emerging visions of schooling.* Eugene, OR: ERIC Clearinghouse on Educational Management.

Cooke, R. (1993). Organization development in schools. In T. Cummings, & C. Worley (Eds.), *Organization development and change,* (5th ed.). St. Paul, MN: West.

Cummings, T., & Worley, C. (2001). *Organization development and change* (7th ed.). Cincinnati, OH: South-Western College Publishing.

Dahl, R. (1957). The concept of power. *Behavioral Science, 20,* 201–215.

De Pree, M. (1992). *Leadership jazz.* New York: Dell Publishing.

Deal, T. E. (1993). The culture of schools. In M. Sashkin & H. J. Walberg (Eds.), *Educational leadership and school culture* (pp 3–18). Berkeley, CA: McCutchan Publishing.

Deal, T. E., & Kennedy, A. A. (1982). *Corporate culture: The rites and rituals of corporate life* (pp. 13–15). Reading, MA.: Addison-Wesley.

Deal, T. E., & Peterson, K. D. (1990). *The principal's role in shaping school culture.* Washington, DC: Office of Educational Research and Improvement.

Deal, T. E., & Peterson, K. D. (1993). Strategies for building school cultures: Principals as symbolic leaders. In M. Sashkin & H. J. Walberg, (Eds.), *Educational leadership and school culture* (pp. 89–99). Berkeley, CA: McCutchan Publishing,

Deal, T. E., & Peterson, K. D. (1994). *The leadership paradox: Balancing logic and artistry in schools.* San Francisco: Jossey-Bass, Inc.

Deal, T. E., & Peterson, K. D. (1999). *Shaping school culture: The heart of leadership.* San Francisco: Jossey-Bass Publishers.

Doerger, D. W. (2002). School culture on the Internet: Considerations for preservice and inservice teachers. *Journal of Computing in Teacher Education, 18*(4), 141–147.

Donaldson, T., & Preston, L. (1995). The stakeholder theory of the corporation: Concepts, evidence, and implications. *Academy of Management Review, 20,* 65–91.

Florio-Ruane, S. (1989). Social organizations of classes and schools. In M. C. Reynolds (Ed.), *Knowledge base for the beginning teacher* (pp. 163–172). New York: Pergamon Press.

Flynn, C. (1976). Collaborative decision making in a secondary school: An experiment. *Education and Urban Society, 8,* 172–192.

Fullan, M. (2001). *Leading in a culture of change.* San Francisco: Jossey-Bass.

Garrison, S., & Borgia, D. (1999). Responding to stakeholders in the educational process and the impact on course design. *Journal of Financial and Strategic Decisions,* (Spring), 1–3.

Geertz, C. (1973). *The interpretation of cultures.* New York: Basic Books.

Gibson, J. L., Ivancevich, J. M., Donnelly, J. H., Jr., & Konopake, R. (2003). *Organizations: Behavior, structure processes.* New York: McGraw-Hill Irwin.

Goleman, D. (1998). *Working with emotional intelligence.* New York: Bantam Books.

Goodlad, J. (1984). *A place called school: Prospects for the future.* New York: McGraw-Hill.

Greenleaf, R. K. (1970). *The leader as servant.* Indianapolis, IN: The Robert K. Greenleaf Center for Servant Leadership.

Greenleaf, R. K. (1996). *On becoming a servant leader.* San Francisco: Jossey-Bass.

Gross, W., & Shichman, S. (1987). How to grow a culture, *Personnel* (September), 52–56.

Gunn, J. (1995). Educational partners and stakeholders, 1895–1995. AVISO. 100th Anniversary Commerative Edition. Fall. See: www.ntsu.ca/issues/av100jag.html. April 28, 2003.

Heckman, P. E. (1993). School restructuring in practice: Reckoning with the culture of school. *International Journal of Educational Reform* 2(3), 263–271.

Herzberg, F. (1966). *Work and the nature of man*. Cleveland, OH: World Publishing.

Jick, T. (1993). *Managing change*. Chicago: Richard Irwin Inc.

Kanter, R. M. (1983). *The change masters*. New York: Simon & Schuster.

Kanter, R. M. (1985). Managing the human side of change. *Management Review*, (April), 5–56.

Kanter, R. M. (1998). *Bell Atlantic and the Union City Schools (A-D)*. Boston: Harvard Business School Publishing.

Kaplan, R., & Norton, D. (1996a). Using the balanced scorecard in a strategic management system. *Harvard Business Review, 74*, 75–85.

Kaplan, R., & Norton, D. (1996b). Strategic learning and the balanced scorecard. *Strategy and Leadership, 24*, 19–24.

Kaplan, R., & Norton, D. (2000). *The strategy-focused organization: How the balanced scorecard companies thrive in the new environment*. Boston, MA: Harvard Business Review Press.

Katzenbach, J. R. (2000). *The path to peak performance*. Cambridge, MA: Harvard Business School Press.

Kotter, J. P. (1996). *Leading change*. Boston: Harvard Business School Press.

Kozol, J. (1992). *Savage inequalities*. New York: Harper Collins.

Lewin, K. (1947). Frontiers in group dynamics. *Human Relations. 1*, 5–41.

Lewin, K. (1951). *Field theory in social science*. New York: Harper and Row.

Lingle, J. H., & Schiemann, W. A. (1996). From balanced scorecard to strategic gauges: Is measurement worth it? *Management Review, 85*, 56–61.

Martin, J. (1982). Stories and scripts in organizational settings. In A. Hastorf & A. Isen (Eds.), *Cognitive social psychology* (pp. 255–306). New York: Elsevier-North Holland.

McCauley, C. D., Moxley, R. S., & Van Velsor, E. (1998). *Handbook of leadership development*. San Francisco: Jossey-Bass.

McShane, S. L., & Von Glinow, M. A. (2003). *Organizational behavior: Emerging realities for the new workplace revolution*. New York: McGraw-Hill Irwin.

Mintzberg, H. (1983). *Power in and around organizations*. Englewood Cliffs, NJ: Prentice-Hall.

Mok, M., & Flynn, M. (1998). Effect of Catholic school culture on students' achievement in the higher school certificate examination: A multilevel path analysis. *Educational Psychology, 18*, 409–432.

Mourier, P., & Smith, M. (2001). *Conquering organizational change*. Atlanta, GA: CEP Press.

Nadler, D., & Tushman, M. (1989). Organizational framebending: Principles for managing reorientation. *Academy of Management Executive, 3*, 194–202.

Nickse, R. S. (1977). *Teachers as change agents*. Washington, DC: National Education Association.

Ott, J. S. (1989). *The organizational culture perspective*. Chicago: Dryden Press.

Peterson, K. D. (2002). *The shaping culture fieldbook*. San Francisco: Jossey-Bass.

Phillips, G. (1993). *The school–classroom culture audit.* Vancouver, British Columbia: Eduserv, British Columbia School Trustees Publishing.

Piperato, D. F., & Roy, J. J. (2002). Transforming school culture. Third International Conference on Conferencing, Circles and Other Restorative Practices, August 8–10, Minneapolis, MN.

Prosser, J. (Ed.). (1999). *School culture* (British Educational Management Series). London: Sage Publications.

Robbins, P., & Alvy, H. (1995). *The principal's companion.* Thousand Oaks, CA: Corwin Press.

Salancik, G., & Pfeffer, J. (1977). Who gets power—and how they hold on to it: A strategic-contingency model of power. *Organizational Dynamics, 5,* 3–21.

Sarason, S. B. (1990). *The predictable failure of educational reform—Can we change course before it's too late?* San Francisco: Jossey-Bass.

Sathe, V. (1983). Implications of corporate culture: A manager's guide to action. *Organizational Dynamics,* (Autumn), 4–13.

Schein, E. H. (1985). *Organizational culture and leadership.* San Francisco: Jossey-Bass.

Schein, E. H. (1991). What is culture? In P. J. Frost, L. F. Mooer, M. R. Louis, C. C. Lundberg, & J. Martin (Eds.). *Reframing organizational culture* (pp. 243–253). Beverly Hills, CA: Sage.

Senge, P. M. (1990). *The fifth discipline: The art and practice of the learning organization.* New York: Doubleday.

Sergiovanni, T. J. (1999). *The lifeworld of leadership.* New York: John Wiley & Sons.

Sergiovanni, T. J. (1995). *The principalship: A reflective practice perspective.* Needham Heights, MA: Allyn and Bacon.

Simon, H., & March, J. (1958). *Organizations.* New York: Wiley.

Sims, R. R. (Ed.) (2002). *Changing the way we manage change.* Westport, CT: Quorum.

Smith, S. C., & Stolp, S. (1995). Transforming a school's culture through shared vision. *Oregon School Study Council, 35*(3), 1–6.

Stevenson, R. B. (2001). Shared decision making and core school values: A case study in organizational learning. *The International Journal of Educational Management, 15*(2), 103–110.

Stewart, D. J. (2000). *Tomorrow's principals today.* Palmerson North, NZ: Kanuka Grove Press.

Stoll, L. (1999). School culture: Black hole or fertile garden for school improvement. In J. Prosser (Ed.), *School culture* (British Educational Management Series) (pp. 30–47). London: Sage Publications.

Stolp, S., & Smith, S.C. (1994). School culture and climate: The role of the leader. *OSSC Bulletin.* Eugene, OR: Oregon School Study Council.

Tichy, N. M., & Charan, R. (1995). The CEO as coach: An interview with Allied Signal's Lawrence A. Bossidy. *Harvard Business Review,* (March-April),, 69–78.

Wachtell, T. (2000). Safer Saner Schools: Restoring community in a disconnected world. http:/www.restorativepractices.org/Pages/safer/sanerschools.html.

Wagner, C. (2000). School culture analysis. Annual meeting of the Manitoba Association of Resource Teacher (MART). (October 20). Winnipeg, Manitoba.

Wagner, T. (2001). *Making the grade: Reinventing America's schools.* London: Routledge/Falmer.

Waller, W. (1932). *The sociology of teaching.* New York: Wiley.

Weick, K. (1976). Educational organizations as loosely coupled systems. *Administrative Science Quarterly, 21*, 1–79.

Woodward, H., & Bucholz, S. (1987). *Aftershock: Helping people through corporate change.* New York: John Wiley.

ABOUT THE AUTHORS

Serbrenia J. Sims is an independent researcher and consultant. She was formerly the Director of Accountability Assessment and Grants Writing for the Williamsburg-James City County Virginia Public Schools and a seventh grade science teacher. She received her Masters and Ed.D. from the College of William and Mary. She has published a number of articles and books on a variety of education and training related topics.

Ronald R. Sims is the Floyd Dewey Gottwalld Senior Professor of Business Administration at the College of William and Mary where he teaches leadership and change management. He provides consulting to organizations in the private, not-for-profit and public sectors. He is the author or coauthor of more than twenty books and over eighty articles on a variety of topics. Two of his most recent books are *Changing the Way We Manage Change* and *Accountability and Radical Change in Public Organizations*.

Managing School System Change: Charting a Course for Renewal, page 225
Copyright © 2004 by Information Age Publishing, Inc.